WHAT IS REVELATION?

AMS PRESS

NEW YORK

" As our understanding can contemplate itself, and our affections be exercised upon themselves by reflection, so may each be employed in the same manner upon any other mind : and since the Supreme Mind, the Author and Cause of all things, is the highest possible object to Himself, He may be an adequate supply to all the faculties of our souls, a subject to our understandings, and an object to our affections."—*Butler, 14th Sermon, On the Love of God.*

WHAT IS REVELATION?

A SERIES OF

Sermons on the Epiphany;

TO WHICH ARE ADDED

LETTERS TO A STUDENT OF THEOLOGY

ON THE

BAMPTON LECTURES OF MR. MANSEL.

BY THE REV.

FREDERICK DENISON MAURICE, M.A.,

CHAPLAIN OF LINCOLN'S INN.

Cambridge:
MACMILLAN & CO.,
AND 23, HENRIETTA STREET, COVENT GARDEN, LONDON

1859.

Library of Congress Cataloging in Publication Data

Maurice, Frederick Denison, 1805-1872.
    What is revelation?

    Reprint of the 1859 ed. published by Macmillan,
Cambridge.
    1. Mansel, Henry Longueville, 1820-1871. The limits
of religious thought. 2. Religion—Philosophy.
3. Rationalism. 4. Revelation. I. Title.
BL51.M33M3   1975   230   76-173061
ISBN 0-404-04276-7

From the edition of 1859, Cambridge
First AMS edition published in 1975
Manufactured in the United States of America

89-11996
AMS PRESS INC.
NEW YORK, N.Y. 10003

PREFACE.

In the Preface to the third edition of Mr. Mansel's Lectures, p. 14, he says:—"It has been objected by " reviewers of very opposite schools, that to deny to " man a knowledge of the Infinite is to make Reve- " lation itself impossible, and to leave no room for " evidences on which Reason can be legitimately em- " ployed. The objection would be pertinent if I had " ever maintained that Revelation is or can be a di- " rect manifestation of the Infinite Nature of God. " But I have constantly asserted the very reverse."

It is not the object of the Sermons contained in this volume to convict Mr. Mansel of any inconsistency on the subject of Revelation. I have understood him to maintain, just as he states, the " very reverse " of the doctrine that Revelation means a direct manifestation of the Nature of God. My wish is to ascertain whether that doctrine which I have

been used to hold and proclaim, or 'the reverse' of it,
is the true one.   If Mr. Mansel had persuaded me
that all I had believed up to this time on that subject
was false, I hope I should have had the honesty to
tell my congregation so, to ask pardon of God and of
them for having deceived them, and to abandon my
clerical functions.   As he did not persuade me,—
as all that he has written has added immense force
to my previous conviction,—I have explained in six
Sermons (the first in the series was preached before
the Bampton Lectures were preached) why, in spite
of the high authorities on the other side, I must still
assert the principle which I discover in the Services
of the Church and throughout the Bible.

In sermons addressed to a London congregation,
I could only refer to Lectures delivered in Oxford.
Pulpit quotations are nearly always unfair; pulpit
discussions on metaphysical topics must be nearly
always most satisfactory to those who do not understand them.   But if I made allusions to any book, I
was bound to justify them.   If I avoided quotations
and discussions in a place for which they were unsuit-
able, it behoved me to prove that I did not avoid
them because I was afraid of them.   The ordinary
resource in such cases is a collection of notes.   Sup-

posing I had wished to illustrate my own statements, to write a comment on my comments, I should have availed myself of that expedient. But I desired to bring Mr. Mansel's book before my readers, to examine that thoroughly. I did not care to choose the weaker or more startling passages of it: unless it was studied as a whole, my purpose would not be answered. My ' Letters to a Student of Theology preparing for Orders' cannot be accused, I think, of treating the subject or the author carelessly or superficially. I have followed his statements and arguments step by step. If they are as decisive and satisfactory as they are said to be, my objections will only make their worth and their power more evident.

I have at least endeavoured to bring the maxims of the Lecturer to a crucial test. They are defences of the truths which my correspondent is to preach. The defence being admitted, what will he have to preach? They are derived from a " Regulative Revelation;" I ask to know what are the rules, and what is revealed. I hear that Germans are utterly silenced. I am anxious to be shown what remains for Englishmen. I could not hope that learned doctors would listen if these questions were proposed to them. I have some confidence in proposing them to young

men who are entering upon the battle of life; I have
known something of their perplexities; I am sure
that some out of their number demand that the
problems should be solved, having found that to stifle
them is death.

I have not been able to avoid in these Letters a
certain vehemence of expression, which if it has ever
taken a personal form, I shall deeply regret. I have
no excuse for entertaining towards Mr. Mansel any
feelings but those of respect. He has treated me
both on former occasions and in this volume with
a courtesy to which I have no claim; he has even
intimated a hope that we are essentially agreed in
opinion. No one can tell how eagerly I should have
responded to that hope, or how grateful I should
have felt to so able a man for having entertained it.
But since the further I read in his book, the more I
perceived that it would be needful for me to abandon
every conviction that was most precious to me before
I could obtain that result, I felt myself obliged by
his very good-nature to state the reasons of my dis-
agreement. I could not state them as if they were
indifferent to me; I could not conceal my opinion
that the existence of English faith and English morality is involved in them. I have the comfort of

reflecting that my words can do no possible harm
to Mr. Mansel. His popularity cannot be diminished by my opposition. Some may be willing to accept it as an additional proof that his blows have
been effectual,—as a pledge that more illustrious
opponents may recoil from them. If I succeed in
inducing a few Christian students and Christian
workers to ask themselves what is Revelation; if I
can convince a few serious doubters that what we
call a Revelation of God, craves to be tried by the
severest tests, is capable of meeting those agonies
of the human spirit which our arguments can never
meet;—I have done what I meant to do.

I had finished my Letters before I read Canon
Stanley's admirable sermon ' *On the Wisdom of
Christ,*' which was preached before the University of
Oxford last November. Some passages in that sermon, especially those on the criticism of the Bible
and on the ' All or Nothing ' doctrine, anticipate
what I have tried to say in my remarks on Mr.
Mansel's last Lecture. The whole discourse proves,
it seems to me, that the true spirit of Butler has not
departed from Oxford.

5, *Russell Square, June* 4.

ERRATUM.

Page 160, line 4, *for* quisquis *read* quisque.

CONTENTS.

Sermons.

Letters.

WHAT IS REVELATION?

I.

THE MAGIANS.

St. Luke ii. 32.

"A LIGHT TO LIGHTEN THE GENTILES, AND THE GLORY OF THY
PEOPLE ISRAEL."

Two subjects which appear incongruous were brought
before us on the day of Epiphany. The Gospel spoke
of the Magians, who were led by a star to the cradle
of Christ. The Epistle spoke of the message which
St. Paul delivered to the Ephesians. What connection is there between these thoughts? What has
a star in the heavens to do with the sermons of a
tent-maker?

A study of St. Paul's words would suggest the
answer to this question; it is embodied in the very
word *Epiphany*. Not a sermon or a star is the subject of the Epistle or the Gospel, but God's manifestation of His Son to the Gentiles. This manifestation
can be as little explained by the discourses which St.

B

Paul delivered as by the shining of an outward lumi-
nary. It is to the spirit within that God makes any
of His discoveries. Only with this spirit can a man
seize any truth, or enter into communion with it.
Newton might have seen a thousand apples fall from
the trees on which they hung; there was one which
led him to perceive the law of the universe. The
object that was presented to his outward eye became
the instrument through which an idea was presented
to the man himself. A universal truth shone through
that special instance. His devout and humble mind
would have acknowledged at once that God had led
him to the one through the other. If afterwards he
studied the speculations of Copernicus and the demonstrations of Kepler, he would have confessed, with all
gratitude to his earthly teachers, that they also were
instruments by which he was guided to the knowledge
of a truth, which would not have been less a truth
for them, for himself, for mankind, if no one of them
had been able to apprehend it. In like manner the
leading of a star, and the labours of St. Paul, are
equally unintelligible, if they are viewed without reference to the object of both; when connected with that,
each may enable us better to understand the other.

I have taken the words of the old Rabbi Simeon,
which have become a Vesper Song of the Church, to
illustrate this subject. The best commentary upon
them which I know, is found in our Collect for the
Epiphany: "O God, Who by the leading of a star

didst manifest Thy only-begotten Son to the Gentiles, mercifully grant that we, which know Thee now by faith, may after this life have the fruition of Thy glorious Godhead, through Jesus Christ our Lord!" One can but follow lamely in a discourse, the movements of the spirit in a prayer; but I shall try to keep the method of this Collect before me, and to examine its different clauses.

I. An Eastern sage, believing in a light which was older than the darkness, and which would at last overcome it, associating this light with the luminous forms that presented themselves to him in a still evening,—trying honestly and earnestly to find out what these were and what they signified to him,—was in these very studies sending up a prayer to the Source of Light, that he might be shown his way, which was bewildered with shadows and deceitful fires. Such a man is surely a most interesting subject for contemplation. Yet how mournful a one he would be if we supposed it was all in vain; if his wishes were self-created, and met with no response; if his life was passed in dreams, and death was the awakening to a certainty that they pointed to nothing! Is not the doctrine of the Epiphany a more cheerful and a more reasonable one? If we take it,—so we are bound to take every record of Scripture, supposing we believe it,—as the instance and exemplification of a law, of the course of the Divine working, is it not good news that God Himself was directing the thoughts of the

student of the stars, and of all other students and
seekers in every direction—that their disappointments
and sorrows and hasty guesses and crude anticipations
were themselves schoolmasters by which He was bringing them,—yes, why do we stumble at the words?—
bringing them to Christ, bringing them to the Light
which was lightening them, and had lightened every
man that came into the world,—bringing them to
know that He was there who always had been there,
—bringing them to understand the deepest moral
truth, the truth that most concerned their own being,
through some common, often-observed incident, and
by its commonness to feel assured that it was a truth
for all as well as for them?

If we think of Him who was born at Bethlehem as
having never lived till he was conceived by the Virgin,
we may lose ourselves in all kinds of speculations
about the miracle of that particular star that led the
wise men to His manger. But if we adopt the Catholic Faith,—the Faith which was set before us on
Christmas Day; if we suppose that the Word who was
with the Father, who had been with the Father before
all worlds, by whom the worlds were made, who had
always been the life and the light of men, was then
made flesh and dwelt among us,—that star will be no
exception to the law which all stars have been obeying.
They needed not to forsake their courses or break loose
from their orbits that they might become instruments
of illumination to the inner spirit of man, any more

than that they might show him his path through the
wood or across the ocean. In each case they were obeying their Creator's high behest, they were glorifying
His calm and settled order, and so were ministering
to the greatest as well as to the humblest needs of His
children. It might have been indeed a wonder to the
wise men, an overthrow of many previous conjectures
and high imaginations, a tearing in pieces of many
plausible schemes of the universe which they had
devised or adopted, when they were led to confess
the glory in a Jewish child, born in a Jewish stable,
which they had looked for either in some Persian
monarch or in some sun of the upper world. But
if there was a breaking-down of theories, like that
which every true man of science, in whatever department he works, has to endure and ultimately to give
thanks for,—what a satisfaction was reserved for the
humbled heart of the truth-seeker in the very mean-
ness of the outward vesture, in the discovery that the
glory was all within, in the assurance that it was not
the less human glory because it was Divine! How
many lines of thought and of hope, which had each
been visible at times, which sometimes seemed to in-
tersect each other, sometimes to be running for ever
parallel without the power of meeting, found their
centre in that cradle! While they confessed how
little the vision corresponded to what, as *wise* men, as
Magians, they should have anticipated and wished,
the conviction would be brought home to them, that

this was what they required because they were *men,*
that here was the Son of Man.

II. At this point then there seems no violent tran-
sition to that general Manifestation of the Only-begotten Son to the Gentiles, which came through the
preaching of St. Paul, or of any who followed in his
steps.   It was as a messenger to men concerning a
Son of God and a Son of Man that the Apostle went
forth.   This was his Gospel; and wherever he went
preaching it, he found that other preachers had been
before him.   The rains and fruitful seasons, filling
men's hearts with food and gladness, had been there.
The sun and stars had been there.   There had been
thoughts of a Deliverer, of a King, of a Judge.
Wherever he went, he had proofs that God had other
ways than by the leading of a star to manifest His
only-begotten Son to the Gentiles; that in every nation and language there were tokens and witnesses
of Him which God Himself was drawing forth, which
His minister was to learn first of the invisible Teacher
in the secret ear, and then to proclaim upon the
housetops.

III. And how is it now, brethren?   Are things altogether changed?   Have we, as some tell us we have,
the Scriptures and the traditions of the Church,
either separately or both together, as substitutes for
that inner manifestation of the Son of God, which
the Scriptures and the Church say came to certain
wise men through the guiding of a star, and to the

bulk of the nations through the preaching of the Gospel? The actual prayer of the Collect would be utterly inconsistent with the words which introduce it,—the desire for *us* could have no connection with the light which came to wise or foolish Gentiles in the old time, if *our* knowledge of God has not the same ground, is not essentially of the same nature with theirs. The Magians had their traditions, and paid them fitting reverence. They studied the stars in conformity with them. But if their traditions had been a thousand times better than they were, they would have said : "Trust God, and not us. He is with you. Follow His guiding." They acted on the conviction that this was their duty. They opened their hearts to God's teaching, and He manifested His Son to them. He led them to the Child. Those to whom St. Paul preached were not merely Gentiles. A Jewish colony was mixed with them. He spoke to both equally. He made use of Gentile traditions and lore. He appealed continually to the Jewish Scriptures, and to the history of the Jewish calling, as authoritative and true. But in both cases equally his object was to lead them to faith in God, in the living Son of God, who had spoken and was speaking to the Gentile conscience, who had spoken and was speaking to the Jewish conscience, not less directly because He had given the Jews a Law, because He had raised up Patriarchs, Kings, Prophets, to rule them, teach them, reprove them ; because He had caused His oracles to be collected and written down as testimonies of His continual presence with them. The Jew fancied that the Patriarchs, the Law, the Prophets, were substitutes for the voice that was speaking to the Gentiles. He put these and the written oracles, as well as the comments and traditions of the elders, between God and himself. Whilst therefore he prided himself on his superiority to the Gentiles, he in truth reduced himself to a lower level than theirs. He renounced the human privilege, of which he could not deprive them. He cut himself off, as far as he could, from the Divine light and the Divine manifestation, using his traditions, using God's Scriptures, to close the passage through which the light of Christ, the Only-begotten Son, was penetrating into his inner man. Therefore is it that St. Paul had to complain so continually, "A veil is on their hearts." It is not taken away in the reading of the Old Testament, though that testifies everywhere of Christ. Only when they turn to the Lord, when they seek Him who is seeking them, will it be taken away.

This example is so certainly meant for us and is so fearful, that there is need continually to press the truth which the Collect suggests. It is the God, who manifested His only-begotten Son to the Gentiles, who does only, who can only, manifest His Son to us. No book can do it, be it ever so divine; no Church authority or tradition can do it, be it ever so venerable. We must know, not the book, not the

tradition, but *Him* by faith. We must trust Him as
we trust a father; that is what the Divine book tells
us to do, that is what the Church tells us to do, and
its authority and its traditions belie their own origin, contradict themselves and become blasphemies,
if they speak otherwise. If we believe in God habi-
tually as a living Person, if we seek Him as a refuge from our own atheism, from our own idolatry,
from that in us which is most utterly contrary to
Him,—our self-will, our pride, our spite and malice,—
we shall know Him, really, as one knows a friend, not
by seeing Him with the eyes, not by getting reports
of Him or traditions of Him from others, be those reports ever so trustworthy, be those traditions ever so
reasonable and credible, but by experiencing His help,
by finding out how much better He is than we are,
and yet how well He understands what we are, and
cares for us. To exchange for this practical faith, which
rests upon God Himself and His own manifestation of
Himself in the Son of God and the Son of Man, a belief in the holy book, is to disobey all the warnings
of that Book, to show that we do not know what is
in it, that we prize it as a name or a watchword,
not for that which it teaches. To exchange for this
practical faith a belief in the Church,—a notion that
the Church will tell us the right thing and will bring
us to Heaven,—is to show that we do not know what
it is to be members of a Church, or what a Church
is good for; that we do not prize it because it leads

us to the Rock on which it stands, to the God who has called it out to be the witness of His revelation of Himself to mankind, of His redemption of mankind, but because we suppose it is ours, and that it gives us some privilege and glory which other men want. This is to exalt ourselves and to deny God.

IV. That is to say, we do not adopt the next clause of the Collect: *"We which know Thee now by faith."* I have been obliged in some degree to anticipate these words, but they deserve a separate consideration. We were willing enough to limit ourselves by objects of sight. The world had a great many to offer us that were very beautiful, that deserved all admiration. But to rest in them was impossible. We overlooked them. If we came to them with a heart free and open for joy, they met it and gave it food on which it could feast for a time; if it brought sorrow, they oftener took their colour from it than gave it a brighter one. And there was an inward aching, a craving of the spirit for that which was like itself, for that which was higher than itself, a craving for deliverance from itself, that all these fair images merely mocked. How delightful was it to escape from them to a friend, to a kinsman! to find an object not of sight but of trust!—one who could exchange thoughts and feelings with us, who actually suffered and rejoiced, who was wiser and better than we! But the sympathy becomes exhausted, or there is a vacancy in the character which had seemed

all satisfactory, or the wisdom perishes, or some jealousy tears the cord in twain. We need more than
this : one altogether better than ourselves ; one whose
sympathy has no stint ; one whose character has no
flaw ; one who will last the same for ever. We want
a Son of Man. The Gospel that there is such a son
of Man, that He knows our conditions of birth, of
poverty, of suffering and death, what has it not been
to Europe for eighteen centuries ! Who knows into
what hovels the sound has penetrated, over what cra-
dles and what coffins there has been an echo of it?
If you suppose the sun's light and heat have only
been felt by those who are acquainted with the right
doctrine concerning the heavenly bodies, you may
suppose also that Christ's power has been limited by
men's acquaintance with the right doctrine concerning His relation to the visible or invisible world. As
the truest astronomy, by declaring what is the unchangeable law of the world, by showing how entirely independent it is of our conceptions and anticipations, refutes the one conclusion, the truest theology spurns with far greater indignation the other.
The theology of St. Paul declares Christ to be the
foundation that is laid for every man, not one that
men by their faith or feelings can lay for themselves.
The theology of St. John declares Christ to be the
Light that lighteth every man, whether the Light is
acknowledged or denied. The Church, in its Creeds,
its Sacraments, and its prayers, proclaims the Incar-

nation and the Manifestation of the Son of God as good news to the world. She prefers to endure the charge of being assuming and dogmatical, than to earn for herself the credit of hesitation and modesty—by refusing to meet the demand of the human conscience and reason—by teaching men to fancy that truth is created by their trowings.

V. But Simeon did not speak *only* of *" a Light to lighten the Gentiles."* He said there *was " a glory "* for the *" people Israel."* The Collect does not only thank God for manifesting His Son. It asks that we, though Gentiles, may have the *"fruition of His glorious Godhead."* These are equivalent expressions. We ask for the whole Church, for the whole Universe, what the Jew believed in for his countrymen.

He felt, and he had a right to feel, that the children of Abraham had been educated for something higher than the sight of the most blessed Child, of the most perfect Man. All their discipline had been to teach them that they could only be satisfied when they awakened up after God's likeness, that to know Him was their great reward. In our efforts to convert them, we have, I should think, been far too inattentive to this consideration. We have not done justice to the feeling which has been working, however confusedly, in their minds, that there must be the revelation of a *divine* glory encircling their nation; that if no such glory is in reserve for it, it has existed for nothing. But if we have failed to meet the secret cravings with which God has inspired Jews, if this has been the cause why so few of them have cast in their lot with us, we have done equal wrong to ourselves and to the other nations of the earth through the same ignorance and misunderstanding. The fruition of the glorious Godhead is as needful for us as for them. Whenever we speak of glory, whenever we think of glory, however paltry our words about it, however low our conceptions of it may be, this unspeakable, inconceivable blessedness is lying behind them. Why else does the thought of glory so naturally, so inevitably associate itself with the thought of departure out of the world? Why is there something painful to us in calculating the petty rewards which we can bestow upon a man who has done any work of deliverance for his country? Why do we almost dread—eagerly as we may desire his return—to hear the vulgar, formal phrases which are all we can devise, to commemorate the toils and sufferings that we think of with most gratitude and affection?* Why is there somewhat calming and soothing in the sadness which follows a brave man to his grave in the very place where his work was done, just when it was done? Solon, we are told, thought those young men blessed above kings, who yoked themselves to the car of their priestess-mother, and when they had brought her to the temple where her services

* The news of General Havelock's death, at Lucknow, reached England a few days before this sermon was preached.

were due, fell asleep for weariness, and (since she had prayed that the Goddess would pour her best gift upon them) woke no more. Such a gift we may surely believe the God whom we worship would bestow on those who have offered themselves as freely for our common mother. Here the hard fighter knows Him by faith. Whatever may be the nature or the weapons of his outward warfare, he must seek the Captain of his host amidst jungles, must watch for Him by the light of camp-fires. It is by his own weakness that he learns the everlasting Strength; by his sins, the perfect Righteousness; by the feebleness and uncertainty of the halo which plays about the head of the noblest of His servants, the substantial glory of which that is the reflection. After this life comes the fruition of His glory. The longing for selfish prizes has ceased; the earthly weakness of desiring to exchange faith for sense has been taken away. What remains is the vision of that Light which fills earth and heaven, the revelation to the inward eye of the Godhead itself, as the eye of the spiritual body will by degrees become capable of taking in all the beauty and harmony of God's works.

Yes! there is in us all a deep sighing for Home, a longing which nothing but this beholding of God can satisfy. The more we know of the faiths of all the nations of the earth, the more we discover it. Even where the desire has been most perverted, it still exists. Buddha taught those who honour his name to crave for annihilation. Though few may understand his philosophy, hundreds of millions have been affected by his practical teaching. That dream of theirs seems to us monstrous at some—which are surely the best—moments of our lives. But how often has it seemed most natural, most desirable! To lose oneself, to forget, to be forgotten : who, after days and months of intense restlessness, may not have counted this the highest of all blessings which the soul can attain? As long as there is about us a floating image of a God of wrath, a God from whose dominion we should be glad to escape, yet a God who would fain curse us with immortality, we shall turn to this as a distant but not impossible hope. Terrible as it may be to us to part with all beautiful things that we have delighted in, with all energies, affections, memories, hopes, the conscience will count this a trifling sacrifice to be delivered from its own ever-increasing burden, from the presence of an irresistible enemy.

But when there comes to the conscience the revelation of a reconciled and reconciling God, of One who has manifested His only-begotten Son bearing the burden which we could not bear, taking away the sin of the world, bequeathing peace, giving repentance, baptizing with the Spirit, all is changed. That which was sought in nothingness, is found in a Father. The death of self is the beginning of a new life, of purified affections, energies, memories, hopes. These have their fruition in God. These realize their glory when He is revealed.   Therefore it is true, as it was of old, that the desire of nations is for a Christ, a Son of Man; but for a Christ, a Son of Man in whom we may see the Father. Therefore it is true, as it was of old, that the star which shall guide the wise men from the East, be they Buddhists, Brahmins, Mahometans, will rest on the cradle where the young Child lies; but will rest there because that Child has come to manifest the glory of GOD.   Therefore it is true, as it was of old, that the preachers of a Gospel to the Gentiles must go forth telling them that the Word who is their Light, took flesh and dwelt on earth, and suffered the death of the Cross, and that they may be signed with the sign of His Cross; but it is because the Wisdom and Power of GOD were revealed at Calvary; it is because the assurance was given there that sinful and dying men shall hereafter behold the face of GOD, and that His Name shall be on their foreheads.

II.

CHRIST AMONG THE DOCTORS.

LUKE II. 46, 47.

" AND IT CAME TO PASS, THAT AFTER THREE DAYS THEY FOUND
HIM IN THE TEMPLE, SITTING IN THE MIDST OF THE DOCTORS,
BOTH HEARING THEM, AND ASKING THEM QUESTIONS. AND ALL
THAT HEARD HIM WERE ASTONISHED AT HIS UNDERSTANDING AND
ANSWERS."

THE manifestation to the Magians, which was brought
before us in the service of Thursday, is recorded by
St. Matthew. This manifestation to the doctors is
only spoken of by St. Luke. We might have expected that the places of the narratives would have
been reversed; that St. Matthew, who wrote for
Jews, would have spoken of that which directly concerned Jews; that St. Luke, the companion of St.
Paul, would have seized upon the fact which has
been always described of as the revelation of Christ
to the Gentiles. But it should be considered that
he who cared especially to set forth a King of the
Jews, would very appropriately notice the search of
the Wise Men for such a King, and the homage

C

which they paid Him when they had found Him.
And I think there was no one fitter to speak of the
way in which the Light of the World burst upon the
minds of the Rabbis in the Temple, than he who
had conversed with the pupil of Gamaliel, and had
carefully studied the process of his illumination.

What the Church seems especially to impress upon
us by bringing these two facts together, and classing
them under the common name of Epiphany, is that
every act of our Lord, from His birth onwards, is to
be looked upon as a disclosure of the glory of the
only-begotten Son of the Father—of Him from whose
Grace and Truth all the grace and truth of men had
proceeded.   So considered, these old records which
some suspect and would like to cast off, are seen to
be most consistent with the tenour of the history,
most helpful in delivering us from confusions respecting that history, and respecting the meaning of
the word Revelation.   We think it natural and reasonable that the Apostles, being endowed with certain miraculous powers, should be able to build up
a Church among Jews and Gentiles.   Had we the
like powers, we have little doubt we might convert
Hindoos and Mussulmans as well as the great body
of those who are Christians only in name.   The
Apostles had no dream that they had any such
charms for acting on the hearts and consciences of
men.   They said that the Gospel itself was the "*power
of God unto salvation, to the Jew first, and also to*

the Greek." They said that what they had to do was
to preach Christ crucified, because in His weakness
and humiliation were made known the power and
wisdom of God. In other words, it was He who was
revealing Himself, through their preaching, to that
eye which was intended to receive the discovery, and
was waiting for it. The story of the Star in the East
leading the Wise men to the King whom they were
asking the stars to tell them of, explains how He
made either words or signs effectual for His own
mighty purpose. And the story of His listening to
the doctors in the Temple, and questioning them,
shows how He compelled a set of men, who were
the slaves of words, or rather of letters, who believed
that all power lay in them, to confess a mightier
power in Him.

I. This is the subject which I think is especially
forced upon us by the Gospel today. There were
met in the Temple a number of grave men, full of
all the learning which could be got from the traditions of the past, full, as they thought, of all the
learning which could be got from the words and lives
of Patriots, Lawgivers, holy men. It was no profane wisdom that they were occupied with. Some
of them might have a little measure of it. All would
value it only as it illustrated the Divine wisdom
which had been imparted to their land, or as a foil
to set off its brightness and purity. They might not
be wholly agreed about the meaning of the words by

which they set such store. The Psalms were open to very different interpretations. They were not at one upon the question where and how this or that prophecy would be accomplished. They might differ even upon the relative worth of different commandments—still more when they compared those commandments, simple, broad, and general, with the accurate rules which had been transmitted to them by elders and doctors. Probably there was no doubt in the minds of the majority that the observance of the commandments was comparatively an easy and vulgar thing, that the practice of those refined rules was the sign of a more exact and scrupulous holiness, at all events a step to it. Some however there would be among them who derided such practices as idle and unnecessary. Ordinary morality, they would say, such as the Commandments prescribed, was what God demanded; the maxims of an ascetic devotion had been needlessly grafted upon these. Amidst all such differences there would be a general impression that whatever there was in the land of religion or acquaintance with the oracles of God, dwelt among them. Age, and the knowledge of what former times had bequeathed, were theirs. They were the shepherds of the people. Whether the sheep went right or wrong depended mainly on their submission to this guidance or their neglect of it.

Into this grave and venerable consistory there enters a Boy just twelve years of age. No one can tell exactly how he came there. But of course it is a promising sign, a sign of early devotion, that he should like to be in the Temple. The great festival is just over. Amidst the numbers who frequented it, it is no wonder if there should be one who has been seized with awe and admiration by those beautiful buildings, or by the sense of that which they denote. This one is apparently a fugitive from his parents. He may have wandered from them by accident, or he may have a thought, if his tribe and the rules of the elders permit it, of giving himself to the service of that place. A friendly Rabbi might think it worth while to question him about his purposes, to ascertain why he was lingering in those precincts.

(1.) So he stands among the Rabbis, not affrighted certainly by their dignity, with no sign of bashfulness, but also with none of forwardness. He is not eager to speak. He wishes to listen. The doctors are conversing about matters which they presume are far above the comprehension of a boy. And there is in the face of this boy nothing which tells of assumption or precocity, rather of quietness and docility. Such a one may be allowed to hear their discourse; it may impress him hereafter, if not at once, with reverence for their persons and their office. And what was that listening of his? In the highest sense, as in every lower one, the maxim holds good, " Everything is received according to the measure of the receiver." We can imagine how

*

glibly the familiar texts would be repeated by one
and another,—how often 'sins' and 'repentance'
would be in their mouths,—how they would debate
about the hope of Israel and the promise of dominion over the Gentiles,—how they would speak of
all God's doings with them, if they did not actually
pronounce the Name which signified his hidden essence. What awful, unutterable meanings lay beneath
these sounds ! And the meaning, not the sound, was
that to which the Boy was listening. That of which
the learned men had only the faintest consciousness,
entered into His inmost being. It was in the fullest sense listening, reverent and awful listening,—
the listening of a child, not the judgment of a man.
It is hard for us to make that distinction ; but if
we believe the Incarnation, we shall try to make it.
We shall believe that the Child was a child, the
Boy a boy ; that the Child was perfect as such, and
therefore did not anticipate its after-growth, which
would imply imperfection ; that the Boy was a perfect boy, and therefore had none of that forestal-
ling of manhood which our consciences and reason
tell us is irregular and untrue. And this is not, as
some would state it, merely in order that we may
do justice to the Humanity of Christ. We cannot
in any other way see how the Divinity manifested
itself through the Humanity, how it addressed itself
to all the conditions and needs of Humanity. We
may make a notion to ourselves of Divinity as un-

limited wisdom and power; but such notions are good for very little. What we want is to know what wisdom and power are in their fullest, highest sense, not to mould and contract them by our understandings, and then fancy we make amends for the contraction by giving them the epithet 'unlimited.'

Do you suppose that those Rabbis, after forty, say, or fifty years, of reading and copying out the Law, of comparing and registering the different commentaries upon it, had ever felt such a presence of Divinity with them, as when they looked into the face of that listening Boy? They could copy the letters, they could overlook the commentaries. If there was something very deep and mysterious beneath them, they could reduce it into Cabbala; they could talk of it as *their* possession, *their* distinction from the multitude. But which of them could penetrate the awe and mystery of that countenance, clear and bright as it was? What spoke to them through that, could be reduced into no Cabbala. They could never say, " *That* raises us above the rest of our countrymen." They must have felt : "That face speaks to us of our " connection with Galilean peasants; it reminds us " that we are of the same flesh and blood with them. " While we look at it, does it not seem as if we were " more glorious to be of the same flesh and blood " with any one that is called a man, than to have " all this learning of ours?" A strange message to

come to men who must uphold their reputation for
sanctity and wisdom before the multitude! Yet
surely a divine message! Surely those listening eyes
were reading their very hearts. Surely they knew
better than they ever did before, that GOD was reading them.

(2.) And then came the *questions.* " *He was sitting
among them,*" it is said, " *both hearing them and asking
them questions.*" Still all is suitable to the boy. He
pronounces on nothing. He does not lay down the
law upon this matter or that. The time may come
when He shall go up into a mountain and open His
lips, and speak as one having authority. But that
time is not yet. He is not above the Scribes, but is
sitting at their feet. He desires to know what *they*
think about this commandment in the Law, about
this sentence of David or Isaiah. At first, no doubt,
the answers are all ready. They can tell that which
one elder or another had written down or expressed
orally to his disciples. They begin to give out the
oracles, perhaps with an air of patronage or condescension, to the earnest youth. Why do the patronage and the condescension disappear? Why is the
well-trained memory at fault? Why is there that
look of puzzle and perplexity, almost of terror, on
the countenances of those who are used to resolve
all riddles, to silence all disputes? The question
has gone beneath commentary and text both. The
second-hand answer does not avail. What, for in-

stance, could it profit to give the best exposition of
the Commandments, if the Child with those deep,
searching eyes said : " He who spoke these commandments calls himself The Lord *thy* God.   What is this
Thy ? Is He indeed the God of each of you ?   He
speaks as if He were a Deliverer out of bondage.   Is
that indeed so ?   Was He only a Deliverer of our
fathers in the days of old, or is he that still, that
now ?   The prophets always describe Him as the
Living God—the God from generation to generation.
What ! is He then actually with us as He was with
them, speaking to us as He spoke to them ?   He is
described as a Father pitying His children, putting
away their sins from them, and yet as hating all iniquity.   Is that so still?   Does He actually seek to
make men right?"

I have supposed, you see, questions which had no
novelty or strangeness in them ; questions which arose
directly out of the language of the Holy Book.   If
these had been all,—if there had been none deeper
than these—deeper than we can think of,—what must
have been their effect ?   No Rabbi can have imputed
captious doubt, premature disbelief to the *speaker.*
May not many a one have been led to suspect *himself*
of doubt and disbelief?   May not many a one have
thought : " It cannot be that the words are to be
" taken in this simple strict sense ; if so, the Book is
" not the one I thought I knew from beginning to
" end?"   May not another have said : " Yes ! thanks

" be to God, that must be what is written. I did not
" perceive it, but so it is. The King of kings can-
" not be far from us. He must be in this place ; and
" though it is the holy place,—the place which He
" chose to put His name in,—I knew it not ?"

(3.) We are told that " *all who heard this child were
astonished at his understanding and answers.*" So
that they must have asked Him questions as He asked
them. No doubt He showed as much willingness to
submit to their catechism as He had shown eagerness to receive whatever they had to impart ; a child,
whichever task he was engaged in,—taught by elder
men, doing what they required. And the answers,
we may be sure, like the questions, would not be
new or rare or far-fetched. They would be startling
because they presented the words of holy men in
their direct, full, original force ; because they did
not make veils for the sense, but drew away a veil
which had concealed it ; because the words came forth
in them as if the men were there in whose hearts
they had been as a burning fire ; because the words
were shown to be not theirs, but His who had
spoken to them, and had declared His own purpose
through them. The answers, I repeat it, were not
veils ; they were a Revelation, or Unveiling ; and that
Revelation, or Unveiling, was not of a System or of
a Religion, but of Him who had said, " Let not the
rich man glory in his riches, nor the wise man in
his wisdom, but let him that glorieth glory in this,

that he *knoweth* Me, that I execute judgment and righteousness in the earth."

It was therefore, as the Evangelist expresses it, the *understanding* of this child which astonished the doctors. We can see what must have been the impression upon their minds. This boy entered into the very sense of the words which they had read and copied and committed to memory. They had never *understood* the words as spoken to themselves. They had drawn conclusions from the words, generalized notions from them. But their hearts had never come into contact with them. They were idols to be worshiped at a distance; not worshiped till all the dangerous life had been extracted from them, till they were as powerless to act or teach or govern as the stocks and stones of the heathen, which had been denounced in them. What a wonder, to see them quick and breathing again in the answers of this Child! What a wonder, to find that He went along, not only with them, but with the very mind of Him from whom they had proceeded; that *He* spoke like one who had been brought up with Him, like a sharer of His counsels!

(4.) Although, therefore, one discovers nothing in the listening or questioning or answering of this Boy which interferes with that growth in wisdom and stature of which St. Luke speaks,—with that gradual unfolding of the human life which was necessary to the manifestation of the Divine life,—there is *that*

foreshadowing of after-years which we generally discern in an individual man when we are acquainted
with the facts of his story, and which we should confidently expect in *the* Man, the Representative of the
Race.   After He had entered upon His ministry,—
when He was exercising the fullness of His power,
when He was denouncing those Scribes and Pharisees to whom He had listened in the Temple,—He was
still unveiling some of the deepest mysteries of the
Kingdom of Heaven, by asking questions of his disciples and the multitude, that being the last, which
awakened so much awe, " *What think ye of Christ ?
whose Son is He ?*"; He was still answering those who
asked Him, " *What was the chief commandment ?*"
" *Shall we give tribute to Cæsar ?*" " *Whose wife will
the woman be hereafter, who had the seven husbands on
earth ?*"   He was again a silent hearer of the charges
against Him in the Sanhedrim, till that adjuration
of the High Priest to declare whether He was the
Son of God brought forth that final answer, " Thou
hast said ; nevertheless I say unto you, Hereafter shall
ye see the *Son of Man* sitting on the right-hand of
power, and coming in the clouds of Heaven."   In all
these ways His earliest acts on earth and His latest
exhibited a divine harmony.   His understanding of
the ways of God was more and more discovering His
name to be that which the prophet had proclaimed,
" *He shall be called Wonderful*, COUNSELLOR."   And
the question to Mary and Joseph, when they sought

Him sorrowing, *Wist ye not that I must be about my Father's business?*" was the preparation for His baptism, and for the final prayer, "Father, glorify Thy Son, that Thy Son also may glorify Thee."

II. But the subject is for us no less than for the Rabbis. I will mention some of the lessons which I think lie in it, and which we need especially at this time.

(1.) And first: There is, in many divines—in many Christians who are not divines—a great fear of questions. "Certain things," they say, "have been settled "long ago. To disturb the settlement is perilous. "If we are humble and modest, we shall be content 'without *knowledge* of divine things. Probabilities, "distant approximations to knowledge, are all to which "creatures such as we are can aspire." Now, brethren, as long as I believe in Jesus Christ, the only-begotten Son of God, our Lord;—as long as I seek for my standard of modesty and humility in Him,—so ong I must protest against the kind of modesty and humility which these disciples of His affect. I find Him beginning His pilgrimage on earth as a questioner. I find Him astonishing the upholders of a long and safe tradition by that method. I find Him sanctioning that as His own sound method of detecting falsehood and laziness, and of urging men to seek Truth that they may find it. Brethren, I believe that Christ has been asking questions from that day to this; that He is asking questions of us all, divines and laymen, now; that the questions come to us in multitudes of shapes, through a multitude of lips;—through children tormenting their parents and teachers about the wonderful meaning of *words* which have become to *them* mere familiar sounds, of *things* which they have gazed at till they have forgotten that there is any life or mystery in them at all;—through men who have been exercised with the puzzles of Philosophy, and want to find some ground upon which they may stand, a ground of reality, not of convention;—through the cravings of men who know nothing of Philosophy, but who have found enough in their own thoughts and in the world to amaze and confound them;—through the frivolous, even, who appear to be engaged in no search at all, who only wish to throw down some system or to build up one for their own fame, but who nevertheless, because they are men, cannot be merely busy in that poor occupation, and will be sure to start some inquiry which we may pursue to its issue if they will not. I am greatly afraid that when we try to silence any of these questions we are trying to silence the voice of Christ, in others and in ourselves; that we do not like Him to sift us and make us understand what in us is of Him, and will bear the fires of His judgment-day; what is wood, hay, stubble of our own, and must be burnt up in those fires.

(2.) I know how liable statements like these are to be misunderstood, as if one wished to discourage

reverence for the past, as if one thought there were
no oracles of God which were stronger and deeper than
all the reasonings and speculations of men. I have
endeavoured to show you today how fair and reasonable these charges are. Just because I would uphold
reverence for the past;—just because I think our
own speculations and reasonings are so much feebler
than the oracles of God,—I dare not stifle one anxious question of men respecting the faith of other
days, respecting those oracles of God. The Rabbis
did not reverence the past. They accepted its decrees.
They had no fellowship with the life and sufferings of
its men. They did not honour the oracles of God.
They were buried under their own reasonings and
speculations. They could not receive any communication as coming directly to the hearts of men from
the Ruler of their hearts. No men needed so much
to become little children, to recover the wisdom of
children. That they might attain that wisdom the
Child came amongst them, listened to them, asked
them questions, answered their questions.

I think that same Child, who has the government
on His shoulders, hears us, questions us, answers us
for the same end. There are those doubtless who
wish to cut us off from all communion with the
past, telling us that it is a chain upon our freedom.
There are those who say the Bible is an obsolete
book, useful in the infancy of the world, unworthy of
such advanced sages as we are. You do not confute

these objectors by arguing against them, by opposing
the weight of opinion to them, by emulating their
hard and scoffing temper. It is not that they question too much, but too little. They have never asked
themselves what they want, what mankind wants. If
they once fairly grappled with these questions, they
would begin to reverence those who wept and bled
that mankind might have what it wants; they would
be filled with shame, as they contrast the tears and
blood with their boasting. They would hear an old
text telling them secrets of their own being, which
the wisdom that mocks at texts has never penetrated.
For they would perceive that they want—that mankind wants—the actual knowledge of God; that for
this men have sighed and cried in every country and
age of the world; that if this knowledge is not to be
had, what is called Self-knowledge is either a miserable delusion or a curse and a horror. So you may
lead even proud deniers to come, as little children,
not only to the Bible, but to that Child whom the
Bible declares to be the firstborn of Men, the perfect
manifestation of God.

(3.) This is the subject with which I began, and
with which I shall end. Do *our* Doctors confess Jesus
Christ to be that perfect manifestation of God? Do
they admit that He came into the world, in very deed,
to show men of the Father? Do they confess that
this was His Father's business which he was about,
from His cradle to His Cross? Nay, that in this He

was occupied ever since the world was made; that
in this He will be occupied for ever and ever? Alas!
in the very highest quarters of English Theology,
we are taught a doctrine the very reverse of this.
The only way, we are told, to confute Rationalism,
to establish Christianity, is to affirm that God cannot
be known; that man is prohibited by his constitution
from seeking such knowledge. The justification for
this startling doctrine lies in the simple proposition,
"We cannot conceive the inconceivable," a maxim
so self-evident, that it must have swept all thoughts
about an invisible world, or a divine Being, before it,
if there had not been a deeply grounded conviction in
human beings, however variously expressed, or however unable to express itself, that unless we can rise
above our conceptions, above ourselves, there is for us
no science of things, no knowledge of persons—fathers,
brothers, friends; that all affection must perish as
well (in the true sense of the word) as all understanding. That inward belief, the loss of which, one has
been wont to suppose, is the loss of every aspiration
after goodness or nobleness, the destruction of any
morality but that which is conventional,—that belief
has given rise to the cry that some Being who is above
all our thoughts and conceptions, but who must be the
ground and standard of them all, would tell us what
He is, and therefore what we are. The faith of our fathers was that God answered this cry which He had
awakened; that He did come forth in the person

of His only-begotten Son, to show men what He
is; that He did send His Spirit into the hearts of
men, that all might know Him, from the least to the
greatest. The confession of this Revelation was their
orthodoxy. They had no notion of a system or
scheme of Religion, apart from a Manifestation of
God to men. I believe, brethren, that any scheme
or system of Religion which has not such a Manifestation for its basis,—any scheme or system constructed out of the Bible, or upon a theory of our own
nature,—will effect nothing for the good of mankind.
I believe the Child who stood in the Temple will destroy it. I believe He has saved and will save the
world, which by wisdom knew not God from that
fatal ignorance, by revealing Himself as His Father's
Wisdom, as the source of all Wisdom in us.

III.

ST. PAUL AT ATHENS.

ACTS XVII. 26–31.

" AND HATH MADE OF ONE BLOOD ALL NATIONS OF MEN FOR TO DWELL
ON ALL THE FACE OF THE EARTH, AND HATH DETERMINED THE
TIMES BEFORE APPOINTED, AND THE BOUNDS OF THEIR HABITA-
TION ; THAT THEY SHOULD SEEK THE LORD, IF HAPLY THEY MIGHT
FEEL AFTER HIM, AND FIND HIM, THOUGH HE BE NOT FAR FROM
EVERY ONE OF US : FOR IN HIM WE LIVE, AND MOVE, AND HAVE
OUR BEING ; AS CERTAIN ALSO OF YOUR OWN POETS HAVE SAID, FOR
WE ARE ALSO HIS OFFSPRING. FORASMUCH THEN AS WE ARE THE
OFFSPRING OF GOD, WE OUGHT NOT TO THINK THAT THE GODHEAD
IS LIKE UNTO GOLD, OR SILVER, OR STONE, GRAVEN BY ART AND
MAN'S DEVICE. AND THE TIMES OF THIS IGNORANCE GOD WINKED
AT ; BUT NOW COMMANDETH ALL MEN EVERYWHERE TO REPENT ;
BECAUSE HE HATH APPOINTED A DAY, IN THE WHICH HE WILL
JUDGE THE WORLD IN RIGHTEOUSNESS BY THAT MAN WHOM HE
HATH ORDAINED ; WHEREOF HE HATH GIVEN ASSURANCE UNTO
ALL MEN, IN THAT HE HATH RAISED HIM FROM THE DEAD."

THE picture of St. Paul at Athens, which is given us
in the Acts of the Apostles, has been filled up with
many lights and shades by the imagination of the
reader. But these are the great outlines which cannot be effaced. He was grieved in spirit when he

saw the city wholly given to idolatry ; he disputed in
the market-place with philosophers of different sects ;
the curiosity of the people to hear some new thing
would not suffer him to abstain from a general statement of his object in coming to Greece, if he had
desired to be silent ; he did actually deliver the most
elaborate of all his discourses on Mars' Hill.

What that discourse would have been if he had
adopted the notion respecting the right method ·of
spreading Christianity, which is most prevalent and
admired amongst us in this day, we can have no difficulty in conjecturing. He would have begun with
offering proofs that all other nations had been left
to follow their own courses, unguided and untended,
while his had been the depositary of a divine communication. There was evidence,—he would say,—
not demonstrative, but sufficient to satisfy men who
were alive to their own perils and their own ignorance, that the Ruler of the world had given intimations concerning His will to the children of Abraham.
These intimations, so far as they concerned His nature and purposes, could not be called strictly true—
for men had no faculties wherewith to receive the knowledge of an infinite Being. But they were such approximations to truth as it was desirable for men to
receive. Precepts founded upon them had proved very
beneficial in the practice of life. Amongst these precepts was one against the worship of graven images.
No reason, of course, was given for it. How can an

infinite Being be expected to give reasons for His acts? How could they be made intelligible to men if they were given? But supposing the Lawgiver possessed infinite power to enforce His decrees, was it safe to set any of them aside?

Then proceeding from the people to the learned, he would show triumphantly how every speculation respecting the gods had proved abortive and ridiculous. He would show that by the very conditions of man's being it must be so; that the dreams of men respecting a Nature so immeasurably transcending theirs, so altogether different from theirs, could have no counterpart in reality. Of course he would deal his blows with perfect impartiality. This would be aimed at the self-confidence of the Epicurean denier, that at the scepticism of the Academic, a third at the physico-theology and stern ethics of the Stoic. If there was any departure from this rule, it would be in the case of some particularly earnest inquirer. It must be a greater victory for the Gospel to expose his blunders and failures, than those of a mere sophist or professional disputer. Then, having cleared the ground of all other opinions and speculations, with what satisfaction would he commend his own religion to the acceptance of the multitude! He would represent it as milder, less national, less dogmatic, than the Jewish from which it had sprung. He would appeal to the common sense of the Athenians whether, in the utter ignorance of divine things in which they were and must be, the prudent course was not to accept a faith which promised inconceivable rewards to its champions, which denounced utter ruin against those who rejected it.

I can conceive only two reasons which can be assigned by those who approve this kind of teaching, why it should not have been St. Paul's. One is, that he was not learned enough to know the opinions of sages, or not logical enough to produce *the* overwhelming argument against them. To such an objection I merely reply, that *I* presume St. Paul to have been sent forth with such weapons as were fitted for the work he had to do; if they think otherwise, they should say so boldly. The other is, that such language might have exposed the speaker to a storm of Greek indignation. But St. Paul, according to the opinion of him we have been wont to entertain, was a brave man, whose testimony would not have been more stern when he was in security than when he was in danger. Nor am I prepared to admit that the kind of discourse I have imagined, would have been more perilous to the Apostle, than those which had drawn down upon him the fanatical rage of Jews at Thessalonica and Berea. If his main object was to proselytize for a certain religion, I am not sure that it might not have induced more Athenians to join him than Dionysius and Damaris. For it would have appealed to passions which St. Paul in his actual speech did not invoke. Epicureans and Academics would have seen great plausibility in the denunciations of the popular worship. Each would have welcomed the sneers at the philosophical system of the other. St. Paul's own countrymen—if any were present—would have recognized in him a champion, not an enemy, of their exclusiveness.

But let us consider now, not what St. Paul might have said, but what he did say, to the people of this idolatrous, philosophical, news-loving city.

I. *" God hath made of one blood all nations of men, to dwell upon all the face of the earth, and hath determined the times before appointed, and the bounds of their habitation."* This was the lesson which the Apostle had learnt by earnest meditation on the calling of his own nation, by his study of the Law and the prophets. God hath formed the nations of one blood, of one family. God hath watched over the bounds, the circumstances, the destiny, of each nation upon the face of the earth. The Jewish nation had existed to be a witness for this universal fellowship among the nations. It had existed as a witness against that which tended to divide them and set them at war. It had existed also as a witness for the special work of each one of those bodies which had its definite geographical limits, its sympathies of kindred and race. It existed to say, " The one living and true God has created you all to be one. The one living and true God has assigned you your tasks. He has never left you alone. No one fact of your history has lain beyond the

circle of His providence. No one thought has been
awakened in your minds without His teaching and
guidance. I, the Jew, the child of Abraham, stand
forth to make that claim on behalf of the God whom
I worship. I stand forth solemnly to repudiate the
doctrine that any nation whatever has a right to deny
connection with any other. I, the Jew, the child of
Abraham, stand forth to declare that you, the men of
Athens, have had a divine vocation, that the God of all
has appointed you to play a distinct and a very remarkable part in His great drama. I declare that
you are utterly wrong when you affirm that the great
deeds of your fathers are to be ascribed to them, not
to Him; that your institutions, your freedom, your
wisdom, are human, so as not to be also in the highest sense divine." This is a wonderful message, very
unlike that one which we heard just now. But I ask
you to read St. Paul's own words attentively, and
see whether they express less than my paraphrase of
them; whether they do not express far more.

II. But *why* has God chosen out the particular
nations? *Why* has He ordered the times before appointed and the bounds of their habitation? Here
is St. Paul's answer: " *That they may seek the Lord,
if haply they may feel after Him, and find Him.*"
According to this explanation of an inspired Apostle,
it was God himself who stirred up the thoughts and
inquiries of men about His Being and Nature. Nay,
every circumstance of their outward position was de-

vised and ordained expressly for the purpose of giving this impulse, this direction, to their thoughts. Certainly, if we believed that, many puzzles in history— oppressive puzzles to those who read it as the history of their fellow-beings—would be solved. One sees how the soil and climate, the temperament of peculiar races, their apprehensions concerning law and government, their internal struggles, their relations with neighbours, have modified all their thoughts and feelings; but especially their apprehensions of the invisible world and of divine powers. If one might assure oneself that a soil fertile or rugged, a climate genial or cruel, the need of rule, the need of freedom, the activity which led to wars, the deeper craving for peace, all had been instruments of giving them some glimpse of a Guide and Ruler,—had led them to grasp at something which is really in Him, some side of His character, some purpose of His will,—the past would become an illuminated, not an utterly dark scroll. How one apprehension should become feeble, distorted,— how others should be rejected for its sake,—how when others asserted their right and necessity, all polytheistic confusions and contradictions should arise,— how they might become fixed in the mind by selfish fears,—how they would be perpetuated by dishonest priests seeking to keep up an impression of their own power, confounding that with the unseen power,— this we can understand without much difficulty from later experience. The hard question is, What was the

starting-point of those thoughts ? and that other, How
were they kept alive in men's minds, when so much
in nature and themselves was confuting them ? To
these questions St. Paul gives his decided reply. This
feeling after God,—which has been discovered, under
some condition or other, in all tribes of the earth,
which has had the most marked tokens of being a
human necessity, and yet which a thousand tendencies
in man have threatened with death as well as with
derangement,—this the Creator Himself has called
forth and sustained ; without His first word it could
not have been,—without His continual presence and
inspiration it must have ceased altogether.

III. Bold as this statement is,—strange as it must
sound to those who have persuaded themselves that
the method of defending the principles of the Old
Testament is to treat all heathen apprehensions of
God as merely traditive or merely imaginary,—it is
less startling than the words which follow them. We
are so familiar with them,—they have so leavened the
dialect of Christendom,—that we do not consider how
awful they are in themselves, how much more remarkable they are for the place in which they were uttered, how they contradict some of our most approved
religious and philosophical maxims. *" Though He is
not far from every one of us. For in Him we live and
move and have our being."* Oh, how often has the
wish presented itself to many of us that we had never
heard these words in our childhood !—we think they

would burst upon us with such overpowering strength
if we were listening to them for the first time. It
is an ungrateful and a foolish wish. We have been
influenced by them all our lives through, in ways we
cannot conceive, and shall not know till the day that
discovers all things. We might not have been more
thrilled by them than any of the crowd were who stood
about St. Paul in the Areopagus; they may break
now through all the frost of custom; they may come
on us like guilty things surprised by a presence that
we have forgotten. But is there not something in
them which we shrink from because we think it may
mislead us into a dangerous Pantheism? Do we not
say to ourselves, " That is an especial peril of this
" time. The passage is no doubt true, as it occurs in
" the Bible. But since it is liable to be perverted,
" *we* had better dwell upon some different announce-
" ment, however suitable that may have been for other
" ages, which were prone to another kind of error."
Now consider. If there was a city in all the world
which was exposed to the assaults of Pantheism,—
not in some other age, but in the very age when the
Apostle visited it,—that city was assuredly Athens.
Each form of idolatry, each form of speculation, was
bearing towards this gulf; each, as it became weak,
was sure to be absorbed in it. If St. Paul had no
divine intimation of the fact, his discourses with the
philosophers in the market-place must have made
him aware of it. He must have seen it in the very

inscription which was the text of his discourse. The
dedication to the Unknown God,—whether it only
indicated a desire in a time of pestilence to invoke
all imaginable or possible assistance,—whether it expressed a sense of some Being who could not be represented as demons or demigods were represented,—
equally declared that the mind of the nation was aim-
ing at an all-inclusive worship, and that as one definite object after another lost its hold upon them,
more and more would be drawn into a lazy acknowledgment of the vague and indefinite. With this
conviction full on his mind, St. Paul uses the words,
*" He is not far from every one of us ; for in Him we
live and move and are."*

I conclude, then, that St. Paul regarded this statement as the one great protest against Pantheism, and
all other evil tendencies to which the Athenian was
liable ; a protest against it, because it was the full and
distinct assertion of the truth which was underlying
Pantheism, and which Pantheism was perverting ; a
protest against it, because no proclamation was so certain, if it was received, to inspire men with awe of
that Personal Being whom Pantheism was denying.
The Apostle then is the standing witness for the
maxim which is applicable to all places and all times,
that you can only combat any prevalent error by seeking for the divine principle of which it is the coun-
terfeit. Till you do that, your cleverest scoffs and reasonings will all serve to strengthen, not to abate its
virulence.

IV. At last the Apostle approaches one of the teachers whom we may suppose he wishes to confute. He speaks, indeed, not of a philosopher, but of a poet; but then poets in the latter days were fond of enunciating philosophical sentiments, as in the earlier days they had done so much to build up the popular mythology. And here is a sentiment of Aratus which may be turned to either account. It may justify the old Homeric notion of men having a divine parentage; it may assert the proud notion of sages, that men by wisdom can make themselves gods; "For we also are His offspring."

Surely, it might be said, the sentiment is all the more alarming because the singular number is used instead of the plural. To speak of a son of the Gods—of Apollo or Venus, was merely to use a phrase which most in that time would have felt to be a fable, or would have explained as a metaphor. To speak of *His* offspring was to mount into a higher region, and to assert for the poor frivolous people who cared only to tell or hear some new thing, that their origin was divine. Could you believe it?—St. Paul adopts the phrase in this aggravated sense; he indorses the words of the poet; he applies them not to his own countrymen, or some portion of his own countrymen, but to his heathen audience. He does not speak of some excepted persons among them; some who had arrived by any process at higher intuitions. He resorts to none of the qualifications which the writer of the

words would probably himself have adopted. He looks
out upon the jeering, laughing mass about him, and
says, "We—you and I—also are His offspring; the
" offspring of that Unknown God, that God who made
" the heavens and the earth, and all things therein,
" whom I have been declaring to you."

V. He does not stop here. He builds an argument
upon this mighty assumption. It is *the* argument
against that idolatry which had pressed so heavily
upon his spirit. Upon it he rests the soundness and
reasonableness of the Second Commandment. *" Forasmuch then as we are the offspring of God, we ought
not to think that the Godhead is like unto gold, or
silver, or stone, graven by art and man's device."* Do
not say that this was an additional motive which he
urges for their abandoning the tradition of their
fathers, the habit of their city. It is the only motive.
He cannot urge them to make that change which involves such a convulsion in the whole moral being,
which cuts asunder so many links of old affection, if
the doctrine of their poet is not true, if they have not
a right to claim God as related to them,—God as, in
the strictest, fullest sense, their Father. I say again,
in the strictest, fullest sense; not in some vague sense,
which is indeed Pantheistical, a sense which represents
Him as the Father of all cattle and trees and flowers, and therefore their Father. The argument would
be utterly worthless and contemptible if that were
his meaning. They might make the Godhead in the

likeness of any object in nature,—they might mould Him according to their conceptions of any of those objects,—if that were all. It was because He was the Father of them, the Father of their spirits,—because they were spiritual beings created in His spiritual likeness, created to feel after Him and find Him,—it was therefore that the conceiving Him under any of these notions of theirs, the casting Him in any material shape, was so degrading and abominable. The whole burning indignation of the Jew against the gods of the hills and the groves comes forth in this assertion, which is nevertheless so full of tenderness for every heathen, and which could only have been uttered by one who believed that God had loved the whole world, and had sent His Son to take upon Him the nature of the dweller in Athens as much as of the dweller in Jerusalem.

VI. The tenderness to heathens,—the justification of God's ways to men in all ages,—the assertion of the ground upon which he had affirmed all to be of one flesh and blood,—comes out fully in the next passage of the discourse. *"And the times of this ignorance God winked at, but now He commandeth all men everywhere to repent."* I will not debate about the force of the word which we translate *winked at,* or inquire whether any better expression might have been found. No doubt it might have been an advantage to preserve the sentence in St. Paul's own form, by using a participle in the first clause. But at least

we may be sure that this sentence does not contradict the Apostle's previous assertion, that God had
not overlooked the different nations of the earth, so
as not to order the bounds of their habitations, and
to direct the search after Him; on the other hand,
that it is incompatible with the headlong and un-
godly conclusion which divines have often sanctioned
respecting the condition of the heathen world, and
the amount of guilt which was involved in its idol-
worship. St. Paul assuredly does not tell the Athenians what Tertullian's higher inspiration and later
revelation enabled him to proclaim with absolute certainty, that their fathers were doomed to hopeless
perdition. That opinion which (it is said) urged the
honest barbarian monarch to refuse baptism, was not
thrust before the Greek; an entirely different one was
suggested to him. But the message to the men of that
generation was not less strong and decisive, because
it involved no judgment upon previous generations.
"*God commandeth you to repent.*" " Since by me He
tells you that the words of your poet are fulfilled,—that
He has sent His Son to claim you as His offspring,—
by me He commands you to cast aside the gods of
gold and silver, made by art and man's device; by
me He bids you to turn round to Him and own Him
as your Father. But not only by me. The message
is to your consciences. The message comes straight
from Him to them. He commands repentance. He
gives repentance to all that will have it. If you are

conscious of separation from Him who is so near to you, He destroys the separation. If you have felt after Him, and not been able to find Him, He will reveal Himself to you. The message is to all men everywhere. The separate gods, the material gods, shall not for ever tear the nations asunder. All in all nations are invited to become brothers with each other, by taking up their position as offspring of the same Father."

VII. But is not that call to repentance fortified by a threat of punishment? If it were, I should produce it, and dwell upon it; for I do not think we can warn people too much of the heavy punishment which they bring upon themselves, by continuing servants of material, sensual, unreal things, and by not taking up their rights as children of a gracious and righteous Father. But though I might like the word if it was in St. Paul's discourse, I cannot introduce it when it is not there. St. Paul speaks of *judgment*, not of *punishment*. He speaks of " *a day in which God will judge the world by that Man whom He hath ordained, whereof He hath given assurance in that He hath raised Him from the dead.*" I am bound to say that the two modes of speaking are wide as the poles asunder, however in our carelessness we may confound them. To proclaim a judgment, is to proclaim an accurate discrimination of acts and characters. To proclaim a judgment of God, is to proclaim that *He* will discriminate who knows characters and acts perfectly. To

E

proclaim a judgment of God by that Man whom He
has ordained, is to declare that He will apply to men
that kind of measure which the Son of Man applied
when He was upon earth. Now *He* said, " *It shall
be more tolerable for Sodom and Gomorrah in the day
of judgment than for Chorazin and Bethsaida.*" He
preached a gospel to publicans and harlots. He said,
" *Woe unto you, Scribes and Pharisees.*" He said to
His disciples, " *Judge not, that ye be not judged.*" In
the face of such language, how could St. Paul dare
to stand up among the Athenians, and tell them that
either they or their fathers would be cast off by God,
who had not cast them off yet? How could he help
telling them that there would assuredly be a judging
and sifting of all nations and all men, inasmuch as
the Son of Man, the risen Head of Nations and of
Men, had come to bind them all to God,—to bind
them all to each other? How could he help saying,
" He whom you have been seeking for,—He who has
" been seeking for you,—will be revealed in the full-
" ness of His glory. He will know what each nation
" has done in fulfilment of the purpose for which it
" was called out. He will know what each man has
" done to fulfil the purpose for which he was sent
" into the world. He will know who have followed
" the light which He gave them, and sought for Him ;
" who have loved darkness rather than light, and
" have chosen death. I, Paul, can pass no judgment
" upon you or any one. I judge not my own self.

" But I know that that judgment will be according
" to the truth. For He who is truth,—He who, dy-
" ing and rising again, has manifested the truth to
" men,—will be manifested in every man's conscience.
" Every eye shall see Him."

My brethren, I have endeavoured in this sermon
to set before you two methods of presenting the Gospel of our Lord Jesus Christ to men. I have not
concealed from you—indeed you are all aware of it—
that the first has very powerful supporters, that it
puts itself forth as *the* logical, *the* safe, *the* orthodox
method. I have been able to say nothing on behalf
of the other, except that it was the method of that
Apostle, who, as we affirm, was God's instrument for
causing His light to shine throughout the world. By
the one course we silence objectors, joining, according
to all precedents, in the same *auto da fé,* the representatives of the most diverse sects and schools, the
most devout and the most scornful, the most earnest
and the most frivolous. By the other, we claim all
the most diverse sects and schools, the most devout
and the most scornful, the most earnest and the most
frivolous, as witnesses for the God and Father who
would lead them all to His Son. By the one, we
magnify immensely the skill of the particular dialec-
tician who argues the case; we depress to the lowest
point our common humanity. In the other, the man
who pleads is nothing, but the race is glorified by its
union with a crucified and ascended Lord. To the

one method we are indebted for an exhibition of a
vast amount of ingenious advocacy, of fine metaphysical reasoning; to the other we are indebted for the
existence of a Christendom.

Such is the testimony of the past. How the future
will speak we wait to learn. Nothing less is involved
in the question, than whether the hundred and sixty
millions in India shall be taught that all their mythology and all their philosophy is folly—or that God has
sent His Son to claim them for His offspring; whether the masses of our own population who have been
alienated from our Churches, shall be told that infidelity is false and foolish, because it holds out a hope
that man may know something of the Infinite—or that
God seeks that all should know Him, from the least
to the greatest; whether each one of us shall accept
every dogma of the Church and Bible because that is
quite as likely to be true as anything else,—or shall
continue to pray to Him who cannot be mocked, that
He will give us in this world knowledge of His truth,
and in the world to come life everlasting.

IV.

THE MIRACLES.

John x. 37, 38.

"IF I DO NOT THE WORKS OF MY FATHER, BELIEVE ME NOT. BUT IF
I DO, THOUGH YE BELIEVE NOT ME, BELIEVE THE WORKS : THAT
YE MAY KNOW, AND BELIEVE, THAT THE FATHER IS IN ME, AND I
IN HIM."

Last Sunday I compared the method which we commonly suppose to be the most ingenious and successful for the defence of Christ's Gospel and the confutation of its opponents, with that which was adopted
by St. Paul, in his speech at Athens. I showed you
that there was not a difference merely between them,
but a direct, formal opposition,—one which could not
be accounted for by any advantages which the Apostle
possessed over us in the mightiness of his gifts, or
which we possess over him in the fact of our being inheritors, for eighteen centuries, of the blessings that
he proclaimed. If the modern course is right, his
divine inspiration was only a means of leading him
wrong; if he was right, we are showing that we have
little appreciation of the treasures which he affirmed

to be ours, by the measures which we take for the
purpose of securing them against invaders.

The causes of this wide departure from the precedents which we profess to esteem most, is to be
sought, I have maintained, in the entirely different
force which he and we give to the word *Revelation*
and the kindred word *Manifestation.* They are, as I
have often observed to you, specially favourite words
of St. Paul's,—words upon which the interpretation
not of single passages but of whole Epistles depends.
It could not be otherwise, seeing that the revelation
of Christ to him was, he declares in the Epistle to the
Galatians, that which enabled him to preach the Gospel to the Gentiles. The records of his own life therefore—the very meaning of that conversion which we
shall be considering this week, and by a necessary
consequence the meaning of the message which he
delivered to the nations—are inseparably connected
with his idea of Revelation. I think the more you
pursue the words which express this idea through his
letters, the more you will feel that he is rigidly accurate in the use of them; that the sense never changes;
that Revelation is always with him the unveiling of a
Person—and that Person the ground and Archetype
of men, the source of all life and goodness in men—
not to the eye, but to the very man himself, to the
Conscience, Heart, Will, Reason, which God has created to know Him, and be like Him. Or to take his
own far better and bolder language,—that which we

considered last Sunday,—that of which his Epistles
contain the exposition and the rationale,—it is the
revelation of Him "*in whom we live and move and
are,*" to creatures who are "*feeling after Him, if
haply they may find Him.*"

Now, if this idea of Revelation has been changed
for another that is wholly unlike it,—if by Revelation *we* understand certain communications made to
us by God, and which we cannot dispense with, because the very constitution which He has given us
makes us incapable of knowing Him as he is, because
by no possibility can there be an unveiling or discovery of His own nature, or character, or purposes to
us,—the whole subject must be contemplated by us,
and must be presented to others, in an aspect which it
never assumes in St. Paul's writings and discourses,
or in any part of the Old and New Testament. So
that we are in the strange predicament of men fighting with prodigious zeal and prowess on behalf of the
authority of books which, the moment we take them
from their shelves and examine their contents, are
found to set at nought the hypothesis upon which we
have rested our apology for them. In establishing
the necessity of *a* Revelation, we have done what we
can to confute *the* Revelation of which these books
testify.

When once such a theory about the nature of Revelation as this has been fully developed (and the unfor-
tunate rage for apologetic literature in the Christian

Church has always fostered it, while the faith, the
practical life, the sufferings of Christians, have been
a continual protest against it),—when, I say, it has
been fully developed, it will find, like jealousy, proofs
strong as holy writ, proofs even drawn from holy
writ, to confirm and justify it. Our Lord's miracles have been especially made to perform this office. 'They are,' it is said, 'upon the face of them,
'strange, exceptional acts. What were they for?
'Why are they recorded? Surely to make the mis-
'sion of Christ credible. Once admit them, and
'you cannot doubt that He spoke with an authority
'which never belonged to any one else. Accept this
'authority, and whatever you find in the book, how-
'ever much it seems at variance with your heart
'and reason, you will be bound to receive as divine.'
I am not now considering the question, how far this
mode of argument in our day has been successful in
its intended purpose. I am not considering whether
it has not kept back numbers from the faith which
it recommends; I am not considering how far appeals to the intellect on the particular question of
miracles are consistent with the demand for a sup-
pression of the intellect afterwards; I merely desire
to meet the question, For what purpose are these
works of Christ, if not for the end these apologists
have imagined? I will not answer them as they
would answer me, in all cases except this, with an assumption of ignorance, 'How can we penetrate the

designs of an infinite Being in any of His doings?'
because I think the Scriptures and the Church have
given the answer, and wish us to profit by it. They
declare that the miracles were for the *manifestation*
of Christ's glory. That is the very expression which
the beloved Disciple uses respecting the miracle at
the marriage-feast; for this reason the Church has
chosen that story and the story of other miracles for
the Gospels on the Sundays after Epiphany. They are
not, according to this teaching, arguments to convince
the understanding that it ought to suspend its own
proper exercises; they are unveilings or manifestations
to the whole man, of the nature, character, mind, of
the Son of Man; and therefore, as He shows us in
the passage of which my text forms a part, of the nature, character, mind, of the Father who sent Him.

I. Our Lord says, in the words I have taken, *" If I
do not the works of my Father, believe me not."* Did
you think St. Paul's words at Athens very inconsistent with some of our current notions? But how
much more startling are these! How continually we
are told that we are evincing the greatest irreverence,
that we are proving ourselves ignorant of the limitations of our own minds, and of the distance between
the Divine nature and ours, if we presume to consider
whether such and such acts have a divine quality in
them, or one that is the reverse of divine. I trust
and believe that those who speak this language are
utterly inconsistent with themselves. I am satisfied

—indeed, I know for certain—that they talk of many of the acts attributed to Siva and Vishnu, and to the gods of the classical mythology, as evil and hateful, and therefore as having no savour of divinity in them. Where did they learn that language? Was it not in the book which told them that God is a righteous Being, just and without iniquity? Have we not learnt it by those reasonings of God with His creatures about the madness and folly of worshipping stocks and stones, about the wickedness of pouring out drink-offerings to false and evil beings? Have we not learnt it from those chapters of Isaiah which we are reading in these Epiphany weeks, those which declare that He is setting forth His true Image, the Image of perfect gentleness and meekness, to confound all the dark images which men have made of Him? And yet, when we come back to the school in which we have received all these lessons, and are assailed by doubters of our own land with the assertion that such and such words or acts or habits of mind should not be attributed to a Divine Being,—instead of asking ourselves, and encouraging them to ask, whether these representations of Him are actually in the Holy Book, or whether the objector has rightly understood them, or whether they really outrage his conscience, as he fancies they do,—we stop him with a preliminary denial of his right to make the inquiry at all. From some high logical or theological tribunal, we pronounce that there is no test in man for ascertaining what is right or wrong in One who claims to be above man; that he may exercise all his faculties in ascertaining whether a certain book has probable claims to be regarded as coming from an infinite and omnipotent Being, none of them in ascertaining what manner of Being He is from whom we say it has come. Has not the disputer a right to turn upon us and say, " All that may be true enough; I dare say it is. It confirms many of my suspicions; it strengthens me in my growing atheism. But how happened it that your logic and your theology fell asleep when you were talking about Vishnu and Siva and Jupiter?"

Now to all this strange and contradictory talk, I oppose not some conclusions of my own reason, but the words of Christ himself, "*If I do not the works of my Father, believe me not.*" Here was a distinct appeal to something in man which *could* recognize whether the works He did were the works of His Father or not. That appeal He was making to men through His whole life upon earth; in those *good* works—so He calls them—which we have changed into mere exercises of irregular power, into violations of the order which He had himself established.

Take, for example, the work at Cana, which the Church brought before us last Sunday. We are told by St. John, who must have witnessed it, that in it Christ manifested forth His glory to His disciples. Of course he means us to recollect his own words in the previous chapter, " *We beheld His glory, the glory as of the only-begotten of the Father,*" which was fullness of grace and truth. A Man was sitting in the midst of them, sharing their joy, feeling with them. He manifested Himself to them as the source of that joy. A change wrought calmly, secretly, unobtrusively, unknown to those whom it would have startled most if they had known it, gave them a sense of creative power such as they had never had before. The occasion was common and earthly. The gift was the gift of an ordinary thing, though of one which symbolized life and gladness. It is in little things, in particulars, that the laws of a universe reveal themselves. The unfolding of a flower may teach us more of the birth and growth of all things than we can obtain by reflecting on the whole Cosmos. And in this one act of changing the water into wine at the marriage-feast, the sense of all good things coming down through a Brother, from a Father, may have been more profoundly awakened in the minds of those fishermen, than it had been awakened in all kings and prophets before them. From what material conceptions of Creation may it not have delivered them ! How they may have risen to the perception, if not at once, yet through the discipline of after-years acting upon that one event, of a Word who giveth life !

That, I think, was in the truest sense a *manifestation.* We may confidently apply our Lord's test to it. If it had not come to the Disciples as a work of the Father, they would not have believed on the Son of Man. They might have believed on a great enchanter,—in one who could play with the powers of nature. They would not have believed in a Lord of their hearts and reins; they would not have believed in a King of nature and of man; they would not have believed in One of whose fullness all had received, and grace for grace.

Take again those acts of healing which have been brought before us in the Gospel today. The first was wrought on behalf of a leper, who met our Lord as He came down from the Mount. The people who heard His discourse on that Mount said, "*He speaketh as one having authority, and not as the Scribes.* He speaks like a King, like one who knows the Law and the Lawgiver, not like one who has to spell the meaning of it out of books." The leper confessed the same fact. "*Lord, if thou wilt, thou canst make me clean.* Thou hast authority; I see that. Thou art the King over men, over me. And Thou hast spoken of a Father who cares for His children, who cares for the unthankful and evil. That has been the burden of thy discourse. Wilt thou not then have regard even to an outcast from the society of men, to one who proclaims himself unclean? Others may cut him off, but wilt thou?" The answer, "*I will; be thou clean,*" is assuredly an assertion of the authority which the leper had ascribed to Him. He assumes a kingly right over the body of this man—a right to restore its health. But so far is He from trying to separate that act of healing from the order of God's government and kingdom, that He sends the man to the priest, the ordinary and appointed judge in cases of leprosy. He is to prove, by the recognized outward sign, that the inward cure has taken effect. He is to offer the gift which the law has prescribed. Here is then not a King now for the first time installed in that office, now for the first time exercising its noblest functions. Here is the manifestation of Him whose goings-forth have been from everlasting; a revelation of Him from whom all powers and methods of healing have been derived. Most strictly then is He fulfilling His own words, *" If I do not the works of my Father, believe me not.* If my works are less regular, orderly, inward, than those of Him who governs all things, who renews the life of all things and all men day by day, *believe me not.* If my works are not works of grace and truth, works which bear witness of a Father who is full of grace and truth, of a Father who is not the destroyer but the restorer of men, who is pursuing them into all the secret places of their sorrow and misery to make them right, *believe me not."*

This manifestation is the proper preparation for the next, of which I have spoken to you more than once. I will not dwell upon it in reference to the Centurion's training in the Roman camp, to the lessons he had learnt there of obedience and government, and the power of words to subdue physical strength and hold multitudes in subjection. I would speak of it as the typical instance of those works of healing which demanded faith, and evoked a faith in the persons who were benefited by them. The notion we have formed of miracles and their object leads us to suppose that this faith was in a Person presented to the eye, and able to do marvels that had never been done before. Our Lord selects, as *His* instance of lively faith, a man who cared nothing for the sight or touch, who confessed an invisible might, who believed that if Christ spoke the word, his servant would be healed. May we not affirm then, without hesitation, that the highest blessing which our Lord conferred on palsied, leprous, blind, deaf, dead men, was that He awakened in them a trust which raised them above what they saw—above themselves? Was not the difference between the nine who went their way, and the one who returned to give glory to God, precisely this, that they received a bodily cure no less perfect than he did, but that he was saved out of his selfishness and ignorance of God, because he perceived that Jesus was doing His Father's works? This, I think, has been the interpretation of earnest readers; it may almost be called the traditional interpretation of Christendom. If we would but hold it consistently,—if, in the case of this miracle or of any other, we would but accept the lessons which it has carried home to suffering and lonely people in all parts of the world,—if we would but consider those lessons worth all the apologies that ever have been written, or ever shall be written, we should be less afraid of taking the words of the Son of God as they stand,—we should not think it dangerous to apply His own test to His own works.

I reserve the consideration of one of these works, that of restoring the man possessed with the devils, for next week, because it strikes directly at one of the leading and most effective reasons for inventing another test than our Lord's, and for discarding that. The Church has connected with that narrative the one respecting the passage over the Lake of Galilee, when Jesus said to the storm, "Peace, be still." There is a great beauty, which all readers have felt, in the association of the tumults in nature with the tumults of the human spirit. There is more than beauty : there is the deepest practical benefit in considering wherein they are alike, wherein they differ, why the same monarch must have dominion over both. I should gladly use the Gospel of next Sunday to suggest this comparison, but as I wish to fix your minds upon the cure of the demoniac for its own sake, I will refer for one moment to the first story now, as an additional illustration of the doctrine, "*If I do not the works of my Father, believe me not.*" The remark can scarcely have failed to strike any one, that our Lord's acts of power do, in a very wonderful manner, gather up the different functions which those who were seeking God, if haply they might feel after Him and find Him, had attributed to separate divinities. Little as the Jews knew of the names of Dionysus, Demeter, Æsculapius, Phœbus, they, like all other people, *felt* as if some distinct benefactor must be concerned in the gift of the wine that made glad the heart, of the common bread, of bodily health, of the light in the eye or understanding. And so, as the disciples were to preach a Gospel to all nations, acts which testified of this union of powers were the most perfect preparation they could receive—initiating them into the faiths of different races, making them in the fullest sense assertors of the unity whereof their own was the appointed witness. To realize, by one special instance, in whose hand was the trident of the seas, was surely a part of this practical discipline which they would appreciate hereafter. But they would only appreciate it hereafter, because the impression He made on them at the moment was not the impression of a wonder-worker, who was exhibiting his power in producing startling effects and a sudden excitement, but of a calm Ruler, the upholder and restorer of peace and order. It was a work which revealed Him who had fixed the bounds of earth and sea. It was a work which, beneath the Creator of the world, revealed the Father of men.

II. The first part of my text is negative,—" *If this is not so, believe me not.*" The second is positive; it is full of instruction, I think also of encouragement. " *But if I do, though you believe not me,*

believe the works." In general, perhaps, the order
was reversed. Jesus was recognized first by the Ga-
lilæan fishermen as the Teacher they had craved for;
to whom the prophets and John, the chief of the
prophets, had pointed them; then the works became
fuller manifestations of His nature and His dominion. The Centurion had learnt his need of One who
could command men by a word, as he commanded the
soldiers that were under him; the power which sent
away his servant's palsy appeared to be the proper
endowment of such a Ruler. But our Lord speaks
of cases in which a belief in the works may precede
a belief in Him, and may lead to it. The works, He
says, may lead men to *know*—actually to *know*—that
the Father is in Him, and that He is in the Father.
What! to know this? Is not this the deepest mystery of the Christian faith? Must it not be received
as a dogma transmitted from other ages, very galling
to the reason, but against which it cannot remon-
strate, because it has no capacity for dealing with the
Infinite? I can only repeat our Lord's words. He
says that men who believe the works as works of His
Father, even before they have learnt to believe Him,
may come to know this truth. And suppose it were
a truth—suppose this mystery did underlie the universe, as we in our creeds profess that it does,—and
suppose that the Church is right in treating these
works as divine manifestations,—must it not be so?
Could they be divine manifestations, and not mani-

festations of this divine relation? Could men feel
them as divine, because the expression of the highest
grace and truth,—feel them as human, because coming
with all human grace and truth,—and not confess a
Father and Son, with an inward reality and certainty
such as no mere dogma or tradition ever earned for
itself, ever pretends to earn for itself?

And yet, brethren, we fear to let our Lord's miracles be exposed to a trial which He claimed for them
and to which such a promise as this is attached!
We think it safer to stifle all examination into their
moral character, lest we should put in hazard the
authority of the documents which contain them! Oh,
poor and heartless policy, which must produce the
results of all policy that is not based on truth! No
doubt, if you invite men to say whether the miracles
of Christ have not in them the tokens of all grace and
truth,—are not such signs of His power as a Father
would give to His children,—you permit them to state
their doubts, their difficulties, their suspicions. Do you
not wish that they should? Do you not know that
there is danger, incalculable danger, in their quelling
these doubts, difficulties, suspicions,—in their not
bringing them forth to the light of day? If some are
merely idle doubts, doubts suggested by the spirit of
scorn, are there not some which God has awakened,
that He may satisfy them? Dare you crush those?
Can you distinguish the tares from the wheat? Cannot you trust God to do it? The truth must be

spoken—our modern way of meeting objections nou-
rishes and justifies all the pride and contempt which
prompts the worst of them; only hinders those from
coming forth which really demand a solution, which,
if there is any moral standard for man, any moral
sense in man, will find one.

And while we consider the effect we may produce
on others, let us not forget the reaction upon ourselves.
History, not speculation, supplies us with an awful
warning. We know, on the testimony of Evangelists
and Apostles, that there were men—religious men—
eager to crush all doubt respecting the authority of
the Scriptures; quite ready to confess miracles that
were merely miracles of power. These men refused
our Lord's test. They would not ask whether His
works were good, whether they came from the Father.
They did not believe they had any faculties for entering on that inquiry. And so they denied both the
Father and the Son; so they came to believe that
Christ healed the sick, stilled the winds and waves,
preached glad tidings to the poor, under the inspiration of Beelzebub, the prince of the devils.

V.

CASTING OUT THE EVIL SPIRIT.

LUKE VIII. 35.

"THEN THEY WENT OUT TO SEE WHAT WAS DONE; AND CAME TO JESUS,
AND FOUND THE MAN, OUT OF WHOM THE DEVILS WERE DEPARTED,
SITTING AT THE FEET OF JESUS, CLOTHED, AND IN HIS RIGHT MIND:
AND THEY WERE AFRAID."

I HAVE chosen a passage from St. Luke's version of
the story which we read in the Gospel of today. In
doing so I am aware that I must remind you of a
conspicuous variation in the Evangelists who report
it. St. Matthew speaks of two men possessed with
devils; St. Mark and St. Luke, only of one. The
peculiarity of the incidents, and the strict agreement
of the geography, leave no doubt that the miracle to
which they refer is the same. Here therefore would
be a legitimate subject for examination, which, if it
were honestly conducted, must lead to good. The
only danger in such cases is the concealment of difficulties, or the distortion of evidence for the purpose
of removing them.

Another question is raised by the narrative, which

may receive illustration from the physician as well as the practical divine, each helping to clear the mind and remove the prejudices of the other. Are there such cases as are described here, in modern times, or were they confined to the age of the Evangelists ? Which argument can hardly fail to introduce the whole controversy respecting the existence and influence of evil spirits.

It is not because I would shun either of these lines of thought that I choose that one which the Church suggests to us by her use of the story in this season of the year. The Gospel for today is intended, no doubt, to give us another of the Epiphanies or Manifestations of Christ. I do not think we shall find such a manifestation less, whichever Evangelist we follow. One as much as another will assist us in the inquiry in which I am engaged: " What, according to the writers of the New Testament, is Revelation or Manifestation ?" If we keep that problem steadily before us, I do not despair of our finding some light upon the others. At all events, we shall not be able to look upon them as mere cruxes and trivialities which may be left to critics ; they will assume a human significance and grandeur.

I. Whatever differences may exist between the Evangelists, there is none as to the character of the malady which affected the one man or the two. All the symptoms of outrageous madness are described, let the cause of it be what it may. *" They came out*

of the tombs," says St. Matthew ; *" they were exceeding fierce; no man could pass by that way."* St. Mark,
speaking only of a single maniac, adds some more
lines to the description. *" No one could bind him,
no, not with chains. Because he had been often bound
with fetters and chains, and the chains had been plucked
asunder by him, and the fetters broken in pieces; neither could any man tame him. And always, night and
day, he was in the mountains and in the tombs, crying and cutting himself with stones."* St. Luke says,
*" He wore no clothes, neither abode in any house, but
in the tombs."* Surely as clear and full a picture of
madness as was ever painted.

II. None of these signs are in themselves rare;
we connect them with facts we have known, with
sights we have seen. If there were no provision for
the care of the insane, there is nothing in the conditions of modern civilization which would make it
impossible or unlikely that such objects as those
which presented themselves to our Lord in the country of the Gergesenes, should encounter us in England. But again, the Evangelists are agreed as to the
origin of this fury. " The men," says St. Matthew,
" were possessed with devils." " He had an *unclean*
spirit," say St. Mark and St. Luke. They do not
however abandon the plural number. The answer,
" Our name is Legion," occurs in both. If this language is disagreeable to our ears, we cannot rid ourselves of it by comparing the documents. It stands

out as strong and clear in one as the other. I need scarcely remind you that it does not belong to a single story or to ten stories. It is characteristic of the Gospels as such. It is not, as I have observed to you before, characteristic of them *as well as* of the Old Testament books. It distinguishes them from those books. The allusions to evil spirits are rare in the one, continual in the other.

III. In another point there is no diversity. It is that for the sake of which I am referring to the story, that which has given it a place among the Epiphany services. "*What have we to do with thee, Jesus, thou Son of God ? Art thou come hither to torment us ?*" is St. Matthew's account of the voice which met our Lord when he approached the madman. "*What have I to do with thee, Jesus, thou Son of the most high God ? I adjure thee by God that thou torment me not,*" is St. Mark's version. St. Luke substitutes "*I beseech thee*" for "*I adjure thee ;*" otherwise he nearly repeats St. Mark. Here again the expressions are familiar to us. We meet them under varieties of form in other narrations. Evil spirits are said always to regard Jesus as their tormentor, because He is come to deliver a man from their dominion.

IV. That which distinguishes this story from others of the like kind—the entrance of the devils into the herd of swine—is also dwelt upon carefully and minutely by each of the Evangelists. However we explain it, we cannot treat it as an interpolation : and it is an evidently hopeless experiment to look for some particulars in one of the three narratives, which may induce us to hold by that as the least difficult.

V. Finally, though the passage I have taken out of St. Luke, which declares the ultimate effect of our Lord's command, has nothing exactly corresponding to it in St. Matthew, it is evidently taken for granted in his account. The men, being delivered from the tyrants that possessed them, would of course be clothed and in their right mind. I wish to keep that result in recollection, therefore I have set it before you in express words; I might have reached it just as well by inference from the first Gospel.

Taking the story then as it stands, and not having any secret for changing it from an account of spiritual bondage and spiritual emancipation into something else, I cannot doubt that a number of persons in our day—of intelligent and devout persons—will turn from it with considerable annoyance and discontent. Any preacher who recalls his own feelings about it at some time or other of his life, will not, I should think, be inclined to judge harshly of such objectors. Least of all—unless his remembrances are of a rare and peculiar kind, or his present convictions very feeble— will he desire that their doubts should not be frankly stated, should not be fully confronted with the facts of experience as well as with the words of Scripture. For if we have any of us been led to accept this record, not coldly and reluctantly, but as one which we

could not bear to part with, which has been a strength
and help to us in dark hours, the process, I suppose,
has been something of this kind.   Beginning to contemplate the subject quietly and at a distance, with
very great indisposition to compromise his reputation
for sense,—asking himself what sort of maniac the
man described in the Gospels might be, and what
natural way of accounting for his frenzy there might
be found,—the inquirer has suddenly had the thought
thrust upon him, " What if *thou* art that man ? What
if the strange fact that he was a spiritual being is
a fact that is common to him and to thee ?   What
if that other strange fact, that his spirit was under
the yoke of unlawful intruders, of cruel usurpers,
may also explain what thou hast known in thyself,
and which thou couldst very ill explain ?   Hast thou
not been conscious of a subjection to the tyranny,
not of one ruler, but of divided, contradictory rulers ?
Is not their name Legion ?   Thou hast been wont to
speak of them as impulses, motives, principles : has
that language made the fact clearer ?   They are not
visible ; they assail thy own very self ; from them have
come foul and cruel thoughts and inspirations.   Is it
not horrible to think they *are* thyself, that there is
no distinction between them and thee ?   Is it not a
lie to think so ?   Whether thou hast resisted them,
whether thou hast obeyed, do not the very names Re-
sistance, Obedience, imply that they are not thyself?
But was there no other that thou wast resisting

when thou wast obeying them? Was there no other that thou wast obeying when thou wast resisting them? What says thy conscience? Does it witness of none such? Has He never manifested Himself to thee yet? Is He not manifesting Himself to thee now? In all thy thoughts of good, in all thy struggles with evil, is He not manifesting Himself to thee? And Who else was it that manifested Himself to the maniac in the country of the Gadarenes? Was not that a crucial instance of His nature and His power? Was He not showing His purpose of claiming a spirit that had sunk into the lowest and bitterest bondage? Was not He showing that there are no usurpers over the human spirit so mighty that He cannot overcome them?"

I imagine that a person who has gone so far as this, will find in the final incident of the narrative something to cause him trembling rather than to affront his taste. He will be disposed to say, "Yes! as I see in that fierce madman a man of my flesh and blood,—such a man as I might become if a mightier than I was not upholding me,—so I cannot deny that those swine running violently down a steep place till they are choked in the sea, do set before me the liveliest image of the effect those powers which have swayed me, which are always seeking to sway me, would produce if they were transferred to mere brute natures. They show me that we do not sink *merely* into a condition below humanity when evil has the

mastery over us ; that the depraved Will carries into its
degradation a malignity which gives the animal what
it has not of its own. Surely a lesson which a divine
Teacher would desire to impart, by such an example
as the Gospels speak of, to those whom He came to
claim as spiritual beings ! For," he will go on, " when
one looks at the New Testament again, with the
light thrown upon it from experience, do not I perceive that this is the very character in which Christ
is presented, not in one or two passages, but throughout ? What does it mean, that He baptizes with
the Spirit ? What means the history of the Temptation ? What means every discourse, miracle, parable ? Are they not all testifying of One who is
come to debate the possession of the man, not with
flesh and blood enemies, but with principalities and
powers that are assaulting, if not holding, the very
citadel of his being ? Why does He speak of the
strong man armed, keeping the house in peace ? Why
does He speak of the stronger than he, who takes
from him all the armour wherein he trusted, and spoils
his goods ? "

Now, I repeat it, a man who has learnt by this
process of thought, or by any process of thought like
this, to accept the narrative of the Demoniacs without
change or qualification, cannot be offended with any
one who hesitates about it, nay, who fights every step
of his way before he will surrender his objections to
it. I apprehend that his experience of such a state

of mind will make him far more than tolerant of it. There are many feelings connected with it which he would not for the world eradicate, because they are some of the greatest confirmations of his own faith on this very subject. For instance, the dread of Superstition and Fanaticism. The more deep this dread is,—the more a man regards superstition and fanaticism as horrible evils into which by God's help he will not sink, and which it would be agony to suspect in the Son of Man,—the more hope, it seems to me, there is that he will take in this story in the length and breadth of it. For the direst kind of Superstition is that which connects evil with the Nature of God, and the next direst kind is that which identifies the man himself with evil. And here both are undermined from the foundation. God manifests Himself in conflict with the Evil Spirit in his essence, and in all the forms he may take. God manifests Himself in the very act of distinguishing the man from the evil which has possessed him. The direst fanaticism is that which assumes the being of any man to be the proper habitation of evil spirits. And the second most evil form is, that which supposes that certain special men have a right to claim the Spirit of God as theirs in a sense in which ordinary men may not claim it. And all the petty forms of fanaticism wherein it passes into triviality, such as abound in our day, have their root in the notion that spiritual powers and influences are light topics, for drawing-room gossip. Here at once each of these shapes of fanaticism is laid bare. The Spirit of Christ meets the Unclean Spirit in what appears his last, securest, most legitimate hold, and declares that there he has no right. The maniac is as fit to be the receptacle of His power and inspiration as the highest saint. The whole transaction is full of solemnity and awe ; so that if it be true, and have come from the source of Truth, the stories with which our ears are dinned must be not ridiculous but loathsome.

For all these reasons, then, a believer in the narrative will be exceedingly afraid of using even what may seem to him fair methods of argument for the sake of dispelling scepticism upon it. Something perhaps he may do by calmly stating his own conviction and how he has been led to it. But he cannot be displeased if he should not be the means of imparting that conviction to any other mind. If it has been given him, as he thinks it has, he can trust One who knows all the passages and channels of His creatures' hearts to send it them as they want it. He knows that so far as he tries to drive it home by arts of persuasion or of ridicule or of terror, because it is his, so far he shall be marring the effect of the divine arguments which are so much subtler, and penetrate so much deeper, and carry with them such a different kind of compulsion.

These conclusions are inevitable for a person who regards this story as a revelation of Christ himself, and of His dealings with the human spirit. But I have told you in former sermons that an entirely different notion of revelation from this has been proclaimed in our day as the only one which is consistent with Christian orthodoxy and with common sense. To represent it as the discovery of the true God in the person of His Son, to a creature capable of knowing Him, incapable of freedom and peace without the knowledge of Him, is to incur I scarcely can say what frightful charges. Mysticism is on the face of such a statement; Rationalism lies beneath it; it betrays a profound and fatal ignorance of the nature which God has given us, which can never come into near and close contact with the Eternal, which can only abstract some feeble notion of that from the things of time and sense. What then is Revelation, if not this? It contains, we are told, lessons which it is necessary for us to receive,—which God wishes us to receive,—because though they are not in any strict sense manifestations of what He is, they are necessary for the regulation of our lives. Here at last is something positive. We are not merely told by what standard we *cannot* judge of that which is presented to us. We know what its office is. Be it so. Then let us consider what sort of Revelation has or has not fulfilled that office.

I would still hold fast to the Scriptures in entering upon this inquiry. I would begin with this story of the Demoniac. I am not now engaged with

objectors to it, but with those who say that, being
a part of the Bible, it is to be received like any
other part; that to raise any cavils against it, or to
put any unliteral sense upon it, is perilous. Here
then is a case of moral regulation. A man who was
wild and furious becomes calm and orderly. He sits
at the feet of Jesus clothed and in his right mind.
What has wrought this mighty change? Is it the
announcement to him of some law which God has
laid down for his creatures? Is it the announcement of some punishment which will follow the
breach of that law in some other world? Is it a
series of sound ethical maxims? Is it injunctions
about prayer to God or self-government? Is it anything whatever which we comprehend under the ordinary notion of moral discipline? All these regulations were desirable, assuredly, for a man in the condition of the maniac. But common sense pronounced
them ridiculous. It was obvious that they could take
no effect; that they must be wasted. Far more direct and simple methods were resorted to. He was
chained. But that was as ineffectual a scheme of regulation as the other. The fetters were burst asunder,
the chains were broken. It is just when all mere
regulations, divine and human, are found absolutely
vain to restrain him from being the curse and plague
of his fellow-men that Christ is said to have met
the man himself, to have entered into colloquy with
that which could hear no laws, could be restrained

by no force,—to have emancipated and reformed that. And here is the result: not a new excitement substituted for the old; not religious paroxysms taking the place of other paroxysms, but quietness and order: he is in his right mind.

Here is one instance, and, as I have shown already, a type-instance, of Christ's acts towards a class of human creatures. But let us pass to a case of a directly opposite kind. Saul of Tarsus, instead of being a maniac, is the most correct of men, reverencing the law,—as touching all the commandments which are contained in it, blameless. He has been trained to regard the Revelation given to his fathers as a regulative one. Precisely in that character it has been set before him by the doctors at Jerusalem. The thought of its being anything but this,—of its being in any sense an unveiling of God himself,—the promise of a more perfect unveiling,—may now and then have disturbed him as he pored over some passage in the Psalms or the Prophets. But he has dismissed it—angrily dismissed it. God has been pleased to give his nation a revelation. It consists mainly of a law, though it has also pleased God, in compassion to the ignorance of His creatures, to set before also a system of worship and sacrifices which it would be very unsafe and criminal for them to neglect. He hears of a set of men who are apparently teaching another doctrine than this; who, if he has not mistaken them, proclaim that a crucified man has

manifested or unveiled the Divine Being to men. All
regulations, all limitations, have been burst through;
these wretched fanatics are actually assuming that
the Invisible has come nigh to His creatures,—that
there is a way by which they may ascend to him. St.
Stephen's speech perhaps first discovers to him the
extent of their departure from all the maxims which
he holds sacred. There every step in the Jewish
History is treated as a step towards the revelation
of that Just One of whom his countrymen had been
the betrayers and murderers. There those countrymen are charged with having resisted the Holy Ghost,
who in all ages has been striving with them. There
the vision of a Son of Man at the right-hand of
God is openly announced in language which could be
nothing less than blasphemy in the ears of one who
looked on God as immeasurably distant from man.
He becomes more and more furious; still it is fury
against the opposers of a regulative Revelation. Then
comes the crisis in his life. That regulative Revelation,—the system of laws, precepts, ordinances,
which God Himself has appointed for the good of his
nation,—prove utterly ineffectual; instead of their
helping him or raising him, he finds himself crushed
under the weight of them. It is only when the same
Lord who bade the unclean spirit depart out of the
maniac in the country of the Gadarenes, claims to
be the Lord and Deliverer of his spirit, that he becomes clothed and in his right mind.

What kind of work he did then, what sort of revelation of God he proclaimed in the city which was
most unlike Jerusalem in its speculations and its
worship, I considered in a former sermon. And if we
followed up the discourse there by an examination of
his Epistles, we should come, I think to these two
conclusions :—1. That he is everywhere announcing
an actual revelation and manifestation of God's righteousness to the spirit of man as the deliverance from
a mere law—a regulative Revelation—which had
never reached, which never could reach, the spirit
of man. 2. That he speaks of the Spirit of God as
holding converse, not with the spirit of the maniac
in the country of the Gadarenes, not with the spirit
of him, the Apostle of the Gentiles, but with the
spirit of man, from generation to generation; that he
regards the assurance that such a Spirit shall be with
us, witnessing to us, sustaining us, making us partakers of the Divine Nature, as the great assurance of
the Gospel, apart from which it would have no power
whatever to improve the lives of men or the condition of the world.

Brethren, was St. Paul right or wrong in this an-
ticipation ? Has the Gospel of Christ produced any,
even the slightest, amelioration in human society, except so far as it has carried this message home to the
hearts of human beings ? It has done singularly little
in the way of outward regulation.   It sent forth no
decrees against gladiatorial exhibitions, against poly-

gamy, against slavery.   If it has wrought, in any period of its existence, any cure of these evils,—if it has
given any new face to society,—it is because a voice
was saying to the unclean spirit that had possessed
it, " Get thee out ;" because Christ himself was felt
to be wrestling with that spirit and overcoming it.
So has it been with every man.   In the latest ages
as in the first, there have been messages of deliverance to the outcast maniacs who could not be bound
with chains ; but through whomsoever they have come,
through the benevolent physician or the sympathizing
sister of charity, they have been recognitions of a
better spirit struggling with the evil spirit ; they have
been tokens from Christ that He can set free the
captive and put down the oppressor.   Decent men
have been changed in later times, as in earlier times,
from self-satisfied and bitter haters into humble
Christians, into zealous apostles of goodwill to men.
But in every case the change has been preceded by
the discovery of the inefficiency of all mere regulations, in whatever form they might come,—as laws of
earth or laws of Heaven,—to make a true man.   It
has taken place when the heart has owned a Son of
God to whom it had been crying, " *What have I to
do with thee?   Art thou come to torment me ?*" as a
friend and deliverer.   It has come when the heart
has perceived that the power which it had thought
far away, in Heaven or Hell, is nigh to it.   It has
come when the man has confessed that the Righteous

God, seeing that he had no righteousness of his own, was clothing them with the righteousness which none can comprehend, which every spiritual being is created to apprehend.

I believe, brethren, it is not true of the Gospel of Christ, that if you take from it its original character, —if you strip it of those claims which Apostles and Martyrs put forth in its behalf,—it may challenge respect on a lower ground, it may claim a sort of useful and recognized position for itself among the other agents of civilization. I know such an opinion prevails in many minds. They say that

"Reft of a crown, it still may share the feast."

You will find it is not so. You will find that if we dare not proclaim Christ as the Deliverer of the spirit of man from its bondage,—if we dare not say that He has come actually to reveal God's righteousness to men,—we had better cease to speak of Him at all. For it is such a one that men want; it is for such a one that in their inmost hearts, even when their language against the Son of Man is loudest, they are crying. It was so in former ages; it is so now. It was so among the most miserable and the most respectable; it is so still. If preachers of the Gospel do not answer the cry,—if they only represent it as one of the regulative processes that are at work in society,—it will be felt to be the feeblest of all these processes; the chain and the prisonhouse will be stronger.

Brethren, the lesson is written in broad and deep characters upon our annals; it is written in characters of blood. I may dare to speak to you, on this thirtieth of January at all events, not of other men's sins, but of our own. We are not commanded any longer to forget the beam in our eye that we may search for the mote in our brother's eye. The Church of England has herself to blame for the event which this day commemorates, because she did not heed that groan which was deep before it became loud : " Give us a Gospel which speaks to us as spirits, for spirits we are. Do not merely deal with us as creatures of time and sense. Do not soothe us with shows, or coerce us with rules and punishments. Tell us if the Eternal has come near to us. Tell us if we may know Him." The voice was not understood. It was supposed that they who uttered it were maniacs, and that chains might bind them. It was supposed that a regulative Revelation, if it were duly proclaimed, would satisfy all reasonable wishes. The experiment was made; you know how it succeeded.

Alas, the fearful lesson of this day was not enough for our warning ! In the following century there was again the cry for a Revelation that should reach the spirits of men, that should present Christ to them as an actual Deliverer from evil spirits, claiming maniacs, robbers, outlaws, for sons of God. There was evidence—clear, undoubted evidence—that those who proclaimed Him in that character, did leave men whom they found possessed with unclean spirits, clothed, and in their right mind. There was evidence as clear and undoubted that effects the opposite of these were the result of their preaching; that fanaticism often followed it—sometimes hypocrisy. These facts were heeded, the others not. The conclusion was drawn, that a preaching which spoke of God as actually coming near to man, of a Spirit working upon his spirit, was not favourable to morality. A regulative Revelation must be proclaimed instead of this, a revelation of things which it was fitting to believe and fitting to do, stamped with the Divine authority, but bearing no witness that man is intended with open face to behold the glory of God, and to be changed into His image. Has that attempt succeeded better than the other? Has not Methodism vanquished you, as Puritanism vanquished you before? Have not you been obliged to adopt its phrases, even some of the phrases which were most reasonably charged with leading to mischievous results, because it proved itself more strong and effectual over men's minds than any mere regulative Revelation ever was or ever can be?

Brethren, must this lesson also be wasted upon us? We have not indeed the same circumstances to deal with that we had in the seventeenth century or in the eighteenth. But we have men to deal with still, —men of all different classes, the criminal and the respectable, the sane and the maniac. Oh! shall we try again that old and worn-out experiment which has proved so helpless with them all? Shall we argue with men about the wickedness and folly of their unbelief? Shall we tell them how they may regulate themselves so that they may present a comely face to the world, distracted by no tumults, perplexed by no doubts? Or shall we speak to them as the Church speaks to them, declaring that God has verily manifested Himself, not to the eye, but to the spirit, and that His spirit is working with their spirits that they may be clean and pure within? Oh! if we could but proclaim that message to men, what would nicknames signify to us? Surely we might bear to be called Mystics or Rationalists or madmen or atheists,—all which titles have been bestowed upon Apostles and Martyrs,—if we could but be Christ's instruments in casting an evil spirit out of the age; if we could but bring one man who has been possessed with a legion of them, to sit at His feet clothed and in a right mind!

VI.

CHRIST'S PARABLES.

MATTHEW XIII. 14–17.

"AND THE DISCIPLES CAME, AND SAID UNTO HIM, WHY SPEAKEST
THOU UNTO THEM IN PARABLES? HE ANSWERED AND SAID UNTO
THEM, BECAUSE IT IS GIVEN UNTO YOU TO KNOW THE MYSTERIES
OF THE KINGDOM OF HEAVEN, BUT TO THEM IT IS NOT GIVEN.
FOR WHOSOEVER HATH, TO HIM SHALL BE GIVEN, AND HE SHALL
HAVE MORE ABUNDANCE; BUT WHOSOEVER HATH NOT, FROM HIM
SHALL BE TAKEN AWAY EVEN THAT HE HATH. THEREFORE SPEAK
I TO THEM IN PARABLES: BECAUSE THEY SEEING, SEE NOT; AND
HEARING, THEY HEAR NOT, NEITHER DO THEY UNDERSTAND. AND
IN THEM IS FULFILLED THE PROPHECY OF ESAIAS, WHICH SAITH,
BY HEARING YE SHALL HEAR, AND SHALL NOT UNDERSTAND; AND
SEEING YE SHALL SEE, AND SHALL NOT PERCEIVE: FOR THIS PEO-
PLE'S HEART IS WAXED GROSS, AND THEIR EARS ARE DULL OF
HEARING, AND THEIR EYES THEY HAVE CLOSED; LEST AT ANY
TIME THEY SHOULD SEE WITH THEIR EYES, AND HEAR WITH THEIR
EARS, AND SHOULD UNDERSTAND WITH THEIR HEART, AND SHOULD
BE CONVERTED, AND I SHOULD HEAL THEM. BUT BLESSED ARE
YOUR EYES, FOR THEY SEE; AND YOUR EARS, FOR THEY HEAR.
FOR VERILY I SAY UNTO YOU, THAT MANY PROPHETS AND RIGHT-
EOUS MEN HAVE DESIRED TO SEE THOSE THINGS WHICH YE SEE,
AND HAVE NOT SEEN THEM; AND TO HEAR THOSE THINGS WHICH
YE HEAR, AND HAVE NOT HEARD THEM."

MANY have given their answer to the question why

our Lord spoke in parables. Owing, it has been said, to the limitations of the human intellect, it is impossible for us really to know anything of divine, eternal things; they can only be presented to us through very imperfect likenesses derived from nature or the transactions of men. That is a general reason applicable to one human being as much as another. Then there is a special reason, drawn from the circumstances of our Lord's life on earth. He was instructing ignorant fishermen. Such wisdom as it was possible for men of this class to receive might, it is said, be expected to reach them best through stories and apologues. Or thirdly : Why should not the parables be veils purposely contrived to hide sacred truths from the gaze of the profane multitude ?

The Disciples were not less perplexed than any in later times have been on this subject. They took what appeared to them the simplest mode of freeing themselves from the perplexity. They said to our Lord, " *Why speakest thou to them in parables ?*" He replied at once. The answer is contained in the passage I have read to you. Let us consider how far it accords with any of those we have invented for ourselves.

I. " *To you,*" He says, " *it is given to know the mysteries of the Kingdom of Heaven.*" I need not remind you to whom He is speaking. They were those ignorant fishermen for whose sake He is supposed to have devised this kind of teaching. They are told expressly that they can dispense with it, that they are capable of a high knowledge. Yes, knowledge. He says it is given them to *know* the mysteries of the Kingdom of Heaven. Do not let us dismiss that phrase till we have examined it. We oppose the Kingdom of Heaven to the Kingdom of Earth. We call the one eternal, the other temporal or transitory. That is ordinary language; none, whatever their theory may be, object to it. Only they say: What is eternal is mysterious, inconceivable. Our Lord admits that it is. He speaks of *mysteries*. But He speaks of knowing mysteries. He means apparently what St. Paul meant when he says, " *Eye hath not seen, ear hath not heard, neither hath it entered into the heart of man to conceive the things which God hath prepared for them that love Him.*" But He affirms that the Disciples—taken from the commonest order of men, sharing in their ignorance—have a capacity for *knowing* these mysteries, these eternal things which cannot be conceived.

Does it strike you that there is a force in the word ' given,' which I have neglected? Does it seem to you to take these simple men out of the common roll of men, and to signify that they had a privilege altogether special, not the least appertaining to their race? " *To you it is given; to them it is not given.*" I admit all the value of the expression. It is of incalculable importance for the understanding of this passage, —and of every passage in the New Testament. But before you decide that it can bear that sense which has just been suggested, reflect on the next sentence.

II. *"For whosoever hath, to him shall be given, and he shall have more abundance; but whosoever hath not, from him shall be taken away even that he hath."* Here a Universal Law is announced as the explanation of that gift to the Disciples, and of the difference between them and others. *Whosoever* hath. *Whosoever* hath not. Is it not assumed in that universal statement—is it not affirmed—that every man whatever has received certain things which the Bestower will increase if he hold them fast; but which he may let go and be left utterly bare? And what are these things? If there is the least connection between this verse and that which precedes it,—between the difficulty and the solution,—they are *mysteries of the Kingdom of Heaven.* These are the treasures—not lying far from any man—to which these fishermen had not foregone their claim, which no one can relinquish without abandoning his rights, without renouncing his manhood.

III. For thus He goes on, *" Therefore speak I to them in parables : because they seeing see not, and hearing they hear not, neither do they understand."* Seeing, hearing, understanding, these are admitted powers of human beings. They are *gifts,* in the truest, deepest meaning of that word ; they should be owned as fresh gifts every morning. They are *felt* to be gifts by those who have suffered any temporary blindness, deafness, derangement of intellect. But still they are gifts to *men;* to be without them is a fearful penalty, the exception to a rule. To have them and not to exercise them is wilfulness. Is it not intimated to us that there is something exactly corresponding to these organs of sense in the spirit of man; that an eye is *there,* which may be opened or may be closed; an ear is *there* which may be awake to take in a voice that is speaking to it, or may be stopped; a capacity for profiting by the vision, for yielding to the voice, which may be continually expanded, or may continually become more contracted?

Would you say that this eye of the spirit was less truly and essentially *human* than the eye of the body? Would not you call it far *more* truly and essentially human? Would not you say that that *appertained* to the man, that this was a part of his very being? Would not you say that that might be extinguished and he still remain; nay, that the loss might bring with it, as it certainly brought to Milton, an abundant compensation; that for the other to be put out is for the man himself to perish? Supposing this were meant, you would recollect at once expressions which would illustrate it, and would appear to be of precisely the same character. Such as these:—" *The light of the body is the eye. If therefore thine eye be single, thy whole body shall be full of light; but if thine eye be evil, thy whole body shall be full of darkness. If therefore the light that is in thee be darkness, how great is that*

darkness!" The verity of this description, when we
apply it to the external world, commends itself to us
all. And oh! have we never thought—have we never
known—that it must have the other application also,
and that that application was the primary one? Have
we never been brought to confess that the light of
the sun cannot be *the* Light, the Light of the world,
the Light of men,—that there must be an older, a
more penetrating, a more universal Light than that,
because there has been something in us which has
quailed before it, which has wished to quench it?

But if there is this correspondence between the
organs of the spirit and the organs of sense,—if experience assures there is,—does not that explain to us
the meaning and power of the parables? May not all
sensible things, by a necessity of their nature, be testifying to us of that which is nearest to us, of that
which it most concerns us to know, of the mysteries
of our own life, and of God's relation to us? May it
not be impossible for us to escape from these witnesses? They may become insignificant to us from
our very familiarity with them; nay, we may utterly
forget that there is any wonder in them. The trans-
formation of the seed into the full corn in the ear may
appear to us the dullest of all phenomena, not worthy
to be noted or thought of. The difference in the re-
turns from different soils, or from the same soils under different cultivation—the difference in the quality
of the produce, and the relation which it bears to the

quality of the seeds,—may be interesting to us from the effect such varieties have upon the market,—from the more or less money we derive from the sale;—not the least as facts in nature, facts for meditation. The relation between a landholder or farmer and those who work for him, between a steward and his employer, between a shepherd and his sheep, all in like manner may be tried by the same pecuniary standard; apart from that, they may suggest nothing to us. Thus the universe becomes actually "as is a landscape to a dead man's eye;" the business in which we are ourselves engaged, a routine which must be got through in some way or another, that we may have leisure to eat, drink, and sleep. Can any language describe this state so accurately and vividly as that of our Lord in the text? Seeing we see, and do not perceive; hearing we hear, and do not understand.

But is He not declaring to His disciples why He *spoke* in parables to the Jewish people? and am not I alluding to parables which are not spoken so much as acted,—acted before us as well as before them? I will not evade the question. St. Matthew says in this chapter:—"*All these things spake Jesus unto the multitude in parables; and without a parable spake He not unto them: that it might be fulfilled which was spoken by the prophet, saying, I will open my mouth in parables; I will utter things which have been kept secret from the foundation of the world.*" Were it true that these secret processes of Nature, that

the transactions of human beings, had been, from
the foundation of the world, the lesson-books out of
which God was instructing men, and revealing Himself to them,—were it true that these lessons had been
perverted and misunderstood, changed into excuses
for idolatry, as if He were made after the likeness of
natural things or of man's caprices—what force then
would be in this application of the prophet's sentence !   How truly would Christ fulfil the words by
withdrawing the veil which had been covering these
common facts, by showing what was behind them !
How wonderfully He would be proving that He knew
the mind of the Father from whom He came,—that
He had indeed been as one brought up with Him !
If this is not the import of the parables, does not St.
Matthew's quotation sound inflated and exaggerated ?
How did mere apologues, intended to make truths
more lively, or to recommend them to the ignorant
(I say nothing of the other supposition, that they were
intended to *conceal* truths), " *declare things that had
been kept secret from the foundation of the world* "?

But the greatest satisfaction of our doubts upon this
subject is derived, I think, from a comparison of this
part of my text with the passage in the fourth chapter of St. Mark's Gospel, which corresponds to it.
" *Unto them that are without* "—this is his version of
our Lord's answer—" *all things are done in parables.* "
To those who never dwell on that which is within,
—upon that which concerns their own selves,—but

live merely in the outward world, these things,—the things of the Kingdom of Heaven,—become only in this form of parables. I use the expression ' *become,*' as the most literal rendering of γίνεται, but I cannot think that our translators were wrong or unhappy in the phrase which they chose in preference to it. The divine things are not merely spoken through parables, they are *done* in parables,—the parables are about us, only, through the want of a light coming from within, we do not recognize them.

IV. But though on this ground I cannot look upon any parable as less really concerning one age than another, I do not for a moment deny that our Lord's words in the next clause had a special reference to the last age of the Jewish commonwealth. "*And in them is fulfilled the prophecy of Esaias, which saith, By hearing ye shall hear, and shall not understand ; and by seeing ye shall see, and shall not perceive. For this people's heart is waxed gross, and their ears are dull of hearing, and their eyes have they closed : lest at any time they should see with their eyes, and hear with their ears, and understand with their heart, and should be converted, and I should heal them.*" Such words intimate very clearly that the incapacity for discerning anything not material or sensual, which Isaiah lamented in the Jews of his day,—which he was told would make them heedless of all his warnings and of all his consolations, till the armies of the Assyrians had laid the land waste, till there was

H

great forsaking in the midst of it, and many cities
were left without inhabitant,—was reaching its climax in the days of our Lord's Incarnation ; all the
Divine discipline which had been used for the correction of it, having been turned into a justification of it. In that day was fulfilled (or had come to
its full maturity) all the coarseness, the covetousness,
the pride, which had been corrupting and undermining the nation in former times, but had not then
reached its vitals. For now there was no more the
consciousness of wrong-doing which there had been
in the days of hill-altars and of temples to Baal.
*" Had we been in the days of our fathers, we would
not have murdered the prophets,"* was the comfortable
conviction of a people who were just about to murder
the Prophet of Prophets. No past lessons, therefore,
were of the least avail. How did they concern men
so free from all the crimes and wrong tendencies of
their ancestors ? They had the Holy Book in their
possession ; no heathen could claim it ; all its sounds
and letters were familiar to them ; they could repeat
them, argue from them, comment upon them,—only
they were mere sounds, mere letters. Hearing they
heard, and did not understand ; seeing they saw, and
did not perceive. No living voice came to them out
of that which was read continually in the synagogue.
No vision of a divine Presence or a divine Deliverer
shone through the writings that testified of nothing
else. And so idolatry—taking no shape, protested

against and vehemently abhorred—crept inwards, took
possession of the whole being of those who held idolaters to be accursed of God. The gold upon the
altar became the measure by which they judged of
the sacrifice that was offered upon it; the gold of the
Temple was really for them the Presence that dwelt
in it. To a race bound in these chains, our Lord
spake of a Shepherd who went into the wilderness
to seek after a sheep that was lost, of a Father who
ran and embraced the prodigal when, after eating his
swine's food, he had thought of the house from which
he went out. These were parables of human duty, of
human affection, witnessing to hearts that were open,
of some divine Shepherd who might lay down His life
for the sheep, of a Father who might make a mighty
sacrifice to bring back His children to Himself.
These were witnesses that a care as actual as the
care of the human shepherd, that a love as actual
and personal as the love of the human parent,—
only free from all their limitations and partialities,
—was about them in their daily walks. But if the
shepherd was regarded merely as a servant hired to
see that certain articles of merchandise were not lost
to their owner,—if they, the shepherds of the people,
were hirelings after the same pattern,—if the ties of
father and child were changed into suspicion upon the
one side, dread on the other, a calculation of worldly
interests and advantages on both,—what would these
Parables be to them ? They would prove their truth

even in these cases. It would be seen that the analogy between the human and the divine is not an imaginary or artificial one, but exists in the nature of things. For even such a shepherd, even such a father as they were, would they take God to be. They would worship a self-seeking tyrant under the name of the God of Abraham; and the true God of Abraham would manifest Himself by casting them forth as enemies alike of Him and of His creatures, to be a spectacle and a bye-word among the nations.

V. This terrible test of the veracity of these parables was not however to be the only one. *" Blessed,"* says our Lord to the fishermen about Him, *" Blessed are your eyes, for they see : and your ears, for they hear. For verily I say unto you, that many prophets and kings have desired to see those things which ye see, and have not seen them ; and to hear those things which ye hear, and have not heard them."* What was this blessedness which raised these poor men, these ignorant men, above David and Isaiah ? Was it that they saw the outward face of Jesus ? So did Caiaphas and Pontius Pilate. Was it not that One had apprehended them, whom they confessed to be the Lord and Master of the spirit within them,—who was speaking to that, illuminating that, delivering them from their own miserable conceptions, raising them above any judgments of God deduced from the objects of sense, educating them to know Him as He is ? Was it not that they were under the teach-

ing of One who repulsed no questions, listened to all
doubts, bore with all confusions, showing them that
it was no will of His Father that there should be
veils over their hearts when they heard His words
or contemplated His works ?   Was it not that a
sense of a union between men and God was dawning
upon them, through all the acts and discourses of
Him who called Himself the Son of Man ?   Did not
that name testify to them that He who was speaking to them in the ear in closets, must be indeed the
King of all human hearts, and that as such they
were to declare Him to all nations ?   Was not this
Revelation of the actual glory of the Unseen God in
a man, that which kings and prophets had longed to
see ?   Was not the message that He is the Lord of
Gentiles as well as Jews,—is the head of every man,
—what they desired to hear ?

And so I think we find the explanation of a fact
which has, perhaps, sometimes puzzled us.   Why did
not the Apostles, trained as they were in our Lord's
school, when they went forth among the hardened
Jews, amongst the idolatrous Gentiles, make more
use of Parables?   Why do we find so few in their
discourses or their letters ?   I apprehend that when
they preached of a Son of God and a Son of Man, of
One in whom God was reconciled to men, in Whom
God was showing forth His glory to men, they were
going to the very root of this teaching; they were
enabling mankind to profit by it as they had profited

by it. For if once we receive that fact of God's union
with our race in the Person of a Mediator as the interpretation of all other facts,—as the kernel mystery
of the Universe,—we cannot suppose that we rise to
conceptions of God through the things of time and
sense, we cannot help supposing that through these
things He is speaking to us. The Apostles who bore
witness that a Spirit had been given to dwell among
men, because the Son of Man was glorified at the
right-hand of God, and that this Spirit testifies with
the spirits of men that they are Sons of God, could
not suggest the thought that men must ascend to the
mysteries of the Kingdom of Heaven by an earthly
ladder. They must invite all to enter into the mysteries of that Kingdom as they had done, through a
sense of deep want, through the infinite need of a
Deliverer from their sensuality and their darkness.
They must declare that their Deliverer, their Illu-
minator, was the Deliverer and Light of all, and that
none need walk in darkness,—that any man might
awake out of sleep, and see that Light which would
one day fill the Universe. But this testimony, so far
as it was received, converted all Nature, and all human
acts, from dead letters into divine hieroglyphics, from
instruments of idolatry into preachers concerning the
Unseen and the Eternal.

Such preachers they have been to the humble and
meek, who have asked Christ, as the Disciples did,
to tell them why He spoke by parables, and to in-

terpret the parables which they have found in every
street and alley, as well as in every hill and stream.
We are told, brethren, that they have been deceiving
themselves. No real knowledge of the Eternal is
possible; our conceptions are bounded by the finite
and the visible. My answer is:—If that is the reason, no knowledge of the seen and the temporal is
possible. Slavery to our conceptions, as the teacher
of experimental science has shown us, is the hindrance to any real, solid acquaintance with the mysteries of Nature. When we try to bind her with
the forms of our intellect, she will give us no faithful answers; she will only return an echo to our
voices. Here is another proof of the analogy between
things sensible and spiritual. The same enemy blocks
the entrance into both regions. The determination
to measure all things by ourselves, to bring everything under the conditions of our intellect, makes us
exiles from the Kingdom of Heaven and the Kingdom of Earth. That determination in other days was
called, Pride; in ours (words alter their meaning so
strangely) it claims to be owned as the profoundest
humility. We dare not presume to burst the shackles
which God has imposed upon us; we dare not dream
of ascending above the world in which He has seen
good to place us; that we do not is the great sign
that we accept Christianity with childlike submission.
We prove our allegiance to the Gospel by affirming
that it is *not* given us to know the mysteries of the

Kingdom of Heaven; that the parables of Christ are
not real revelations of it.

For this strange method of vindicating the faith
and confuting its opponents, the venerable authority
of Bishop Butler is sometimes pleaded. The man to
whom some of us owe the first suggestion of the thought
that there is an actual analogy between the things of
Earth and the things of Heaven, between what we see
and what we do not see, between the temporal and
Eternal,—the man who courageously adopted the
words of Origen, with whose mystical tendencies his
cautious intellect could have no sympathy, as the
text of his book and the exposition of its design,—
this man, because, through the coldness of his age,
he gave a somewhat negative form to his argument,
using it rather to refute opponents than to establish a
principle, is now supposed to have employed his clear
logical faculty chiefly for the purpose of undermining
the hopes which he had himself raised, and of maintaining the melancholy proposition that the general
scheme of the Universe is not on the whole much better
or more intelligible than the particular scheme of
Christianity, and that we should not be *more* ignorant
and perplexed than we are, if we had not been obliged,
under terrible penalties, to believe in the Bible. That
it was the intention of this earnest and devout thinker
to make good such conclusions as these, I can never
convince myself; that such an intention has been
imputed to him by admiring disciples, is one proof

more how little in general we gain, how much we may lose, by abandoning our own positions that we may dislodge assailants from theirs.

But it is a comparatively light question, whether we are doing justice or gross injustice to luminaries of our own; whether, as the orator says, we are honouring them in their noonday, or bringing forth our hymns and symbols at the moment of their eclipse. It *is* a very great and serious question indeed, whether our patronage of Christianity is not subverting the revelation of Christ. It is a most serious question for ourselves, whether the mysteries of the Kingdom of Heaven, the eternal realities, are indeed near to us all, and whether we may know them, or whether we may allege that they are far from us, and that by the very nature of our vision it is impossible for us even with the divinest telescopes to discern them. It is a very serious question whether we have any message or not concerning the mysteries of the kingdom of Heaven, to those who are as poor as the fishermen of Galilee were ; or whether we can only appeal to some vague fears which are in them, of a Kingdom of Hell, —not being allowed to tell them that the horror of the Kingdom of Hell consists in the absence of all knowledge of God's Righteousness and Truth and Love. These thoughts must press very heavily upon those who preach ; I trust they press also upon some who hear.

Oh, let us desire for ourselves that we may, as

humble men, as little children, receive the mysteries of the Kingdom of Heaven ; that we may not
substitute an acknowledement of the Scriptures for
a study of their contents, contempt of doubters for
faith in Christ, and so become—as the Jews of old became from the same causes—deaf to the teachings of
the Spirit within, blind to the parables of the world
without !

VII.

PRACTICE AND SPECULATION.

1 PETER i. 13–18.

"WHEREFORE GIRD UP THE LOINS OF YOUR MIND, BE SOBER, AND
HOPE TO THE END FOR THE GRACE THAT IS TO BE BROUGHT UNTO
YOU AT THE REVELATION OF JESUS CHRIST; AS OBEDIENT CHILDREN,
NOT FASHIONING YOURSELVES ACCORDING TO THE FORMER LUSTS IN
YOUR IGNORANCE; BUT AS HE WHICH HATH CALLED YOU IS HOLY,
SO BE YE HOLY IN ALL MANNER OF CONVERSATION; BECAUSE IT
IS WRITTEN, BE YE HOLY; FOR I AM HOLY."

I HAVE chosen these verses as a fitting conclusion to
the subject upon which I have been speaking to you
during these weeks of Epiphany. I have been trying
to ascertain what that Revelation of Jesus Christ is,
of which the writers in the New Testament speak so
continually. Is it, as the word seems to intimate,
the actual unveiling of a Person to the conscience,
heart, reason of human beings? Is it, as the Church
appears to say, the unveiling of the character and
nature of GOD to a creature who is formed to know
Him? Or is it the announcement of certain opinions
and maxims and rules of life to a creature who is
formed *not* to know Him, and who, *because* that is

his condition, must receive whatever, on probable evidence, he can guess to be divine? This has been our question—nearly the most important one with which it is possible for men to occupy themselves. The metaphysical arguments by which the latter opinion has been defended, I have touched upon very slightly. They involve subtleties which the hearers of sermons cannot be expected to follow, which they are likely to judge of rather by their wishes than by their convictions. I have contented myself with suggesting the inquiry whether these arguments, if they are truly stated, do not prove the impossibility of all knowledge whatever,—of that which refers to earth as much as of what is heavenly or eternal. My business has been to show you that the Bible at all events solemnly repudiates the maxim which has been put forth in its defence; repudiates it by all the anticipations of the holy men and prophets of the Old Testament; repudiates it through every work and parable of Christ which is recorded by Evangelists, through every discourse which was delivered by Apostles.

There is, however, one justification of this doctrine which I have hinted at, but not yet fully discussed. It is said that practice, not speculation, is what God desires of men; that His Word sets before them objects of fear and objects of hope; that He tells them what kind of men He would have them be, instead of tempting them to lose themselves in endless mazes of doubt that they may ascertain what He is. To all these propositions I give a hearty assent. I wish you to see how they bear upon the controversy;—for they have, I am satisfied, a direct bearing upon it. What that is, we might have gathered from the Epistle which was read today. But as that Epistle is taken from St. John, and as those who show any special reverence for St. John are said by some to exhibit fatal symptoms of the disease which they call Mysticism, I prefer to take my text from St. Peter,—whom all will admit to be the most practical, the least speculative of teachers,—who in this passage of his Epistle especially, is setting forth the hopes and fears which he would wish his disciples to keep in mind, and the maxims which were to guide them in the fight of life.

I. It will at once occur to you that the expectation which St. Peter speaks of here, is that expectation of the appearing or manifestation or unveiling of Jesus Christ which sustained the Christians of the first age, and which all the Apostles, none more than St. Paul, encouraged by their words and by their example. I have often spoken to you of the opinion which prevails so widely in our day, that this hope was disappointed,—that what they looked for as close at hand was deferred to an immense distance of time,—that there has been no fulfilment of their longings even yet. I have often declared that if that were so, their whole message to mankind, and the lives which illus-

trated it, would seem to me utterly perplexing and
bewildering. For this hope was certainly the staff of
their being; if it was false, the acts and thoughts
which were inspired by it and determined by it, must
also have been false. I could not hope that such
statements would produce much effect upon those
who believed the Apostles to have been generally
under the influence of a delusion ; I desired that they
might be weighed by those who suppose that they
were the heralds of a truth to mankind which is as
needful for this age as it was for theirs.

Now our inquiry respecting the word Revelation is
closely connected with this subject. If it denotes—
wherever it is used, to whatever time it is referred—
the removal of a veil which had hidden the eternal
God from men ;—if from the hour in which men were
created such veils had been removing ;—if the sin of
man, which had seemed to cut him off from God, had
been a means of discovering the nature and essential character of God, by His warfare with it and
forgiveness of it ;—if no one step in Jewish history, or in any history, could be regarded by holy
men except as the instrument of such a discovery,
as setting forth something of the divine power and
righteousness ;—if the one desire of those holy men
was for the complete rending asunder of that which
had hidden from all nations the light in which
they were intended to walk, and in which alone they
could see themselves or see each other ;—if the Son

of Man did, while he was on earth, by all His acts,
discourses, parables, declare the Kingdom of God to
men, did manifest to men the Father;—if, when He
had overcome the sharpness of death, He opened
the Kingdom, and discovered the inner mind of the
Father to all who believed in Him, who received
Him as the well-beloved Son;—if this unveiling of
His Kingdom to men was precisely that which the
Apostles were appointed to preach, and did preach;—
if they preached it to a world which contradicted all
they said, and treated it as ridiculous;—if the spectacle which that world presented seemed to make it
ridiculous to themselves, so that to keep the faith
that it was not all a dream for which they were
giving up the traditions of infancy, old friendships,
all that belonged to life, and life itself, was often
unspeakably hard, and would have been impossible if
the partaking of God's nature had not been the one
only refuge from the curse and plague of their own,
—what encouragement could they hold out but this:
' There will verily be a revelation of the Son of Man
' and of the Son of God to the Universe; it will be,
' whether we look for it or not; it will be attested
' by that doom upon our own holy city and temple of
' which our Lord spoke when He was upon earth, and
' which He denoted as a revelation or appearing of the
' Son of Man; but if you look for it,—if you brace up
' your spirits to the expectation of it,—if you resist
' whatever dulls or stifles that expectation within you,

' —then this unveiling will indeed be to you the satis-
' faction of all your longings, and of all the longings
' of past ages. It will be this blessing to you, because
' it will be not for you, but for the world; because it
' *will be as the lightning, which lighteneth from one*
' *part of heaven, and shineth even to the other.*' You
will see how consistent this language was with all
their other language; how little the use of it was
affected by any ignorance they might have of times
and seasons, or of the exact nature of the change
which was to take place in the condition of the outward world. If what they expected was not a full
unveiling of the Eternal Mind,—of that which is the
same yesterday and today and for ever,—points of
chronology would have been of the most vast importance to them; a mistake about such points would
have been fatal to their hopes. If what they expected was not the full manifestation of Him of
whom the things of time and sense are all testifying,
but about whom no conclusion can be deduced from
them,—their conception of those things would have
determined the degree and character of their hopes.
As it was, the invisible things were no more limited
by the narrowness of their intellects than the vision of sea and sky is limited by the size of the eye
which took it in. Faith, not in some notions or communications about God, but in God himself, made
them inheritors of His righteousness, capable of entering into His infinite love, and of losing themselves
in it.

II. And therefore the practical exhortation, " *Gird up the loins of your mind, be sober,*" had its proper ground in this hope; by this hope it was changed from a mere verbal exhortation into an actual stimulus and power for work. Only the spirit can entertain such a hope as this; those to whom St. Peter wrote were capable of it only so far as they were living in the spirit. They must therefore continually be 'girding' themselves up to the conviction that they were spirits, that Christ had claimed them as spirits, that they could by His grace have all the rights of spirits. They must assure themselves day by day that the Spirit was working with their spirits, that they might not sink, as they were always inclined to sink, under the dominion of low, vagrant, fleshly impulses. Do you think that such an expectation was likely to intoxicate these early Christians with a sense of their own consequence? St. Peter thought it was the one thing which could keep them sober,—sober in the commonest application of the word, by restraining them from indulgences that make the senses their masters; sober, as raising them above the fumes of self-conceit and vanity. For he that is always looking beyond himself and above himself, who is aspiring after the revelation of a Goodness and a Truth which are not in himself, is flying from conceit and vanity, is regarding them as his torments and curses. Himself is his prison-house; Christ has come to set him free from it.

I

Till he has escaped from its bondage altogether, and
has entered into the glorious liberty of the sons of
God,—the liberty from selfish objects, selfish aspirations, selfish limitations,—he cannot be satisfied.
No one had had deeper experience of this truth than
the Apostle. Fisherman as he was, not to think himself above his Master and Lord, not to trust his
own power of going to prison and death, had been
the hardest of all things for him. It was, no doubt,
a battle with him still. And he looked for victory
in that battle by exercising the same hope to which
he encouraged all his fellow-Christians. If he had
any different expectation from theirs,—any dream of
some private or special reward, such as he had entertained when our Lord was upon earth,—he would
soon have lost all that he had learnt from His Cross
and His Resurrection.

III. This is the next point on which I would fix
your attention. The Apostle is addressing a society
of men. He sets the same hope before them all.
There is no discrimination of characters, no attempt
to ascertain which were leading sinful, which were
leading exemplary lives. Why so ? Because the hope
was itself the great test of what they were. Because
the hope itself would be the means of raising those
of them who would be raised. Because the raising
would consist in their casting away partial and selfish ambitions, to entertain a common ambition, ambition for an object in which all might share. Because

hereby it was shown that the Church is a communion of spirits, not a communion of mere creatures of flesh and blood, and that so far as they were pursuing a spiritual object, so far were they attaining the unity of a Church.   Here then we have the Apostle's mode of educating men, by high rewards of glory, immortality, eternal life, to gird up their loins, and to be sober. Here we have his way of terrifying them with the thought of future damnation.   What could be such a damnation as to lose that glory, immortality, eternal life,—as to be left without the knowledge of God?

IV. But this glimpse into the method of his teaching does not give us an adequate conception of its practical character, or of the principle on which it rests.   We must turn to the next passage : " *As obedient children, not fashioning yourselves according to your former lusts in your ignorance ; but as He which called you is holy, so be ye holy in all manner of conversation.*" He refers here to a former condition of mind into which there was a danger of their relapsing, if there was not that strenuous effort, that girding up of the loins of the mind, that sobriety, that hope to the end, which he had urged upon them.   He describes this former state as one which was produced by their ignorance.   I will not take for granted what this ignorance was.   I will turn to one or two passages which may explain it.   The first occurs in the fourth chapter of the Epistle to the Ephesians, the seventeenth and eighteenth verses : " *This I say therefore,*

*and testify in the Lord, that ye henceforth walk not
as other Gentiles walk, in the vanity of their mind,
having the understanding darkened, being alienated
from the life of God through the* IGNORANCE *that is in
them, because of the blindness of their heart."* There
can be no doubt, I think, that when the Apostle who
told the Athenians that they were living, moving,
and having their being in God speaks of an alienation from the life of God, he means an unnatural
separation from Him to whom they ought to have
been united; that by blindness of heart he denotes
the loss of a vision which they were created to enjoy.
And if so, what other ignorance can he have thought
of than ignorance of God? to what other cause than
the absence of an actual knowledge of what He is—
of His nature and character—is the vanity of mind,
the moral evil of the heathen traced?

Perhaps, however, a passage from the Apostle of
the Gentiles may not suffice to illustrate one from the
Apostle of the Circumcision. Take then the opening of St. Peter's own second epistle : " *Simon Peter,
a servant and an Apostle of Jesus Christ, to them that
have obtained like precious faith with us through the
righteousness of God and our Saviour Jesus Christ :
grace and peace be multiplied unto you through the
knowledge of God, and of Jesus our Lord, according
as His divine power hath given unto us all things that
pertain unto life and godliness, through the knowledge
of Him that hath called us to glory and virtue : where-*

by are given unto us exceeding great and precious promises : that by these ye might be partakers of the Divine nature, having escaped the corruption that is in the world through lust." Twice in this short passage is the knowledge of God assumed to be the ground of all good to man. Grace and peace proceed from that knowledge. Whatever belongs to life and godliness, whatever leads to glory and virtue, comes through that knowledge. And see whether this is a mere phrase which admits of different interpretations, which may be explained to mean anything or nothing. St. Peter leaves us no excuse for thrusting in our interpretation. He gives his own : Knowledge of God is that which enables us to become *" partakers of the divine Nature."* If there is not a way of ascending out of our nature into the pure and perfect Nature, he intimates that we have not received that which is necessary to life and godliness, that we have not learnt how we may escape the corruption which is in the world through lust.

I need not tell you that if I had followed up my quotation from St. Paul by an examination of the Epistle from which it is taken or any other of his Epistles, I should have found language exactly answering to this. To put on Christ, to put on the new Man, to be clothed with the righteousness of God, are not only expressions which occur continually in his writings, they are *the* expression of his own inmost mind, they come forth in the midst of his most earnest practical exhortations, they determine the character of his ethics. But, as I have chosen this sentence to make the purpose of my text more evident, I would leave this point to speak of the word "*called*," which occurs in both the passages of St. Peter;—in our text, "As He that hath *called* you is holy, so be ye holy in all manner of conversation;" and in the second Epistle, "Through the knowledge of Him that hath *called* us to glory and virtue." The idea of a Calling is always present to the mind of the Apostle. How could he have entered so thoroughly as he did into the meaning of his nation's existence if it had not been? But what hindered that belief of a calling from being the hard, exclusive belief to him which it was to his countrymen? *This* hindered it. He attached a much fuller and deeper meaning to God's calling than they did. He supposed that a spiritual Being was in very deed calling out the spirits of men to behold His image, to be partakers of His Nature. It was no formal election of a set of favourites of Heaven, who were to earn rewards from which the rest of the world were excluded. It was the election of a people to know what are the rights of men, that they might be witnesses to all men of *their* rights. It was the election of a people to testify that God Himself is leading his creatures out of darkness to light, out of vague notions and conceptions of what is right and holy, to the knowledge, and so to the possession, of His righteousness and holiness.

V. *Because it is written, Be ye holy, for I am holy.*
Here is the immutable morality of the Bible. It
is uttered by Moses; it is repeated by St. Peter. Nothing that has happened in the interval between
them has in the least affected it ; everything that
has happened has brought out its meaning and power
more perfectly. The protecting care and faithful-
ness of the unseen God were unveiled to Abraham ;
he became the faithful man in his care of his family and his flock. A vision of God's foresight was
given to Joseph ; he could teach Pharaoh to foresee.
The *I am*, the Absolutely Righteous one, the guard
of Law and Order, unveiled Himself to Moses, that
name sustaining, not swallowing up, the old name
of the Friend of Abraham, Isaac, and Jacob ; so he
could be the just Lawgiver, the teacher and patient
guide of the people. A divine King caring for men,
feeling with men, yet punishing them for their transgressions, was discovered to David ; so he grew to be a
king after God's own heart. Every prophet confessed
his word speaking in his heart; so he was able to speak
and not be dumb. The prophets felt that God was
caring for the whole nation, and suffering on account
of its sins; so they were able to feel themselves parts
of the nation, and to suffer for its sins. The prophets felt that God had promised to bring all nations
into His family ; so they could long that He should
make Himself known to all nations. Just so far as
they had an apprehension of God's nature, just so

far as they were partakers of that, just so far did they
exhibit the gentleness, purity, truth, which the consciences of men recognize as truly human. And
when the Apostles saw in Jesus of Nazareth Him of
whom Moses and the Prophets did write, then they
knew that this must be so, and why it must be so.
They could doubt no longer that all practical goodness in men corresponds to a goodness in God and is
derived from it, because they owned the Son of Man
as the perfect concentration of that goodness. They
were sure that He had united His divine nature to
the human, that the human might share the divine.
They could solemnly protest against all attempts of
men to establish a righteousness of their own by obedience to the law, or by any acts, as hopeless and immoral; they could preach the Righteousness of God
as manifested to all men in Christ, that all might
with their spirits believe in it, know it, be conformed
to it; and that those who did confess it might let
their light shine forth to the world.

That practical morality,—morality, whether you regard it on the negative side or the positive, as resist-
ance to evil, or as the being good and doing good,
—is connected by the writers of the New Testament
with the actual Revelation of God and the actual
knowledge of God,—I have endeavoured to show. A
less agreeable task remains. I must put it to your
consciences and my own whether our morality has
not been speculative rather than practical, whether we

have not been full of vague, restless doubts as to the
ends we should set before ourselves, as to our relations with other men, as to our standard of character
and of duty, just because we have not believed, or
have believed so weakly, that God has revealed His
own holy nature to us, and that we may be partakers
of it; that He has taken knowledge of us, in order
that we may take knowledge of Him.

Brethren, I cannot help perceiving that the hope and
expectation of any good to come is exceedingly weak
among us all.   There is a dread of an *evil* that may
be threatening the world or threatening ourselves ;
in some minds, a dread of anarchy and infidelity; in
others, a dread lest God should visit them for their
own particular sins when they leave the world.   But
I cannot find that the first dread acts at all as a
check upon infidelity. I cannot find that the second is
effectual against any great temptation, far less against
the daily and continual temptations to harshness,
uncharitableness, injustice.   Least of all does either
of these dreads serve to bind us more closely together
as members of a Nation or a Church.   They isolate
us from each other ; they make us afraid lest every
person we meet should be doing something to rob
us of a comfort which we feel that we hold very
loosely; they make us suspect that intercourse with
our fellow-men on earth may lessen our chances of
heaven.   And so, it having become little more than
a calculation of chances, men begin to reckon up

what it is safe to retain, or worth while to give up, for the sake of obtaining a future good, or for the sake of evading a future misery. Which consideration, as the future misery and the future good are so indefinite, ends generally in our taking what lies before us; not expecting much enjoyment from that, but being ready to bear it, since nothing better has been provided for us.

No man is at all times in this state of mind. Properly speaking, it is not a *state* of mind; it is an oscillation of mind, which, while it lasts, may allow us to be credulous or sceptical, impatient of everything, or eager to place ourselves under absolute authority. And there are moments, I am certain, when other thoughts altogether different from these visit him who is most under the influence of them. There come dim recollections of our being told that we are children of God —or if we are only too familiar with the sound of these words—a suspicion that they may have a meaning;— a meaning for ourselves and a meaning for the multitudes from whom we are trying to distinguish ourselves. And with those words come others stranger and more mystical, but still the words of an Apostle— *" If children, then heirs, heirs of God and joint heirs with Christ."* What can that mean? If it did mean that we, even we, are created to be partakers of the Righteousness, the Love, the Truth of God,—that we have not and cannot have any righteousness, love, truth of our own which can entitle us to any reward from God, but that these are His own rewards,—that these are offered us without money or price,—that these we may be claiming even here,—that these we enter upon as our full inheritance hereafter,—oh, what a difference it would make in our moral state! What a hope would be kindled in us,—a hope which cannot make ashamed,—a hope which we can boldly set before every human being! How little we should care then to convict men of their infidelity! With what shame and sorrow we should confess our own! How we should say to all:—A message has been brought us to which we have none of us given credence—or only a beggarly credence. Is it not the message which meets your questionings and longings as well as ours? Does it not present itself to you as that which in lonely sad hours you have been crying for? Oh, if it does, let us begin to hope together! You have the same right to do it as I have. There is no difference between us, except that I have offended more against God, by professing to hold that which I have not held, —by repeating words without giving them their natural force. But now let us forget the things that are behind. You do not like our pride and self-glorification. Encourage us to hate them, for they keep us from that glory and virtue which are for you, as well as us, through the knowledge of that God who has called us—who is calling us—to be like Him.

And here also would be the remedy for those uneasy thoughts about their own lot in the world to come, which haunt so many gentle and so many ungentle minds; which often lead them to neglect plain practical duties, which aggravate the very sins that give occasion to them. What would they wish to have in this world, or in any other world? Is it not Righteousness, Love, Truth? Is it not the want of these which they feel so bitterly? Yes, surely; because they are seeking them in themselves, and not in God, in whom alone they dwell. Because they are dreading Him as one who requires these things of them, instead of trusting Him as the Righteous, the True, and the Loving,—who invites them to know Him, and so to possess His own infinite treasures.

Brethren! it is because I find here the one escape from the evils by which we are surrounded,—from the lusts of an evil nature,—from the restless speculations of our intellect,—that I have contended so earnestly against those who would take this hope from us. I do not for a moment say that they intend to take it from us. I know well that what men deny with their lips, they may hold in their heart of hearts. I am quite sure that some who, whilst they speak as logicians, seem to tell us that the love of God, which was manifested at the Cross of Christ is not really the same love which is to dwell in our hearts,—that the words which describe its nature are merely accommodations to our conceptions,—I can quite believe that those who use this language, which appears to me so frightful, have a far stronger hold than I

have upon that love, and are exhibiting far better
fruits of it in their lives. Nor ought we to forget that
Logicians, as such, are occupied with the individual
soul, which, as St. Paul tells us in the first Epistle
to the Corinthians, *is* subject to all those conditions
and limitations that make the knowledge of spiritual
things impossible. Schoolmen may naturally think
that it is their business to investigate these conditions and limitations. And therefore we should have
no cause to complain, if they did not intrude into
another region,—if they did not deny the existence
of that *Spirit of man* within us, of which the same
Apostle speaks—that Spirit which acknowledges no
such fetters, but claims fellowship with the Eternal,
and is never satisfied till the Spirit of God has
called it forth to know the truth which alone can
make it free. Of such a human spirit the student
in the poet's legend who was worn out with his books
of Jurisprudence, Medicine, and Theology, and was
ready in his despair to take the poison-cup, became
conscious, when he heard the children singing their
Easter Hymn of the risen Christ. He felt it again
when he went forth into the spring air among the
common people and cried, ' *Here I am a man, here
I dare be one.*' The legend goes on to tell that
he committed that human spirit to the guidance of
an evil, mocking spirit, and so fell into guilt and despair. Not for that terrible possibility which each
one of us may have felt at times to be a possibility

for himself, are we to suppress the lesson which the Apostle of the Gentiles and the Apostle of the Circumcision conspire to teach us. They were alive—how much alive, St. Peter's second Epistle will tell us—to the danger of men acquiring a devilish nature; they were all the more earnest to tell them they were intended to be partakers of the divine Nature. They felt that it was impossible, since the appearance of Christ, to conceal either the glory or the peril of humanity; that if we would awaken men to the last, we must speak to them of the other. There is a middle region, through which we may pass, but in which we cannot dwell. It is a region of clouds, with none of the brightness of Heaven or the firmness of earth. In that region all is speculation; there is no practice. It may be a region of dry logical formulas, or of emotions, sensations, individual feelings. But it is one which we are called to leave by the actual sorrows and miseries that we witness,—by the sense that we are kinsmen with the lowest and worst, as well as with the noblest of our race,—by the voices of friends who, on earth, learnt that there must be an actual Kingdom of heaven, and are beckoning us to seek the home which they, we trust, have found,—by the voice of God Himself bidding us eat the flesh of His Son and drink His blood which are given for the life of the world. That life, that eternal life, is said by the Church to stand in the knowledge of God. When we partake of the sacrifice of Christ, we partake of the mind of God. To know Him is, in the words of the Apostle, to know that love which passeth knowledge. Think not that those who seek that knowledge,—who believe that the Supper of the Lord is the pledge and assurance that all men need it,—that it is offered to all,—will have less of awe and trembling as they enter into the presence of God, than those who stand afar off and affirm they have no capacity for such a gift. Love is far more awful than power. The beloved Disciple who spoke most of knowing God and dwelling in God,—when the High-Priest of the Universe was actually revealed before him, fell at His feet as one dead. Those who most join in St. Paul's prayer for other men and themselves, that they may comprehend with all Saints what is the height and length and breadth and depth of the Divine mystery, are most sure to exclaim with him, "*Oh, the depth of the riches both of the wisdom and of the knowledge of God! How unsearchable are His judgments, and His ways past finding out! For who hath known the mind of the Lord, or who hath been His counsellor? Or who hath first given to Him, and it shall be recompensed unto him again? For of Him and through Him and to Him are all things; to whom be glory for ever. Amen.*"

NOTE.

The passage in the First Epistle to the Corinthians which is alluded to in p. 125, is that from the ninth to the sixteenth verse of the second chapter, inclusive. I shall refer to it in my Letters, in noticing Mr. Mansell's Lecture which gets its text (or motto) from that chapter.

The allusion in the next paragraph is to the speech of Faust when he hears the song ' Christ ist erstanden,' ending with the line—

> " Die Thräne quillt, die Erde hat mich wieder ;"

and to the one in the next scene ending—

> " Hier bin ich Mensch, hier darf ich's seyn."

(Goethe's Werke, 12ter Band, 12mo. pp. 46 and 54.)

LETTERS

TO A

THEOLOGICAL STUDENT

Preparing for Orders.

ON MR. MANSEL'S

BAMPTON LECTURES.

LETTER I.

---◆---

My dear Sir,

I do not wonder that you are spending a portion of the time which remains to you before your examination in the study of Mr. Mansel's Bampton Lectures. You have heard, on good authority, that they expose triumphantly different forms of unbelief or half-belief which exist in Germany and in England. This exposure is not, you are told, like many that have preceded it, made by a man who has only a second-hand acquaintance with the writers whom he condemns, or who condemns them with the zeal and passion of a Theologian. He is a scholar, and has mastered the books against which he warns us; he is a philosopher, and places his warnings on a philosophical ground. His maxim, you are assured, will be as effectual for future Rationalists and semi-Rationalists as for those who flourish in our day. It will be effectual for crushing the questionings that have arisen or may arise in your own mind. It in-

forms you of the Hercules' Pillars beyond which you
cannot, by the very conditions of your intellect, sail
in quest of truth.   How desirable to have such a
monitor !   What a help to a student in divinity, who
must find himself often amidst the quicksands of
written controversies !   What a help to a preacher
of the Gospel, who must encounter the doubts, old
and new, of his lettered or unlettered hearers !   Such
are the motives which will induce you and very
many in your position to hail the appearance of a
book which is said to be the latest expression of Oxford learning and Oxford orthodoxy, which promises
to become the *Ductor Dubitantium* for the nineteenth
century.

You have been a little startled, I suspect, by the
criticism upon these Lectures which appeared some-
time ago in the 'Times' newspaper.   No greater
homage could be paid to Mr. Mansel's ability and
success than the writer of that article was willing to
bestow; he had the knowledge of the subject, which
makes compliments valuable.   But without meaning
in the least to qualify his praise, he pointed out, with
the skill and conscientiousness of a logician, certain
results which followed inevitably from Mr. Mansel's
doctrine.   Others, he said, besides Hegel and the
Germans, our natural enemies, must be crushed beneath it.   *Thomas-à-Kempis* he especially instanced
as one who must henceforth be cast aside as simply
ridiculous.   With him, it was suggested, a number

of divines will perish who are not accused of his mystical tendencies. Where, you have asked your-self, will this prophecy carry us? ‘Am I quite pre-pared, were that all, to part with the Imitation of Christ, the most cherished book of devotion through-out Christendom, dear to Romanists, to Protestants, to Quakers,—the companion of the sick in hospitals, of the solitary prisoner?’

I should doubt the fairness or lawfulness of this inquiry into the consequences of a principle before you had thoroughly examined the principle itself, if I did not perceive that you were already bribed to accept it by the hope of other consequences which look particularly tempting to you. You should not refuse to try the Lectures by their own merits, be-cause if you yield to their arguments, you must aban-don some portions of theological literature which you have been used to consider precious,—even some con-victions which have wrought themselves into your heart, and which come forth almost unconsciously in your language. But since you are prepared to ad-mire Mr. Mansel from the hope that he will enable you henceforth to hold your Theology far more com-fortably, with little disturbance from without or from within, you are not wrong in considering *what* it is that you will rescue from these dangers, what treasures you will have to surrender as the price for keeping the rest in security. I wish you to approach the investigation of his doctrines, and of the deduc-

ductions from it, without an unfair bias for or against
either.   It will not be amiss, therefore, to calculate
a few of the losses we must reckon upon if we bring
Mr. Mansel's powerful weapon into ordinary use; the
gains you know already from higher judges.

(1.) First, then; I cannot doubt that the critic in
the 'Times' was altogether right, and very felicitous,
in his selection of Thomas-à-Kempis as a victim who
must at once be sacrificed.   Did you ask yourself, as
you read, *why* he could not use the shibboleth which
the Bampton Lecturer demands of all theologians?
Is it on account of any qualities which appertain to
him as a monk or as a Romanist?   Is it for that
defect which the Dean of St. Paul's* notices in
him, that his devotion does not lead enough to active exertion,—that he does not tell us we are to
imitate Christ as Him who went about doing good?
Whatever of monastic or mediæval notions may have
mingled with his faith, whatever of justice there may
be in Dr. Milman's criticism,—these are not the
offences which bring him within the scope of Mr.
Mansel's law, which subject him to its extreme penalties.   His crime consists in his assuming that
there is a divine Teacher of man's spirit; that it is
possible for man's spirit to have converse with that
Teacher.   All that is expressed in books of divinity
by the union of the soul with Christ, by living intercourse with Him, is impossible in the very nature

* 'Latin Christianity,' vol. vi. pp. 303-306.

of things, if Mr. Mansel's mode of confuting infidels is the right one. *Non meus hic sermo.* I am merely indorsing the statement of a highly intelligent admirer ; one which I think Mr. Mansel would not himself disclaim.

(2.) When the objection to Thomas-à-Kempis is stated in this way, I scarcely know what divines of any age are not within the peril of it. The Jansenists must give up all their great authors ; the Puritans the best of theirs. You are well read, I doubt not, in Leighton's Commentary, as well as in those ' Prelections' which Professor Scholefield edited so carefully ; those, I mean, that were addressed to an assembly at Edinburgh, not altogether unlike the one which Mr. Mansel addressed at Oxford. These must fall upon the same ground with à Kempis, and upon other grounds, to which I may allude hereafter. In these cases it is not the theoretical part of the divinity which must be rejected ; it is what the writers believed to be the essentially practical part, that which concerned the moral reformation of themselves and their hearers. And note this. Just the part of their teaching which brings them within Mr. Mansel's condemnation, is that which had fallen into oblivion in the last century, and which the conscience of England, the conscience of the most earnest and religious men in England, has demanded again with a voice so loud and imperative, that all the modern discourses even of those who are naturally

disinclined to the use of its favourite language, are
coloured by it.

(3.) For, next, all that history of mental and spiritual experiences which exists either in the old Ha-
giographies or in the Puritan biographies, or which
has been brought forth among us since the days of
Wesley and Whitfield, must be expelled from the li-
braries of Christians, or at least must be treated as
merely fictitious. All these assume an actual living
knowledge of God to be possible for men. They
assume the conversion of the soul to consist in its
awakening to that knowledge. Do you remind me
that there is much in the narratives of such conversions which even those who attach most value to
them trace to an enthusiastic or morbid temperament? I grant you that there is. But I think those
who have most earnestly considered such stories, and
have most brought them to the test of that self-knowledge which Mr. Mansel regards as the exclusive test
of truth, have treated that as the fantastic element in
them which concerns the senses and apparitions to
the senses. This they could refer to the conditions
of the writer's body or to his external circumstances;
whereas just the part which, according to Mr. Mansel, we must discard as delusion, is what they would
confess as sound and true—that which concerns the
internal and spiritual apprehension, the recognition of
the Eternal Being.

(4.) Again, there is one eminent theologian whose

fate we have not to gather from the inferences of any of Mr. Mansel's supporters or disciples. The following passage from himself decides the question:—

" 'God,' says Augustine, 'is not a Spirit as regards " 'substance, and good as regards quality; but both " 'as regards substance. The Justice of God is one " 'with His Goodness and with His Blessedness; and " 'all are one with His Spirituality.' But this asser- " tion, if it be literally true (and of this we have no " means of judging), annihilates personality itself, in " the only form in which we can conceive it. We " cannot transcend our own personality, as we cannot " transcend our own relation to time; and to speak " of an Absolute and Infinite Person, is simply to use " language to which, however true it may be in a " superhuman sense, no mode of human thought can " possibly attach itself." (*Bampton Lectures, 2nd ed. p.* 85.)

Now I would put it to Dr. Pusey, to the Dean of Westminster, to any person differing as widely from them as they differ from each other, provided he has devoted as much attention as they have to the writings of St. Augustine, whether the conclusion which is thus peremptorily announced, that "we cannot " transcend our own personality, as we cannot tran- " scend our own relation to time," annihilates a single passage of this Father; whether it does not annihilate the very man himself? If you cannot wait for their decision, read 'The Confessions,' read any passages which you may stumble upon by chance from the first book to the last, and then ask yourself whether every part of his experience, everything which raised him from a Manichean into a Christian, even from an animal into a man, is not associated with the conviction that he could and did transcend his own personality and his relation to time, that he could and did apprehend the Personality of God.

(5.) Augustine then must perish, and with him all that have thought and written in his spirit: a blow, I need not tell you, to nearly all the most powerful of the mediæval thinkers, even to those who did not follow Augustine in his Platonism, but belonged to the Aristotelian period. How Anselm is treated by Mr. Mansel we shall know by-and-by. Bernard has, of course, no chance of mercy at his hands. If Aquinas is not absolutely scorned, Bonaventura must be. The disciples of Luther might perhaps endure this violence to Schoolmen. They will be foolish if they do. Of all persons *their* Master has the least hope of escaping the new proscription. He hated the logicians precisely because they denied that faith was a way to a direct personal knowledge of God. His Reformation consisted in the assertion that there is a Gospel from God to men, revealing His Righteousness to them, announcing that Righteousness as the foundation of their own.

(6.) But may we not at least retain the Creeds of the Church? We may retain them to this extent:

all objections to them can be proved utterly futile,
because it is impossible for men to know anything
certain about the Nature of God. But these Creeds
profess to tell us something certain about the Nature
of God. Nay, they assume that certainty to be the
deepest certainty, the ground of all other. Must not
they and their antagonists die by the same rule?
Has not Mr. Mansel demonstrated the futility of
both ?

(7.) I cannot tell what your feelings are about alterations in the Prayer-book. You may dread them
less than I do. But are you prepared—is any Dis-
senter in England prepared—for the changes which
Mr. Mansel must demand in it—which the University of Oxford must demand, if the Bampton Lecturer is the faithful representative of her sentiments?
Mr. Mansel has handled with great severity one of
Schleiermacher's doctrines, " as involving something
like hypocrisy in every act of prayer" (Note 16 to
Lecture IV. p. 360). He has therefore a righteous
horror of anything approaching to such hypocrisy.
He could not mean to impute it to so devout and
honest a man as Schleiermacher was in the judgment
of those who differ from him most; he only dreaded
that which might ' involve' it ; might cause it in other
minds if not in his. How much then must the Lecturer tremble at the thought of our using such phrases
as these, " *We who know thee now by faith*," " *In
knowledge of whom standeth our eternal life.*" What

'hypocrisy' must be 'involved' in such language—
what hypocrisy we must be propagating in our Con-
gregations—if we have thoroughly persuaded ourselves
that to know the Infinite and Eternal is impossible!
And yet one of these prayers is read every morning;
and the habit of thought which it indicates may be
traced through the whole Liturgy. Can we be parties
to such an imposture? Must we not purge our consciences of it, if we do not wish to bring down a curse
upon ourselves and upon our land?

I shall not now speak of the revision—not of our
translation of the Bible, but—of the Bible itself, which
will be necessary if the doctrine of the Lectures is
true. That is the subject of the Sermons I have
sent you. That subject will recur again and again
in the course of these Letters. I confine myself now
to some topics which should press very heavily on
the consciences of us who are offering up prayers in
the Church, and who are inviting men to enter into
actual communion with God. They need not press
so heavily upon yours if you, before you take the
irrevocable step of binding yourself by vows of Ordination, consider solemnly whether you can really,
in a simple sense, use the words which the Church
puts into your lips,—whether they are to you honest
words or deceitful words. I conjure you, as you
value your own peace, as you care for the souls that
will be committed to you, not to evade that inquiry,
but resolutely to grapple with it, arming yourself for

any consequence to which it may lead you. I rejoice in the publication of Mr. Mansel's book nearly
as much as its most vehement admirers can rejoice.
I look upon it more, not less, than they do as a critical event in the history of the English Church.
For the question must now be asked of each one of
us,—Do you take those words about knowing God
which occur in books of devotion, in old divines, in
the Prayer-book, in the Bible, literally or figuratively,
—in a less exact sense than you would use the word
know as applied to some other subject, or in the most
exact sense, the one which determines its use in reference to any other subject? Because we have not
given a distinct answer to this question in our own
minds, because we have used one kind of language
on our knees before God and another in our arguments with men, our discourses to the people have
been confused and unsatisfactory; they have not understood whether we came to them with good tidings,
or with ill tidings, or with no tidings at all. Thank
God for any one who understands his meaning, and
so can compel us to understand our meaning ! Thank
God for any one who compels two principles that
have long fought blindly in the twilight to come forth
and meet each other in the open day !

I am glad, also, that those two contradictory principles concerning the knowledge of God cannot be
brought into conflict without discovering two contradictory methods in which the Bible may be presented

to the acceptance of mankind. For those who say that no knowledge of the Eternal is to be had, and that the Bible offers us something in place of it, must regard every search which men have made after such knowledge with suspicion,—must delight to register their mistakes, their inconsistencies, their disappointments. If, in the height of their pride or in the agony of their failure, these seekers have uttered words like the east wind,—words in which reproaches, often just, against men were mixed with unbelief of God,—all these must be preserved and triumphantly proclaimed, there being, it would appear, some comfort or some virtue in recollecting that creatures of our flesh and blood have given us an excuse for condemning them. Scorn of their folly in attempting to reach some height which they could not attain is, however, in these days, a more favourite indulgence than indignation at the worst moral perversity. A man may grovel in the stye without attracting any special notice from the modern defender of Christianity; if he aspires by an irregular method after righteousness, no laughter is too loud for his punishment.

He who holds that the Bible testifies from its first page to its last that God has created men for the knowledge of Himself, and is kindling in them a thirst for that knowledge, a discontent with anything which comes short of it,—cannot by possibility listen without the profoundest interest to every cry of men after it in one age or another. He must not ask first what they have failed to attain, but what they have been permitted to attain. He must be glad to learn from their blunders as well as their successes : perceiving in the first the likeness of his own; in the second, the guidance of God. He may not expect their opinions or conclusions to do much for him; their struggles and questionings and glimpses of light he will cherish, and be thankful for. All will appear to him to be pointing to a full-orbed Truth which is not in them but in God, and which He has manifested in the Eternal Word, the only begotten Son. The remembrance of hard and proud words spoken against those who were crying out for Truth will be always the bitterest in his life, that which recurs to him with the keenest sense of having grieved the Holy Spirit of God, of having brought upon him the curse of a brother's blood. And if he may look upon that sin as blotted out in the blood of the great Elder Brother of the whole family, he must ask that hereafter he may regard the Sermon on the Mount as if it were not an interpolation in the Divine Book, —that he may accept it as the law of his discourses and acts, not only in his daily life, but *even* when he is contending for the faith once delivered to the saints.

Yours very truly,

F. D. M.

LETTER II.

———◆———

My dear Sir,

In Mr. Mansel's preface you will find these
words:—" It is to a philosopher of our own age and
" country that we must look for the true theory of
" the limits of human thought, as applicable to the-
" ological, no less than to metaphysical researches,
" —a theory exhibited indeed in a fragmentary and
" incomplete form, but containing the germ of nearly
" all that is requisite for a full exposition of the
" system. The celebrated article of Sir William Ha-
" milton, on the Philosophy of the Unconditioned,
" contains the key to the understanding and appreci-
" ation of nearly the whole body of modern German
" speculation. His great principle, that 'the Un-
" 'conditioned is incognizable and inconceivable, its
" 'notion being only negative of the Conditioned,
" 'which last can alone be positively known or con-
" 'ceived,' has suggested the principal part of the

"inquiries pursued in the present work; and his "practical conclusion, 'We are thus taught the sa-"'lutary lesson, that the capacity of thought is not "'to be constituted into the measure of existence; "'and are warned from recognizing the domain of "'our knowledge as necessarily coextensive with the "'horizon of our faith,' is identical with that which "is constantly enforced throughout these Lectures." (p. viii.)

Our attention is drawn in this passage to a very remarkable article published originally in the 99th No. of the 'Edinburgh Review' (Oct. 1829), included afterwards in a volume of 'Discussions on Philosophy and Literature, Education and University Reform,' which appeared in the year 1852. Obtain, if you can, the Essay in its latest form. The notes which have been added at the bottom of the pages are very important for the illustration of this particular subject. The accompanying Dissertations are scarcely less important for the illustration of the writer's mind. But at all events, do not study Sir William Hamilton merely in the pages of his Oxford disciple; if you take that course, you will not appreciate either his philosophy or Mr. Mansel's theology.

I do not give you this caution because I think Mr. Mansel has perverted the doctrine of his Edinburgh teacher, but because that doctrine, as it stands 'in his quotation, I apprehend would be simply unintelligible to the majority of those who turn to his Lec-

tures as to an armoury which will supply them with
weapons against unbelievers.   Hence I fear they will
be involved in practical dishonesty.   They will not
care what the ground of the argument is.   That they
will leave to Mr. Mansel, taking it for granted that
so profound a logician knows all about it.   Nay, I
am not sure that their want of comprehension of his
fundamental maxim will not lead them to regard the
conclusions which he has deduced from it with more
devout   astonishment,   and   more   perfect   credence.
" These   great   words, *unconditioned, incognizable*," so
they will reason, " must be sufficient to demolish the
German speculations.   We may receive the practical
advantages of the demolition in the security of our
own opinions."

No such satisfaction to easy inquirers was contemplated by Sir William Hamilton.   He did not overlook the fact that there was a relation between his
maxim and the controversies of theologians.   But he
was nearly indifferent to the use which adverse divines might make of it.   The theological hints which
are contained in his notes are of great worth from
their sincerity, from their not being adapted to fit
into any system, sometimes from their startling bold-
ness, sometimes from—what you would less expect in
so accurate a thinker, such an abhorrer of contradictions—their   obvious   inconsistencies.   But the substance of the Essay has an interest of another kind.
What   strikes   one   in   Mr. Mansel's   quotation   as   a

piece of dry technical logic, insignificant till we can
see its effects in the downfall of some party foe, is
taken out of its folds and translated into life. It suggests an historical examination of English, Scotch,
French, German habits of thought. It is not merely
destructive, for Sir William Hamilton appears as the
patriotic champion of Reid and his doctrine of consciousness, if the schools of other countries are to be
swept utterly away.

The Essay is a criticism on M. Cousin's *Cours de
Philosophie*. It explains, with a clearness and can-
dour which the subject of it generously acknowledged,
what the design of M. Cousin's work—properly speaking, of his life—was; how he had rebelled against
the sensualism which Condillac had developed out of
Locke; how much he had been influenced for a time
by the philosophy of Reid, which had expanded the limits of experience as they were settled by Locke and
his French followers, but had confined itself rigidly
within those limits; how he had yielded to the influence of certain Germans who held that the pursuit
of the Absolute is *the* pursuit of Philosophy; how he
had attempted to reconcile the two in an Eclectical
or Catholic Philosophy of his own. Sir William
Hamilton's object is to show that this experiment is
hopeless; that all which Cousin had learnt from the
Germans was mere delusion; that for the mind to
discover that which is beyond its own conditions, is
simply impossible. He thus enumerates the opinions

which may be entertained respecting the *Unconditioned* as an object of knowledge or thought :—" 1°, The Un-" conditioned is incognizable and inconceivable; its " notion being only negative of the conditioned, which " last can alone be positively known or conceived.— " 2°, It is not an object of knowledge; but its notion, " as a regulative principle of the mind itself, is more " than a mere negation of the conditioned.—3°, It is " cognizable, but not conceivable; it can be known " by a sinking back into identity with the absolute, " but is incomprehensible by consciousness and re-" flection, which are only of the relative and the " different.—4°, It is cognizable and conceivable by " consciousness and reflection, under relation, differ-" ence, and plurality. The first of these opinions we " regard as true; the second is held by Kant; the " third by Schelling; and the last by our author." (p. 12.)

The mere statement of the opinion of so eminent a man as Sir William Hamilton, that these experiments are utterly unreasonable, would of course carry great weight with ignorant people like you and me. But, moreover, how much there is in our own minds which seconds his decision ! He appeals directly to our common sense. He asks whether the notion of thought passing beyond the boundaries of thought is not absurd upon the face of it,—whether we can conceive the inconceivable,—whether we can know that which we do not conceive ? Set such questions be-

fore any number of civilized persons,—say in a London drawing-room,—and what answer could you expect but just as much laughter as the courtesies of
society permitted? What need, as Sir W. Hamilton
sometimes asks himself,—and Mr. Mansel frequently
echoes him,—of debating the point? Is it not like
entering into a controversy with lunatics?

I wish you to give this consideration all possible
weight; to observe how ridiculous a pursuer of the
Absolute makes himself in the eyes of these eminent
logicians and in his own; and then to reflect upon
a few other facts which also are vouched for by
Sir W. Hamilton, and are as indisputable as any in
history.

I. The first is expressed in these words :—" From
" Xenophanes to Leibnitz, the Infinite, the Absolute,
" the Unconditioned, formed the highest principle of
" speculation." In other words, from the beginning
of the most earnest Greek philosophy,—of that Eleatic school of Greek philosophy to which the discovery of the science of logic is commonly attributed,
—down to the commencement of the eighteenth
century,—after Bacon and Locke had written,—the
most thoughtful and vigorous minds were devoting
themselves to that pursuit which it would seem that
only madmen can engage in. This conclusion is deduced, not from any statement of mine, but from one
which I have given you in the very words of Sir W.
Hamilton.

II. But a time came shortly after Leibnitz, when one might have hoped that this running after visions would have been stopped for ever. That which was not effected by the sensualism of Locke, was on the point of being effected, Sir W. Hamilton thinks, by Kant's ' Critique of the Pure Reason.' If there should chance to linger in any Scotch or English mind the notion which was very prevalent at the beginning of this century, that the philosopher of Königsberg was himself a dreamer or an idealist, the following sentences from one who did not speak of him from hearsay, but from study, may suffice to scatter it.

" In his first *Critique*, Kant undertakes a regular
" survey of consciousness. He professes to analyze the
" conditions of human knowledge,—to mete out its
" limits,—to indicate its point of departure,—and to
" determine its possibility. That Kant accomplished
" much, it would be prejudice to deny ; nor is his ser-
" vice to philosophy the less, that his success has been
" more decided in the subversion of error than in the
" establishment of truth. The result of his examina-
" tion was the abolition of the metaphysical sciences,
" —of rational psychology, ontology, speculative the-
" ology, etc., as founded on mere *petitiones principi-*
" *orum*. Existence is revealed to us only under spe-
" cific modifications, and these are known only under
" the conditions of our faculties of knowledge. 'Things
" in themselves,' Matter, Mind, God,—all, in short,
" that is not finite, relative, and phenomenal,—as

" bearing no analogy to our faculties, is beyond the
" verge of our knowledge. Philosophy was thus re-
" stricted to the observation and analysis of the phe-
" nomena of consciousness; and what is not expli-
" citly or implicitly given in a fact of consciousness,
" is condemned, as transcending the sphere of a le-
" gitimate speculation. A knowledge of the uncon-
" ditioned is declared impossible; either immediate-
" ly, as a notion, or mediately, as an inference. A
" demonstration of the absolute from the relative is
" logically absurd; as in such a syllogism we must
" collect in the conclusion what is not distributed in
" the premisses: And an immediate knowledge of the
" unconditioned is equally impossible." (p. 16.)

With such a champion arising in the very country
of the enemy, what might not have been expected?
But hear the result :—

" Kant had annihilated the older metaphysic, but
" the germ of a more visionary doctrine of the abso-
" lute, than any of those refuted, was contained in
" the bosom of his own philosophy. He had slain the
" body, but had not exorcised the spectre of the ab-
" solute; and this spectre has continued to haunt the
" schools of Germany even to the present day. The
" philosophers were not content to abandon their me-
" taphysic; to limit philosophy to an observation of
" phenomena, and to the generalization of these phe-
" nomena into laws. The theories of Bouterweck (in
" his earlier works), of Bardili, of Reinhold, of Fichte,

" of Schelling, of Hegel, and of sundry others, are just
" so many endeavours, of greater or of less ability, to
" fix the absolute as a positive in knowledge." (p. 18.)

What have we been told here? In the eighteenth
and nineteenth centuries, after a denial, by Hume,
not only that the Absolute and Eternal could be
known, but that there was an Absolute and an Eternal,—after all the efforts of Reid and his school to
vindicate the results of experience from what seemed
Hume's inevitable inferences,—finally, after Kant's
annihilating criticism, which seemed to leave no scope
for Metaphysic, in its old sense, ever again to lift
its head,—there has been more eager search after
that which passes the limit of experience, more feeling that somehow that *must* be the business of human search, than even in the period between Xenophanes and Leibnitz. The kind of ridicule which
Sir William Hamilton has poured upon such inquiries, was poured upon them in every age. Schelling knew such jokes from his boyhood; Hegel must
have learnt them from doctors and jesters old and
new. Yet these men, whose dialectical faculty has
never been disputed,—is not disputed by Mr. Mansel,—acquainted with history, interested in the condition of humanity,—amidst the falls of thrones and
empires, in the country which most felt the shock
of the French earthquake,—could not be withdrawn
from these wild inquiries,—could not be prevented
from drawing a multitude of disciples after them, or

from influencing more or less decidedly the politics,
the religion, even the ordinary life of Germans who
knew little of the nature or course of their speculations !

III. A line which Sir William Hamilton adopts
from an old author with whom his extensive reading
had made him acquainted,—

"Gens ratione ferox et mentem pasta chimæris,"

may perhaps account satisfactorily to some minds
for these phenomena in Germany.   But what is
the occasion of this Dissertation?   The passing of
the same delusion into France,—that country from
which all dreams of the Absolute seemed to have
been banished since the days of Malebranche,—that
country which is called by our learned author, "the
metaphysical antipodes of Germany."   He was led
to notice it because some of its most dangerous
symptoms appeared in a man who had passed under
the healthful discipline of Reid and Stewart, who
busied himself, as we all know, in the most practical
questions concerning the education of his own country
and of other countries, to whose "learning, elegance,
distinguished ability," his Edinburgh critic bears
abundant testimony.   And it was not a monomania.
"Two thousand auditors" (I quote again from the
Essay, p. 2) "listened all with admiration, nay with
"enthusiasm, to the eloquent exposition of doctrines
"intelligible only to the few; and the oral discussion

"of philosophy awakened in Paris and in France an "interest unexampled since the days of Abelard."

IV. A madness spread over so many countries and ages, resisting so many remedies which were suggested by the wisest men, starting up again when it was least expected, is a fact demanding investigation. I cannot think that Sir William Hamilton has investigated it. He has merely announced it. Mr. Mansel may perhaps tell us something, in the course of his book, about the causes and growth of the disease which he proposes to extirpate. But we must recollect that his book itself adds one more startling fact to those I have already enumerated. It is not only France which has taken the infection. If he did not believe that England, practical England, was liable to the same danger—if he did not discover indications of it in Oxford, in spite of the number of influences which are likely to counteract it there,—he would not of course have devoted so much of time and toil to the subject of his Lectures. How have *we* come within the reach of this temptation? How is it that neither the religious culture of Oxford, nor that more thorough and continual discipline of the Stock Exchange to which we are subjected in London, has been effectual to ward it off? It is a point which is worthy of the deepest study. Shall I try to give you one or two reasons which have occurred to me, and which I should like you to ponder?

(1.) You may be surprised when I say that the

earnest attention of Englishmen to physical studies—
and to mathematics as the chief instrument for arriving at any clear and sound acquaintance with physical studies,—has somewhat deadened the force of
the ridicule which Sir W. Hamilton would bestow on
those who from Xenophanes to Schelling have tried
to surmount the conditions of their own minds. For
that effort which is said to be monstrous when it is
made in the search of metaphysical truth, is the very
one which Bacon taught the student that he must
make if he would advance one step in the knowledge
of Nature. The Schoolmen, who had done such good
work in ascertaining the terms under which we judge
and name things, had wished to limit Nature by
those terms. Therefore, Bacon said, all her secrets
were hidden from them. Was it not the business of
the 'Novum Organum' to show men how they had
failed to enter into the true meaning of the objects
which they pretended to examine, because they had
made their senses and the notions of their understandings the measures of them? Was it not the
purpose of that book to point out a method of investigation by which we might rise not only above
the conceits of our individual minds, but above those
which belong to us as members of a species? The
possibility of such a method was easily recognized by
the Mathematician. He was rather inclined to affirm that it was not new at all, but the· one to which
he had always been accustomed, the method of as-

cending from a particular case to the affirmation of
a universal law. The Logician, trained to the opposite method, of descending from general propositions
to individual cases, rebelled against the lesson, nay,
has never heartily admitted it to this hour, though
compelled to pay it a conventional respect. Sir William Hamilton, a Logician in the most thorough
and exclusive sense, was too consistent and too honest not to avow his abhorrence of Mathesis.* No
wonder he thought Mathematics 'not an improving
study,' likely to 'induce credulity,' likely also to 'induce Scepticism.' A brave man doubtless, reckless
of popularity, ready to overthrow the discoveries of
generations past, or the prospects of generations to
come, rather than sacrifice his consistency. One
cannot but honour him for his sincere, cordial,
'unconditioned' hatred of that which had no meaning for him. It is amusing to hear such denunciations connected with the cultivation of humility;
but that boast too is instructive, as the fierceness
of Sir W. Hamilton's contempt for some scientific
men of European reputation, and for some scholars
not thought wholly despicable, at least on this side
of the Tweed, is also instructive. The rules of the
Logician could not bind the man. The victims of
his scorn may have sometimes laughed that such a
man should be, and have oftener wept that Atticus
was he. Those who contemplate him from a distance

* See 'Discussions,' p. 257.

may be thankful for all contributions to the illustration of a mind so remarkable in its weakness as well as in its strength. But since Sir William Hamilton has not succeeded in his raid against English Mathematics, he has not succeeded in persuading Englishmen that there is not a way, and a most legitimate way, in which men may ascend above the conditions of their own intellects, in which they *must* do it if they are not to account the belief ridiculous that the earth moves round the sun, as well as every other belief in that which is, instead of that which appears.

(2.) But if our experimental studies, which we generally regard, and I think rightly regard, as a great protection against some of the worst tendencies of the German mind, makes us indisposed to accept *that* protection against them which Sir William Hamilton and Mr. Mansel would offer us, I believe there is another influence which works still more powerfully in the same direction. The Bampton Lecturer would speak of the reverence for the Scriptures which we acquire in our nurseries, and which our public Schools and Universities at least design to foster, as one of our great national possessions, which especially distinguishes us from Germans, and which we are jealously to watch over. I entirely accede to this opinion; only expressing my conviction that we are not guarding the treasure, but endangering it, if we make it an excuse for boasting of ourselves, or for

triumph over any other country. But this reverence
for Scripture is that which, in my judgment, makes
it impossible for us to look upon Sir W. Hamilton's
dogma as conclusive against the search after the Absolute which he shows to have had such an attraction for the most thoughtful men. I will not repeat
what I have said already, or anticipate what I may
say hereafter upon this subject. I will merely refer
you to one or two of the passages in Sir W. Hamilton's notes, in which he gives his own theological application of his position. The first occurs in a note
to p. 15. "True, therefore, are the declarations of
"a pious philosophy :—'A God understood would be
"'no God at all;'—'To think that God is, as we can
"'think him to be, is blasphemy.'—The Divinity, in
"a certain sense, is revealed; in a certain sense con-
"cealed : He is at once known and unknown. But
"the last and highest consecration of all true religion
"must be an altar Ἀγνώστῳ Θεῷ,—'To the unknown
"'and unknowable God.' In this consummation, na-
"ture and revelation, paganism and Christianity, are
"at one; and from either source the testimonies are
"so numerous that I must refrain from quoting any.
"Am I wrong in thinking, that M. Cousin would not
"repudiate this doctrine?" Now it cannot help striking any person brought up in our English reverence
for Scripture, that Sir W. Hamilton is here, not by
inference, but in direct terms, contradicting St. Paul.
He affirmed that the altar to the Unknown God was

not the last and highest consecration of true religion. " *Him whom ye ignorantly worship*," he said, " de-" clare I unto you."

I am not the least anxious to strain this point, or to use it as the ground of a charge against Sir William Hamilton. Every one knows what an excuse it would have been, if it had occurred in any German philosopher, for raising the cry that he wished to set aside Christianity as an obsolete and imperfect religion, and to " consecrate " a higher system. But God forbid that I should make a man an offender for a word, even if that word is the legitimate deduction from a proposition which is used for the purpose of making all other men offenders, and is vaunted as the basis of all orthodoxy ! I rejoice to believe that Sir W. Hamilton meant to be a pious philosopher ; I rejoice to discover in this very passage a wavering and uncertainty of mind, showing that the spirit within him demanded that resting place in the Absolute and Eternal, which he said that men were not permitted, by the conditions of their intellect, to seek after.

A still stronger evidence that it was so, is contained in a note to the 19th page. After quoting a line from Manilius, " None can feel God who shares not " in the Godhead," (which is used as a statement, though Sir W. Hamilton thinks an inadequate statement, of that kind of Pantheism which Schelling at one period of his life advocated,) he goes on to say :

—" Manilius has likewise another (poetically) laud-
" able line, of a similar, though less exceptionable,
" purport :—

> ' Exemplumque Dei quisquis est in imagine parva ;'
> (' Each is himself a miniature of God.')

" For we should not recoil to the opposite extreme;
" and, though man be not identical with the Deity,
" still is he ' created in the image of God.' It is, in-
" deed, only through an analogy of the human with
" the Divine nature, that we are percipient and reci-
" pient of Divinity. As *St. Prosper* has it:—' Nemo
" possidet Deum, nisi qui possidetur à Deo.'—So *Se-*
" *neca :—*' In unoquoque virorum bonorum habitat
" Deus.'—So *Plotinus :—*' Virtue tending to consum-
" mation and irradicated in the soul by moral wisdom,
" reveals a God ; but a God destitute of true virtue
" is an empty name.'—So *Jacobi :—*'From the enjoy-
" ment of virtue springs the idea of a virtuous; from
" the enjoyment of freedom, the idea of a free ; from
" the enjoyment of life, the idea of a living ; from
" the enjoyment of a divine, the idea of a godlike—
" and of a God.'—So *Goethe :—*

> ' Wär' nicht das Auge sonnenhaft,
>   Wie könnten wir das Licht erblicken ?
> Lebt' nicht in uns des Gottes eigne Kraft,
>   Wie könnte uns das Göttliche entzücken ?'

" So *Kant* and many others. (Thus morality and reli-
" gion, necessity and atheism, rationally go together.)
" —The Platonists and Fathers have indeed finely

" said, that ' God is the soul of the soul, as the soul
" is the soul of the body.'

'Vita Animæ Deus est ; hæc Corporis. Hâc fugiente,
Solvitur hoc ; perit hæc, destituente Deo.'

" These verses are preserved to us from an ancient
" poet by John of Salisbury, and they denote the com-
" parison of which Buchanan has made so admirable
" a use in his *Calvini Epicedium*." (p. 19, note.)

This interesting, if somewhat startling, passage exhibits a noble struggle in the heart and mind of a
man after a living God, a God nigh and not afar off.
By the light of it we must study that passage which
Mr. Mansel has taken as the text of his lectures;
" We are thus taught the salutary lesson that the ca-
" pacity of thought is not to be constituted into the
" measure of existence, and are warned from recog-
" nizing the domain of our knowledge as necessarily
" co-extensive with the horizon of our faith." The first
half of this proposition brings out with great clearness the philosophical question which is at issue between Sir W. Hamilton and his opponents. Have we
anything in us which can apprehend that which *is* ?
Are we merely circumscribed by that which we think ?
In other words; is the opinion of one man or of all
men that which determines what we know? This is
a fair way of stating the case. We may play with
the words Absolute and Infinite for ever; but here
is the problem which applies to the least things as
much as the greatest. Can we come into contact with

M

the meaning, the substance, the reality of anything in earth or Heaven? Have we nothing in place of that knowledge but a semblance or appearance which is presented to us? Now here I think our child's faith in the Bible comes in to give its vote, whatever that may go for, in favour of those philosophers whom Sir W. Hamilton and Mr. Mansel condemn. This faith certainly has assumed the Bible to be a book which witnesses against the appearances and notions of men about the Being of whom it speaks,—which testifies that He wishes us to rise above all appearances and notions, and to believe in that which He actually is. And if it be so, then this same child-like reverence for the Bible would lead us to look at the second clause of Sir W. Hamilton's sentence in quite a different light from that in which it presents itself to his admirer. Our faith may have a very wide horizon, far beyond the limits of our conceptions. But *the* Being will be the limit and the object of it. It will not be concerned with a multitude of opinions about Him. It will be in direct affiance to Himself. It will be always craving for the knowledge of Him, just as the eye craves for the sight of any of His visible works. I could almost venture to adopt Sir W. Hamilton's own question to Cousin, " Am I wrong in thinking," that he who made those quotations from St. Prosper, from Seneca, from Plotinus, from Jacobi, " would not repudiate this doctrine?" Am I wrong in thinking that so far as here on earth he repudiated it, he did so because he had not quite accepted St. Paul's statement of the way in which *the* eternal Being has met the seekings of His creatures after Him?

In one of his discussions, that on the Philosophy of Perception, p. 39, Sir William Hamilton has said, "Plato has profoundly defined man, 'the hunter of "truth;' for in this chase, as in others, the *pursuit* is "all in all, the *success* comparatively nothing. 'Did "'the Almighty,' says Lessing, 'holding in his right "'hand *Truth*, and in his left *search after Truth*, deign "'to proffer me the one I might prefer;—in all hu- "'mility, but without hesitation, I should request— "'*Search after Truth*.'" I love Plato's definition as much as Sir W. Hamilton does. I should agree with him and with Lessing, if I did not believe that the revelation of Truth was at once the awakening and the satisfaction of the search after Truth; because it is the revelation of Him who is Truth to the crea- ture who is made in His image. This is the ground of my conflict with Mr. Mansel. He seems to me to crush the search after Truth, all that is expressed in the word *Philosophy*, by crushing at the same time the discovery of Truth, all that is expressed in the word *Revelation*. I do not believe that the heart of Sir W. Hamilton would have gone along with him in this experiment, whatever excuse may be found for it in his formal dialectics. I am sure that neither the practical sense nor the reverence of the English

mind will go along with him. There is one reason
more, besides those I have given, why it should not.
It is not only philosophers, Greek, German, French,
English, from Xenophanes to Hegel, who have been
busy in the search after the absolute. That eminent
Oriental scholar, whom Oxford has done herself so
much honour by adopting among her sons, Mr. Max
Müller, will tell us that Buddhism, the most extensive religion in the world, is just as much as Hegelism a search after the Absolute, may just as much
as Hegelism terminate in Nothingness. Is the best
message we can send from the West to 300,000,000
of people, " You have been dreaming a dream; we
" can show you that all you have been living for
" does indeed mean Nothing"? Or may we say this?
" The search after the Absolute becomes a contra-
" diction when we try to comprehend it in a notion
" of our own minds. But the Absolute Himself has
" stirred you to it, because it has been His purpose to
" reveal Himself to you."

Faithfully yours,

F. D. M.

LETTER III.

MR. MANSEL'S PREFACE.——BUTLER.

My dear Sir,

I think we shall save time in the end, if we dwell a little longer upon Mr. Mansel's Preface, before we proceed to his Lectures. He has introduced us to an eminent Scotch Philosopher. I have tried to show you what good we may derive from him, and where he fails us. The next paragraph brings before us an English Divine, with whom we are acquainted already; whom we both, I trust, regard with reverence and gratitude. "But if the best theoretical expression of "the limits of human thought is to be found in the "writings of a philosopher but recently removed from "among us; it is in a work of more than a century "old that we find the best instance of the acknow- "ledgment of those limits in practice. *The Analogy* "*of Religion, Natural and Revealed, to the Constitu-* "*tion and Course of Nature,* furnishes an example of "a profound and searching philosophical spirit, com- "bined with a just perception of the bounds within

" which all human philosophy must be confined, to
" which, in the whole range of similar investigations,
" it would be difficult, if not impossible, to find a pa-
" rallel.   The author of that work has been justly
" described as ' one to whose deep sayings no thought-
" ' ful mind was ever yet introduced for the first time,
" ' without acknowledging the period an epoch in its
" ' intellectual history;' and it may be added that
" the feeling of admiration thus excited will only be
" increased by a comparison of his writings with the
" pretentious failures of more ambitious thinkers.
" Connected as the present author has been for many
" years with the studies of Oxford, of which those
" writings have long formed an important part, he
" feels that he would be wanting in his duty to the
" University to which he owes so much, were he to
" hesitate to declare, at this time, his deep-rooted
" and increasing conviction, that sound religious phi-
" losophy will flourish or fade within her walls, ac-
" cording as she perseveres or neglects to study the
" works and cultivate the spirit of her great son and
" teacher, Bishop Butler." (pp. ix., x.)

Mr. Mansel could not more happily have distinguished Sir William Hamilton from Butler, than by
speaking of one as a theorist and the other as a practical man.   They are admirable specimens of two
diametrically opposite kinds of intellect.   With an
immensely wider range of reading, perhaps with far
greater metaphysical power, Sir W. Hamilton's na-

tural dwelling-place is evidently amidst notions and opinions. Whatever subject he contemplates, he must reduce under some notion ; till he can do so, it has no interest, scarcely any existence, for him. Bishop Butler is impatient of notions ; he would translate them all into facts if he could. It is among facts that he lives ; he cares for nothing else. What he wants is to find out their meaning ; he would go into the depths or the heights for the sake of ascertaining that. He would never be tempted to forsake the firm ground of earth by the finest theory that was ever invented.

Mr. Mansel therefore has good reason for thinking that he has here found a man who is exceedingly unlike Schelling or Hegel, or even Cousin. But he has not a right to say that he has found a man who will run in the same team with Sir W. Hamilton. If by saying that one has " expounded the limits of human " thought," and that the other is " the best instance " of the acknowledgment of *those* limits in practice," he merely means that Butler, in his judgment, is not a madman,—since all in his judgment *are* madmen who attempt to transgress the limits of thought which Sir W. Hamilton has marked out,—the admirers of Bishop Butler must accept that compliment with becoming gratitude. But if he means that Butler has alluded anywhere to those limits of thought, and has signified his intention of confining himself within them, the passages in his writings which contain that announcement should have been produced. I cannot find them. His work is of the tentative, experimental kind. He begins from what he sees, not from some definition of what he could or could not conceive. He does not descend from Generals, but ascends from Particulars. He will start from the very lowest probability; but what he is feeling after is something fixed and certain. I then " should be " wanting in my duty to the University to which I " owe," not so much as Mr. Mansel, but very much, " if I did not declare at this time .my deeply- " rooted conviction that Oxford cannot cultivate the " spirit of her great son and teacher, Bishop Butler," if she confounds two methods of study which are so entirely unlike as these,—if she accepts the dissertation on the Unconditioned as the measure and rule by which she is to try the ' Analogy.'

Wishing as heartily as Mr. Mansel can do, that the students of Oxford should continue to reverence Butler, and should receive even greater benefits from him than any which they have received hitherto, I cannot conceal from myself that there are serious difficulties in the way of the accomplishment of this desire. They are difficulties which may be overcome if we state them fairly to ourselves; if we believe that Butler, like every great and generative thinker, has the power of adapting himself to circumstances and conditions which he did not contemplate, and which did not exist in his day; if we suppose that the principles which he enforced are not dependent upon the accidents of the moment to which he applied them, or even upon the peculiarities of his own temperament,—but will prove their force most when they are loosened from phrases which he adopted chiefly from compliance with the habits of a dry and dreary period, and which have not borne the test of later experience. Above all, I think those who look upon Butler as a great apologist for the Scriptures, will not suppose he has failed in his object, if the Scriptures themselves should be found to tell more than he could tell. In trying to state the difficulties to which I have alluded, and to point out how they may be removed, I shall not be speaking at random or from guess; I shall be giving the results of my own personal experience, as well as of my experience among young men of your class. I set them down in the conviction that both you and the Undergraduates of Oxford may attain a sounder religious philosophy through Bishop Butler than can ever be attained through the Bampton Lecturer.

1. Mr. Mansel has wisely quoted the entire title of Butler's book. The ellipsis, *The Analogy of Natural and Revealed Religion,* often makes us forget those pregnant and important words, without which the others have no significance,—*to the Constitution and Course of Nature.* I can answer for myself, that what I owe more than anything else to Butler,

and to Butler, so far as I can trace and define obligations, more than to almost any other man, is the sense of being in such a Constitution,—one that I did not create, and have no power to alter, but with which I must be in conformity, or suffer the penalty of being at war with it.

It is not the force of the comparison one thinks of first; it is not the conclusiveness of the argument. What facts are these by which you are illustrating your Religion, natural or revealed! How profoundly important *they* are to me? This is a thought which startles and frightens a man before he has time to calculate the effect of what he is reading on the mind of an opponent. I do not wonder that any one who has felt this should speak of his first acquaintance with Butler as an "epoch in his life." His rapid and brilliant Irish namesake would never, I am persuaded, have used that language about any one who had merely supplied him with a new illustration or argument. His own wit would have produced hundreds of these for or against any cause, on the plaintiff's side or the defendant's. It is quite a different thing when one is forced to ponder the path of one's own life,—to know what it is that wit and argument cannot devise or change. That remains with us as part of an everlasting history when arguments that seemed to us very decisive, have faded from our recollection, or even have proved fallacious.

Any one who cares to know the man Butler,

should study the 'Sermons on Human Nature' as
much as the 'Analogy.' Both, I believe, will make
the same impression upon his mind. In one as much
as the other, Butler is proving himself a *constitu-*
tional writer, in the fullest sense of that word. He
is helping us to understand what the sense of the
word is by bringing us gradually into an experience
of the fact which it denotes. How we become partakers of that experience is as hard to say as it is to
trace the steps by which one is familiarized to a tree,
or a face. By slow, repeated strokes, each of which in
itself is scarcely perceptible, the conviction is wrought
into you. The seriousness of the writer's own conviction has had more share in communicating it to
you than any skill of which he is master.

2. Butler was well aware of one obstacle to the reception of this belief. Our frivolity, our delight in
our own conceptions rather than in the observation of
facts and the reflection upon them, *this* kind of danger was constantly present to his mind. He speaks
of men's levity and impatience of trouble with sorrow, sometimes almost with bitterness.* But there
was a hindrance to the acceptance of his teaching
which he was not prepared for, which no man living
just at his time, and with his education, could fully
appreciate. What is it that commonly awakens a

* See especially the Preface to the 'Sermons,' one of the most
important of all documents for the understanding of Butler's character.

man *out* of his frivolity? What is that fact which presents itself to him when he begins to think earnestly? It is the sense of his own evil; what is commonly called—and I do not think there is any better phrase to describe it by—the conviction of sin. Not the perception of an order at all, but of a disorder; not an interest about the laws of the universe, but about my own very self; this is what takes possession of me. All religion, it seems to me, has to do with this. I cannot understand what it means if it is not occupied about this fact of which I have become so terribly conscious, if it does not explain that fact to me, and make known to me some other fact concerning myself which may render that less intolerable. Nature gives me apparently no information about it. Sea, sky, air,—each say, "The se-"cret of thy trouble and of the deliverance from it is "not in me." I resort to the Bible only because I have been told it is there. Slowly out of the words of some Prophet or Evangelist or Apostle it comes. The dream is told as well as the interpretation.

Now a man returning to Butler in the midst of this experience, or when he has just attained the result of it, feels what can only be described as a bitter discontent. He may pursue the study as a school-task; he may prepare himself for an examination in the Analogy; he may hope that it will serve his turn hereafter in combating the objections of infidels. But all personal sympathy with it is gone.

He does not understand its nomenclature. The religion which it speaks of does not look like the religion with which he is occupied in his closet. He begins to regard it as an artificial, outward thing, which has acquired, unfortunately, the same name with the real inward thing. There is a bewilderment in the equivoque; he submits to it, reluctant and protesting, supposing that there must in the nature of things be one religion for the schools, and another for the man himself. Yet he feels more in Butler than in any of the writers upon evidences like Paley, the sharpness of the contradiction. He can fancy that arguments about credibility and authenticity lie outside of him. The analogy appeals to himself. And yet it talks to him about Nature, and a constitution of Nature with which he, the sinner, can recognize no fellowship, in which he has the least possible interest. It merely introduces the Bible as containing certain difficulties like those in this constitution of Nature, whereas he has fled to it as a refuge from the only difficulties that have really ever tormented him, or which appear to him of any consequence.

3. That these feelings should exist in some of the most serious readers, must be a great discouragement to any University teacher who wishes to promote the study and cultivate the spirit of Butler. Perhaps the discouragement may be lessened for a time when he perceives amongst other young men, also in ear-

nest,—amongst some of those even who have passed
through this state of mind, a strong reaction against
it. From such he will hear loud denunciations of
what they call merely "subjective" religion, cries as
loud for a well defined religious system which shall
come with the authority of a long tradition, which
is given to all, not submitted to the private judgments of any. Those who demand a religion of this
kind unquestionably turn to Butler with far greater
respect, with far more expectation of finding sympathy in him and support from him, than the class to
which I referred just now. They welcome the introduction to the Analogy with great delight. They
put it forward as the protection against the craving
for certainty which characterizes scientific men on
the one side, the believers in an infallible authority
on the other. ' See,' they say, ' what Butler teaches
' us respecting Probability as the guide of human life ;
' see how he admonishes us that we ought to take
' the safer course, even if the arguments in favour of
' a more dangerous one actually predominate ! Wise
' and excellent counsellor ! What can we do better
' than apply his maxim in determining whether we
' shall accept or reject any of the traditions of our
' fathers ?'

Such preparation is there in these minds for the
study of Butler by their sympathy with some passages in his opening chapter. But what disappoint-
ment awaits them when they actually pursue that

study through the subsequent chapters! All the promise of an appeal to the traditions of the past as a protection against the exercise of the understanding upon the facts of the present is utterly belied. On such a question as that of a future state, I am led to think, not of what has been said about it in other days, but of the deep, awful fact of my own personal being,—of the strong evidence which there must be to show me that that can be dissolved,—of the absence of any such evidence in the world around me or in my own experience,—of the presence of a number of facts in both, which corroborate a conclusion that would be weighty without them. Even when I come to the chapter on Punishment,—where the argument for believing anything whatever on the ground of safety must be strongest,—I am still led along in the same quiet unexcited method to notice, not what has been said or threatened of punishment in another state, but the actual connection between ill-doing and punishment in this state,—the signs which there are of a fixed, unchangeable law in the midst of apparent anomalies,—the warrant there is for believing that that law must fully assert itself some day. This is a method of proof so entirely alien from the notions and habits of those who looked to Butler as the champion of Church authority against the exercises of a profane reasoning, that their expectation must be numbered among one of the main hindrances to the " study of his works and the cultivation of his spirit."

4. But these students may reckon, like the others, that if the 'Analogy' does not meet their own especial wants, it may at least furnish them with effectual weapons against different prevalent forms of avowed unbelief. That all-inclusive argument, *There are not more difficulties in our hypothesis than yours;—Without Natural and Revealed Religion you would still meet with a number of unsolved problems in the Course and Constitution of Nature,*—what mouths may it not stop, what subtle reasonings may it not put to rest? My friend! have you tried? Do you know in yourself, do you know in the case of others, what it can effect? It is well that you should understand before you take Orders, or—permit me to say it— in your ministrations to your brethren, in your own heart, there will be a hollowness greater than you can guess. You have worked through the Analogy, you have strengthened your knowledge by reading all the books of Mr. Rogers, and many others who support the same thesis. You can produce the confutation of this and that objection at a moment's notice. But what if you are met with agreement, not objections? What if the unbeliever should say to you, —*You are quite right. I am tormented with perplexities, difficulties, anomalies in the course and Constitution of Nature. They haunt me by night and by day. The condition of millions of human beings in this country, in every country of the world, their physical condition, their moral condition, crushes*

me; it has taken away from me all faith that there is an Order in the Universe, or that there is a God of Order. I thought, perhaps, as you spoke of a Revelation of God, that might have helped me out of my infinite darkness, that might have given me some light and hope. I find from your own confession that it will not. You wish me to receive your Revelation because it leaves me where it found me—not more hopeless, more Atheistic than I was before. I thank you for the offer, but it is not what I want.

Or what if you are met with such an answer as this, coming from a person of quite another class? *There are unsolved problems, you say, in the Constitution and Course of Nature. No doubt there are, thousands and ten thousands of them. But a number have been solved. We are always hoping for the solution of more. It is the work of the lives of us scientific men to seek after the solution. We feel that we are dishonest men when we are not busy in that work, when we are not pursuing it with hopeful earnestness. We start with ignorance,—the sense of our ignorance increases at every step. But that does not hinder us from seeking after truths, after certainties. As long as we float about among hypotheses and probabilities, we are self-conceited enough; as long as we acquiesce in ignorance, we are conceited enough. It is when we demand truth and refuse to abandon the search of it that we become awe-stricken and humble. In your subject, if we understand you aright, the*

N

opposite rule holds. You do not seek for certainties; you are content with hypotheses. Therefore it seems to us there is no Analogy between the Constitution and Course of Nature, and Religion, Natural or Revealed, as you expound it to us.

Now all these very serious hindrances to the study of Butler proceed, you will perceive, from the kind of men whose opposition he would the least have dreaded, upon whose sympathy he would have most counted; from those who are looking earnestly upon the world, and really desiring to do their own work in it. And you, as an Oxford man, cannot be ignorant that nowhere more than in Oxford is each class of these feelings likely to exist,—to exist in great strength and liveliness. In Butler's own day, it was the first home of that Methodist movement which has affected England so mightily ever since. In our day it has been the starting-point of the High Church movement. Numbers there must be groaning over social anomalies and contradictions. Mathematicians and experimental students are vigorously and successfully asserting their claim to be heard there. A splendid Museum is rising to attest the conviction of the University that something is known, that more may be known, of the Course and Constitution of Nature. Are all these influences, so different,—some of them so contradictory,—to conspire in ostracizing Butler?

I am sure they need not. If I had Mr. Mansel's

knowledge and faculty of persuasion, and could get the
ear of one and another young man who was strongly
possessed with any of the thoughts to which I have
referred, I believe I could show him that the more
he was determined not to part with any of his deepest convictions, the greater might be his respect for
the Analogy, the more he might learn from it.

1. I would begin with the man who is absorbed by
the sense of personal evil, and the need of personal
deliverance. I would long for him that he might
never let go that deep, awful truth of which he has
become conscious,—might never care less for the discovery that has been made to him of a goodness and
forgiveness mightier than the sin within him. I
should agree with him altogether that to the Bible,
and not to anything in the order and constitution of
nature, he was indebted for that discovery. I should
agree with him that to the study of the Bible, in its
simple and literal signification, he was called by all
his past experience, by all the deepest monitions of
God's Spirit. Then I would ask him, whether, as
he enters upon this task in this hope, it does not
strike him that he has overlooked some words which
stand out, very prominently, in the Gospels. I mean
these—*The Kingdom of God, the Kingdom of Heaven.* Are not these actually the *most* prominent words
in the Evangelical narratives, those which a literal
student has least right to pass by or to treat carelessly ? Is it not the professed business of the narra-

tives to unfold the meaning of those words, to remove the vulgar apprehensions respecting them which
existed in the minds of the disciples, which are
likely to exist in our minds? That a man in the
eagerness and passion of an inquiry concerning the
condition of his own soul should scarcely see these
constantly recurring expressions, at least not attach
any significance to them, is exceedingly natural. Any
man who knows anything of himself will understand such an oversight, strange as it is. But can
it safely continue? May not the indifference about
words, to which our Lord himself attached so much
importance, be one cause why those facts of personal
experience, once held strongly, become weak in so
many minds,—why they are held rather as recollections of the past than as present truths,—why the
phrases take the place of that which they signify,—
why violent reactions banish even the recollection, or
cause it to be contemned? If we knew what that
Kingdom of Heaven was which is said to be about
us, to be within us, might not we know better, more
deeply, what our own radical evil has been ; why
only a Divine power can extirpate it?

But supposing we begin with very solemn purpose
to consider this language of the Bible, are we not
reminded a little of the language of Butler, of some
of the lessons which he sought to impress upon us?
There is a Constitution belonging to us as men, a
different Constitution from that which is to be seen

in Nature, but not a less real one. There is an Analogy between it and the Constitution and Course of Nature. Does not our Lord say so? What do His parables mean if He does not? Must not we be under the deepest obligation to a writer who tried to fix those truths upon us,—who probably *did* fix them upon us more than we knew,—even if in a particular crisis of our moral history his was not just the kind of assistance that we craved for?

Is there still something in these words, ' Religion, Natural or Revealed,' which grates upon your ear— which does not connect itself readily with our Lord's phrase, ' Kingdom of Heaven,' or with your own sense of what religion is? Well, on the subject of nomenclature I will not dispute with you. I think Butler adopted his from the custom of his age. If it strikes you that the word ' Religion' is better limited to internal life,—if it is for you, as the Germans and Sir William Hamilton and Mr. Mansel would say, merely ' *subjective*,' (remember, that is no word of mine, I dislike it heartily,) I shall not complain. In truth, I am not so careful as some are to ascertain the force of a word which is Roman and Pagan, rather than Jewish and Christian, which has nothing strictly corresponding to it either in the Old or New Testament. I find Evangelists and Apostles speaking not of Religion, but of God. I think, if Butler had lived in our time, he would have much preferred their language to that which he accepted because

it was current in the eighteenth century, and that
it would really have accorded much better with the
meaning of his books. That change would no doubt
involve another, also, I think, very favourable to the
full understanding of his lessons, and to the scattering of clouds which have hidden from us their real
purpose. St. Paul speaks of God as revealing, through
the works He had made, His eternal Power and
Godhead. Having started from that point, he is able
consistently and harmoniously to speak of the perfect revelation in the Son. The phrase, ' Natural
and Revealed Religion,' is, apparently at least, inconsistent with his view of the case ; is it not also in
itself ambiguous and bewildering? Would not many
chapters in Butler become plainer if we took him to
mean that the Author of Nature, whose existence he
assumes, was revealing a part of His mind through
the constitution and course of Nature, was indicating
in that, a revelation that should be more complete
and more directly addressed to man ?

2. But if I make this concession to one class of
serious and devout students, am I not abandoning all
chance of recommending our author to that other
class which appears to demand first of all what they
call an objective Religion,—something given to us, not
merely experienced by us? I should be very sorry if
I thought so. For among these men have I met also
with a devoted purpose, a thorough conviction, which
I should count it a sin to weaken in them, which

I am sure their friends and fellow-sufferers, if not their teachers, should do their utmost to strengthen in them. I tremble when I see those " first affections," even those " shadowy recollections" which once dwelt in them and coloured their lives, passing away,—their life's star "fading into the light of common day." I know the loss must be grievous; and yet I think it is inevitable so long as they fancy that it is a religious system which they are craving for; that it is not rather a City that hath foundations, whose Builder and Maker is God,—a Temple in which they themselves are to be living stones. This is the true High Church longing. Those who become half-conscious that it is *this* they want, and yet retain a confused notion that it is something else which they want, rush to Rome for the satisfaction of a hope which is mixed of the thinnest dream and the firmest substance, fancying that the vague anticipations of the future which she cherishes in them will meet the one, and her present materialism the other. Alas! how many who do not take this course may find in the vagueness of their own thoughts and speculations, in the materialism of ordinary social existence, a drearier *caput mortuum* of all their early expectations than even the Romish confessional and the Romish ceremonial offer to them!

Is there nothing in their old friend and teacher which might save them from this alternative,—which

might point to the actual realization of that which
in their youth was only a fair ideal? Those dry,
hard sermons of his upon Human Nature are founded upon the text, *"For as we have many members in
one body, and all members have not the same office ;
so we, being many, are one body in Christ, and every
one members one of another."* In the opening of
his first sermon you see the man of the eighteenth
century. He feels the extreme beauty of St. Paul's
comparison; he knows how it was drawn out by the
Apostle himself in the Epistle to the Corinthians ;
but he supposes that such passages must have belonged " to the condition and usages of the Christian
world at the time they were written," to " circumstances now ceased and altered." He hovers about
the language with a bashful tenderness ; with an evident feeling that it must be universal; that if ever
language was universal, that is. Yet he is tied and
bound by the usages and conditions of the Christian
world in *his* time. The religion of hoops and ruffles
enchains even his heart and intellect. But what a
noble effort he makes to emancipate himself from it !
What a sense he has that the Apostle was pointing to a fellowship grounded in the very nature of
things, in the very constitution of humanity, which
had nothing to do with hoops and ruffles at all ! He
longs to speak of men as constituted in Christ. His
words often become feeble and contradictory because
he cannot utter what is struggling within him. But

how he may help us to utter it ! How he may enable
us to clear away the difficulties in himself and in us,
in the eighteenth century and in the nineteenth,
which hinder us from acknowledging the one Body
in Christ, and all as being members one of another !
How he drives us to seek a real not an artificial ground
for a society of men—a Church of men—to rest upon !
How, in his slow, clear, calm way, never taking two
steps at a time, he makes us feel that every idea
of our human nature must be inadequate, must be
false, which does not assume a righteous ground for
its thoughts, movements, activities; which does not
treat every departure from that righteous ground as
an act of rebellion on the part of our individual
tempers and inclinations against the Order in which
we are placed, against the law of Love which is holding us together ! How much we gain in the force of
the demonstration by those very circumstances of the
author which make his statement of it scientifically
imperfect !

Most affectionately then I would commend Butler
to these students, in the confidence that if they will
meditate both this work and the Analogy by the
light of that higher wisdom which he and they would
both confess to be in St. Paul, they may attain to
such a grounded belief in a Church—as an actual
family in heaven and earth, named in the Name of
one Father, united in the Person of an elder Brother
who sacrificed Himself for it, inhabited by the Spirit

of the Father and the Son,—as no system, Romish or
Anglican, could ever give them. And will not they
then have an understanding with those who dwell
in their experiences of individual sin, of rebellion
against Christ's law of love, of the blood which
cleanseth away even that sin,—such as they never
had before ?

3. And will not both be able, having the wisdom
which is taught by their different disciplines, to meet
with a kindlier sympathy, with a bolder proclamation, those who demand a revelation which shall explain some of the perplexities in the course and constitution of Nature that have baffled them ?   Will they
any longer assume that miserable attitude of defence
which they pretend they have learnt from Butler,
arguing that the Incarnation and Sacrifice of the
Son of God, the revelation of the second Adam, the
descent of the Comforter, do not make the condition of the universe more dark than it was before?
Have we not faith to put the Gospel of the Son of
Man, who came down from Heaven, and ascended
into heaven, and is in heaven, upon another issue
than this?   Dare we not say, "Yes, we beseech
" you to consider whether this is not the interpreta-
" tion of the anomalies which you see in the world;
" whether you are not told here how those anomalies
" shall be brought to an end; how the law which
" Butler declared to be latent in the constitution and
" course of Nature,—to be visible in the constitu-

"tion of man,—shall triumph over all that has fought "against it"? Dare we not say to the investigator of Nature—" In God's Name go forward; His blessing "be with thee! All the secrets that are hid in His "works He would have thee search out. He rebukes "only the cowardice which hides the talent in the "napkin, because it counts Him an austere ruler. "Work on with ever-increasing courage, and there- "fore with ever-increasing reverence and love. For "there is an analogy,—as Butler has shown us there "is,—between the Kingdom of God in man, His "highest Kingdom, and His Kingdom in Nature. He "has revealed the first in Christ, that we may know it, "and enter into it. He will reveal the other to the "patient inquirer who believes Christ's promise as "Butler believed it, that those who seek shall find."

Blessed shall he be whosoever carries this message into the lecture-rooms and pulpits of Oxford. But- ler's spirit, and a higher Spirit than Butler's, will be his guide and teacher!

Faithfully yours,

F. D. M.

LETTER IV.

— ✦ —

MY DEAR SIR,

Let me entreat you to read Mr. Mansel's first
Lecture carefully, and with the accompanying notes,
before you look at this Letter. Nothing is further
from my wish than that your impression of it should
be determined by my criticism or by isolated passages selected from it. I am too deeply convinced of
the injustice which is done to authors by this treatment—what I had thought on the subject before has
been too firmly fixed in my mind by the perusal of
the Bampton Lectures, and by considering how they
handle the statements and beliefs of eminent men in
all ages and countries—not to be most desirous that
I may not fall into that method of proceeding myself, or tempt any one else into it.

The Lecture is a denunciation of two evils to
which the preacher supposed that his hearers were
exposed. The errors are, *Dogmatism* on the one

hand, *Rationalism* on the other. ' Between these two extremes religious philosophy perpetually oscil- lates' (p. 1). Mr. Mansel's business is of course to ascertain (1st) what each of these evils is, (2nd) what is that middle between them in which Religious Philo- sophy ought to rest from its oscillations. What help the Lecturer gives us for understanding the force of the words which he uses is contained in the following passage :—

" In using the above terms, it is necessary to state
" at the outset the sense in which each is employed,
" and to emancipate them from the various and vague
" associations connected with their ordinary use. I
" do not include under the name of *Dogmatism* the
" mere enunciation of religious truths, as resting upon
" authority and not upon reasoning. The Dogmatist,
" as well as the Rationalist, is the constructor of a
" system; and in constructing it, however much the
" materials upon which he works may be given by a
" higher authority, yet in connecting them together
" and exhibiting their systematic form, it is necessary
" to call in the aid of human ability. Indeed, what-
" ever may be their actual antagonism in the field of
" religious controversy, the two terms are in their
" proper sense so little exclusive of each other, that
" both were originally employed to denote the same
" persons; the name *Dogmatists* or *Rationalists* being
" indifferently given to those medical theorists who
" insisted on the necessity of calling in the aid of ra-

" tional principles, to support or correct the conclu-
" sions furnished by experience (1). A like significa-
" tion is to be found in the later language of philoso-
" phy, when the term *Dogmatists* was used to denote
" those philosophers who endeavoured to explain the
" phenomena of experience by means of rational con-
" ceptions and demonstrations; the intelligible world
" being regarded as the counterpart of the sensible,
" and the necessary relations of the former as the
" principles and ground of the observed facts of the
" latter (2). It is in a sense analogous to this that
" the term may be most accurately used in reference
" to Theology. Scripture is to the theological Dog-
" matist what Experience is to the philosophical. It
" supplies him with the facts to which his system
" has to adapt itself. It contains in an unsystematic
" form the positive doctrines, which further inquiry
" has to exhibit as supported by reasonable grounds
" and connected into a scientific whole. Theological
" Dogmatism is thus an application of reason to the
" support and defence of pre-existing statements of
" Scripture (3). Rationalism, on the other hand, so
" far as it deals with Scripture at all, deals with it
" as a thing to be adapted to the independent con-
" clusions of the natural reason, and to be rejected
" where that adaptation cannot conveniently be made.
" By *Rationalism,* without intending to limit the name
" to any single school or period in theological con-
" troversy, I mean generally to designate that system

" whose final test of truth is placed in the direct
" assent of the human consciousness, whether in the
" form of logical deduction, or moral judgment, or
" religious intuition; by whatever previous process
" those faculties may have been raised to their as-
" sumed dignity as arbitrators. The Rationalist, as
" such, is not bound to maintain that a divine reve-
" lation of religious truth is impossible, nor even to
" deny that it has actually been given. He may ad-
" mit the existence of the revelation as a fact : he may
" acknowledge its utility as a temporary means of in-
" struction for a ruder age : he may even accept cer-
" tain portions as of universal and permanent autho-
" rity (4). But he assigns to some superior tribunal
" the right of determining what is essential to religion
" and what is not : he claims for himself and his age
" the privilege of accepting or rejecting any given re-
" velation, wholly or in part, according as it does or
" does not satisfy the conditions of some higher crite-
" rion to be supplied by the human consciousness (5)."
(*Bampton Lectures*, 2nd ed. pp. 2–5.)

I have left the figures in my extract, that you may
not suppose Mr. Mansel's account of the two opposing terms is his only instrument for " emancipating
" them from the various and vague associations con-
" nected with their ordinary use." Some of these various and vague associations, his readers may think,
cleave to this elaborate exposition. The very words
'philosophical' and 'religious,' which recur so frequent-

ly in this passage, and which are so ambiguous, are
not explained; it is presumed that we must know
what they mean. Perhaps the audience at St. Mary's
did not need the information we want, for if they
comprehended what is involved in " regarding the in-
" telligible world as the counterpart of the sensible,
" and the necessary relations of the former as the prin-
" ciples and ground of the observed facts of the latter,"
they were already great adepts in philosophy; their
minds must have been exercised on some of its hardest
problems.   Yet even they may have needed some
light as to the way " in which the Scripture is to the
" Theological Dogmatist what Experience is to the
" philosophical," since it is generally supposed—and
Mr. Mansel seems himself to confirm the opinion—that
Experience is a ground which is common to the theologian and the philosopher, and that the dogmas of
one are as much affected by it as those of the other.

But, as I said, the mystical numbers in the text
show that Mr. Mansel has not trusted exclusively nor
principally to definitions.   They point to the persons
who are condemned for Dogmatism or Rationalism,
or both.   I will enumerate them just as they occur,
without reference to their chronology, their sect,
or their importance.   Wolf,[a] Paulus, Wegscheider,
Schleiermacher, Hegel, Strauss and certain spiritualists ;[b] Anselm,[c] Gerhard,[d] Chemnitz,[e] Jowett, Greg,

<hr>

[a] Note 3 to p. 4.   [b] Note 4 to p. 5.   [c] Notes 6, 7, 8, to p. 10,
and 11 to p. 11.   [d] Note 9 to p. 10.   [e] Note 10 to p. 10.

Mackay,[f] Socinus, Froude, Priestley, Maurice,[g] Kant, Coleridge,[h] Wilberforce, Damascenus, Schaller, Gö-schel, Dorner, Marheinecke,[i] Occam,[k] Fichte, Parker, Emerson, Leechman, Foxton (with others previously sentenced),[l] Baden Powell,[m] Schelling, Plotinus, An-gelus Silesius (with others previously sentenced),[m] Bruno Bauer, Feuerbach, Comte.[n]

This list, drawn from a few pages, proves surely the extent of Mr. Mansel's reading, and his right to the title of Public or University Prosecutor, which his friends have vindicated for him. I have collected it that I may suggest the question which most con-cerns us : How are you and I to be delivered from these curses of Dogmatism and Rationalism which we know, upon such high authority, are always threat-ening us? Suppose you agree that all those whom the Bampton Lecturer cuts off as exceeding on this side or on that, or as mixing the two evils in one, are guilty of the charges brought against them,—sup-posing you had the opportunity which he possessed, of telling a large congregation that such and such men were Dogmatists, such and such Rationalists, and that neither were in the least free from the enor-mities of the other,—would that be an absolute se-curity against any taint of Dogmatism in yourself? Might not you possibly be driven now and then to

[f] Notes 13 and 14 to p. 11.   [g] Note 15 to p. 11.
[h] Note 16 to p. 13.   [i] Note 17 to p. 13.   [k] Note to p. 17.
[l] Note 22 to p. 17.   [m] Note 29 to p. 30.   [n] Note 30 to p. 30.

explain the grounds upon which you rested your conviction that you were right and they were all wrong?
and might you not, in submitting to that necessity,
find yourself dropping all unawares into Rationalism?
I submit these topics to your consideration, wishing
you always to recollect what terrible dangers those
must be which could have induced Mr. Mansel to
undertake the painful task of passing judgment upon
divines and philosophers of all schools and ages,—
that you may spare no pains in discovering some
adequate precautions against them.

In the eloquent peroration to his eighth Lecture
(p. 266), Mr. Mansel announces the oracle, *Know
thyself*, as the one guide to all safe thought upon any
subject. In cases like this, that oracle has taken
even a more distinct and awful form, as it has issued
from a more sacred shrine. "*Cast first*," it has been
said, "*the beam out of thine own eye; then shalt
thou see clearly to take the mote out of thy brother's
eye.*" This principle, being so exactly in accordance
with the maxim of the Lectures, must, we are bound
to assume, have been diligently weighed by the Lecturer. Before he proceeded to charge any one else
with Dogmatism or Rationalism, he went through, we
may be sure, a laborious process of inquiry, to ascertain what seeds of them there might be in himself.
But his performance of that task, and his success in
it, cannot absolve us from a similar one. I, at least,
who have been warned by Mr. Mansel in some of the

notes to which I have referred, that I have caught the infection of one or both diseases from greater men, am bound to look diligently for the signs of them in the only region in which I may truly judge of their nature or their effects.

I have not far to search for either. If you do not recollect moments in your past life when you have deserved the name of *dogmatical,* when you knew that it must have been applied to you by those who were about you,—especially by those with whom you were disputing,—when you knew they had a right to apply it,—if those moments do not come back to you with a sense of unspeakable shame,—oh, friend, how I envy you! But I do not envy you, if you are not aware with what fierceness that temptation may come back at any moment,—if you do not feel that it is one against which there is need constantly to watch. Now no one, I believe, who has this experience, need be ignorant in what the vice of Dogmatism consists, whence it springs, whither it may lead.· *My* opinion about this or that class of facts, the conclusion to which *I* have been led,—whether I have accepted the general judgment of the world about them, or have dissented from it,—has a worth in my eyes which raises it not only above every other man's opinion, but above the facts themselves. For *this* do I throw down my gage, this will I maintain against the Universe. Is not the world justified in saying that I am very disagreeable, very insolent?

Can I refute the charge? But what if, because that is the case—and I know it is the case—I should resolve to cast all my dogmatism aside? What if I should appear in quite a new character, yielding to everybody, maintaining no ground for myself, admitting that one conclusion is just as likely as another? Such a reaction against our own dogmatism most of us may have known; the more dogmatical we have been in one period, the more likely we are to exhibit that change in another. Is not the verdict of mankind just in condemning this state of mind also? Is it not just in demanding that a man should have something to hold by, in pronouncing him worthless if he has not?

There is then—it is not a question, but an admitted fact—something good at the bottom of this Dogmatism; there is something very evil in the exercise of it. Do you serve me much if you tell me that I am not to be *too* dogmatic; that a little dogmatism is well, but that *ne quid nimis* is the maxim of life? You do not serve me at all. You insult me with a pompous, unpractical rule, which fails me every moment I want to use it. My conscience, and the conscience of mankind, witnesses that Dogmatism, in the sense of maintaining a notion because it is mine, is *altogether* detestable. It does not admit of degrees; there cannot be too little of it; there ought to be none. My conscience and the conscience of mankind witnesses that Dogmatism, in the sense of stand-

ing by a principle, is altogether good; there cannot be too much of it; my want of it is my sin.
Here is a distinction which must somehow be sustained. But how is it to be sustained? Every one
is aware of the difficulty in his own case; every one
knows that he has transgressed, and does transgress
continually the boundary; every one therefore has a
call to be compassionate when he sees or suspects
that his neighbour transgresses it. Every man knows
perfectly why he commits this transgression, and
what would be the escape from it. He knows that
he is a Dogmatist in the offensive, immoral sense,
whensoever he confounds that which *seems to him* or
to any man with that which *is*; that he is a Dogmatist in an honest and true sense whensoever he swears
with deliberate purpose that something is, and that
from that no man and devil shall tear him away.

You see how rude and poor my way of arriving
at the force of this word is in comparison with Mr.
Mansel's. But you and I are not schoolmen; we
are roughing it in the world. We have to look upon
all questions as they bear upon the actual business of
life. I know that Mr. Mansel's account of Dogmatism must strike every one as far more profound and
philosophical than mine; but I am thinking of it
as a great sin which I have to avoid for the sake of
my own being,—as a great moral habit which I must
preserve for the sake of my own being. My words
will be nothing to you if they do not meet your

mind, and point out something which you must fly
from, and to which you must cleave ; if they do,
perhaps they may be some help to you hereafter, if
not now.

Well, and Rationalism ! Is this ' Know thyself' of
Delphi and Oxford not applicable to the investigation
of that tendency also? I can attest in my own experience the truth of Mr. Mansel's assertion that Dogmatism and Rationalism are not necessarily in contradiction; that these habits of mind in their most
evil form may dwell together, nay, *must* dwell together. I have listened to the words of some wise man,
a lecturer on Moral Science, it might be, or on Physical. I have been asking myself the reason of his
statements ; I have not had my ears open to take in
what he said, just because I was busy with that question. I have looked at a picture which other people
admired, which it would have done me good to admire.
I have asked for the reason why I should admire, and
that occupation of mind made it impossible for me to
receive any blessing from the picture. This restless
rationalism pursues us though our lives, into every
corner of them; those who have been and are tormented by it themselves, may not be quite as ready
as those are whose consciences are clearer, to cast a
stone at other sinners; but they will be most ready
to receive hints about the way in which the evil
may be overcome, and to assist their fellows with any
hints which they have found beneficial.

There is one remedy which most of us have tried
with more or less of hope. The reaction against Rationalism is at least as fierce in a man's soul as the
reaction against Dogmatism. When our eyes have
been straining themselves with looking into vacancy,
the natural inclination is to close them, to go to
sleep if we can. When our reason has been acting
as if it had power to create its own objects, the natural inclination is to say, ' We will have nothing
more to do with it. Tell us what you please; we
will take it upon trust. *Logical deduction, moral
judgment, religious intuition,* all are equally hateful
to us. We want nothing but the repose of authority. Give us that, and our souls will be at peace.'
So you have got rid of Rationalism.

And it *is* peace—if a solitude and peace are the
same; peace till the Conscience of which Butler
spoke awakes; peace till some words like those of
St. Paul, " *Christ shall give thee light,*" tell it that
at least it is not obeying Him when it is denying its
own function, when it is refusing to act. Then comes
a very strong conviction that the last state was worse
than the first, that the most eager and profitless questionings and debatings were better than dreary inani-
tion, that one condition betokened a dim belief that
God must be, the other a practical denial of Him.
For we insult ourselves and we insult mankind if we
say there was not a truth at the bottom of our Rationalism as well as of our Dogmatism. In the one

case as much as the other, the discovery of the truth is the only way to the clear acknowledgment of the falsehood.

God teaches me to assert; for there is that which I did not make by my thought, belief, reason, and which I cannot unmake. I glorify my assertions, and so actually constitute my belief, thought, or reason, into a ground of things. God teaches me to question, that I may separate the one from the other, that I may not accept Opinions for Realities. I turn my questioning into an excuse for denying Realities. So I come round to the same point again. My Rationalism becomes impotent Dogmatism, as my Dogmatism becomes the most hopeless Rationalism.

I have tried to test these words by common experience, not mixing at first any theological associations with them. That I suppose was Mr. Mansel's original intention. If he could have fulfilled it, his treatment of the subject would have been more orderly and satisfactory; perhaps a little fairer to his opponents. But he did not find it possible. He could not produce the moral effect which he desired to produce on his hearers, unless he instantly connected Rationalism with a special mode of treating the Scriptures, unless he sometimes contracted and sometimes expanded the definition of it, in order that it might reach all who differed from him, and might by no possibility touch himself. I have shown you that I do not protest against either of his definitions because it includes me. I demand that each of them should include me. A Dogmatist and Rationalist in their worst sense, I know that I am liable to be. A Dogmatist and a Rationalist in their best sense, I desire to be.

But though I think that this method of determining the signification of the words would have been pronounced the honest and reasonable one by Sir William Hamilton, though I am satisfied Butler would have adopted it, I am anxious that it should be applied to the same use to which the Bampton Lecturer applies his. He plunges at once into the doctrines of the Atonement and the Incarnation, testing by the ways in which they have been treated the dogmatic and rationalistic tendencies. I will follow him, trembling indeed, but only on account of the awfulness of the subjects, not the least because I shrink from stating my own convictions respecting them, or from saying what there is in his statements which from the bottom of my heart I repudiate. It is no time for concealing what one believes on any great questions, least of all upon those which form the central subjects of my preaching, as they will do, I trust, one day of yours.

The following sentences bring the first of these subjects directly before us :—" Thus, to select one ex-" ample out of many, the revealed doctrine of Christ's " Atonement for the sins of men has been alternately " defended and assailed by some such arguments as

" these. We have been told, on the one hand, that
" man's redemption *could not* have been brought
" about by any other means :—that God could not,
" consistently with His own attributes, have suffered
" man to perish unredeemed, or have redeemed him
" by any inferior sacrifice :—that man, redeemed from
" death, must become the servant of him who re-
" deems him ; and that it was not meet that he
" should be the servant of any other than God :—
" that no other sacrifice could have satisfied divine
" justice :—that no other victim could have endured
" the burden of God's wrath. These and similar ar-
" guments have been brought forward, as one of the
" greatest of their authors avows, to defend the teach-
" ing of the Catholic Faith on the ground of a *rea-*
" *sonable necessity.* While, on the other hand, it has
" been argued that the revealed doctrine itself can-
" not be accepted as literally true ; because we cannot
" believe that God was angry, and needed to be pro-
" pitiated :—because it is inconsistent with the Di-
" vine Justice that the innocent should suffer for the
" sins of the guilty :—because it is more reasonable
" to believe that God freely forgives the offences of
" His creatures :—because we cannot conceive how
" the punishment of one can do away with the guilt
" of another."—(*Bampton Lectures,* 2nd editiou, pp.
10, 11.)

One remark respecting this passage will strike
you immediately. It is the foundation of ten notes,

condemning a large portion of those writers whose names I have given you already. And yet the Lecturer does not waste even a single line in telling us what "that revealed doctrine of Christ's Atonement for the sins of men" is, which they have assailed and defended. He must be perfectly aware that more than one able series of Bampton Lectures has been delivered for the express purpose of ascertaining what it is and what it is not. He must be aware that in those able treatises some notions which have attached themselves in the minds of many men to the revealed doctrine of the Atonement, are dismissed as untenable. Whether it ought to be received with these additions or without them, in what terms it should be stated or presented to men generally, we are not told. Nevertheless a number of actual men, living or dead, are held up as examples of mischievous Dogmatism or mischievous Rationalism for their way of attacking or maintaining it. Of all outrages upon philosophical method, and upon ordinary English justice, which are to be found in our literature, I believe this is the most flagrant. Mr. Mansel must have had a very strong suspicion that if he *had* stated the " revealed doctrine of the Atonement" according to his notion of it, a number of the most earnest, the most confessedly orthodox and Evangelical clergymen in England, would have said either, 'We do not accept it in that sense;' or, 'That method of setting it forth does not satisfy us;' or, ' Such

an explanation may do very well for the schools,
but it is not the doctrine we preach in our pulpits to
sinners.' It was therefore convenient to leave the
whole subject in vagueness. In virtue of that vagueness he is able to deal his blows right and left; he
can at least frighten his readers with the belief
that there is something which they ought to eschew,
though he is unable or unwilling to tell them what
they should embrace.

But, my dear Sir, however convenient this course
may be to a University Doctor, it is not convenient,
it is not right, for those who believe that they are actually entrusted with a Gospel, and who must give
account to God for the way in which they discharge
the trust. We must be able to say what we mean
when we declare that " *God was in Christ reconciling
the world to Himself, not imputing their trespasses
unto them ; and that He has committed to us the word
of reconciliation.*" It cannot be our chief business to
find out what mistakes men have made in arguing
about our message on one side or the other. What *is*
the message itself? that must be our question. From
whom does it come? To whom is it addressed? That
it is a message of peace from a Father to His children ;
that that Father is a righteous Father, and that the
children have been unrighteous because they have
been separated from Him ; that the peace is made
in the body and blood of a righteous Son, one with
the Father, who has given Himself for men ; that

the peace is carried home to men's hearts by a righteous and reconciling Spirit,—is this heterodox doctrine? Because if it is, it is what I mean, so help
me God, to live and die in declaring to those among
whom I minister; what I am ashamed that I have declared so little and with so cold a heart; what I hold
has the mightiest power to reform and renew human
society. This is what I understand by the doctrine
of the Atonement; this is what I believe Saints and
Martyrs understood by it. In it, I hold, is revealed
the goodness and truth and long-suffering of God.

Wherein do I suppose that this statement differs
from any that Mr. Mansel would make? I have
very imperfect means of judging, as he has kept his
counsel about that which he believes, and has only
been communicative about that which he deems dogmatical or rationalistic. But I should suppose that
he would construct from different passages of Scripture a doctrine which he would call the doctrine
of the Atonement, and that he would object decidedly to my saying that the passages of Scripture
are far more distinct and intelligible than all that
has been constructed out of them or on them, and
that they declare not a doctrine about Reconciliation, but the actual Reconciliation of God with Man
in the person of His Son. Perhaps I ought not to
assume this point at present, for you must remember
that he has not yet given us his application of the
doctrine of the Unconditioned. This present Lecture

is only preliminary to the series. The holocaust of
writers in the Notes is doubtless offered to the genius
of Sir William Hamilton; but he has not yet been
brought forward himself to determine what is included in the horizon of our faith, what are or are not
the possibilities of a Revelation. Nevertheless, I think
we shall find presently that I have stated the Lecturer's meaning fairly, and therefore that what I
have said of the Atonement must necessarily subject
me to his condemnation.

Assuming this difference then, I wish to show you
how it bears upon the question of Dogmatism and
Rationalism. I am tempted, of course, to dogmatize
upon this as upon every subject; that is to say, to
put certain notions of mine concerning the Atonement before my hearers, in place of the Atonement
itself. The hindrances to my doing this are, first, the
strength of my conviction that it is very horrible
to intercept the direct communication between God
and His creatures which I believe the Bible bears
witness of; secondly, the conviction that just what
I and all men want, is to be delivered from our notions and conceits about Him, and the relation in
which we stand to Him, which notions and conceits
have led to infinite disorder and unrighteousness;
thirdly, to the discovery that the more I introduce
these notions and conceits into my teaching, the more
I am out of harmony with the practical teaching
of the Bible, and unable to profit by it,—the less I

am able to do justice to the various thoughts and
speculations and reasonings of men who are seeking
after righteousness through communion with a righteous God. The Revelation of God Himself, as the
Reconciler and Atoner of man, is, it seems to me,
the substitute for Dogmatism, which tries to measure
and confine Him by our narrow and carnal notions.

To escape from Dogmatism about the Atonement
is also, I think, to escape from Rationalism about it.
The unveiling of a Charity such as I could form only
the faintest dream or conception of,—of a God who
makes a perfect sacrifice for the sake of reconciling
to Him those who have wandered from Him, takes
from me all excuse for measuring and circumscribing
Him by any thoughts and notions of mine. Of course
I try again and again to do so. I make all sorts of
silly experiments to bring this love down to my level.
I devise arrangements and form imaginations to account for it, and to determine the limits of it. But
the more the Atonement itself, in its own mighty
power,—not as a doctrine, but as the Sacrifice of a
Divine Person,—is brought home to me and over-
powers me, the more I am driven out of this false
and wretched Rationalism ; the more I am content
to let God manifest Himself to me as He has done
in His Son, as He promises to do in us all by His
Spirit. And this because I become in the truest and
fullest sense a Rationalist, because a spirit that was
asleep in me before, is awakened, to perceive a length

and breadth and height and depth of Divinity which
could, so far as I know, only reveal itself in that way,
and which must open the eye that was created to
discern it.

How does this way of contemplating and presenting the Atonement affect one's judgment of those
whom Mr. Mansel declares to have made shipwreck,
either as Dogmatists or Rationalists? I would take
an instance of each kind. I do not know whether
you are a reader of *Anselm*. I own myself to be
a very affectionate and admiring reader, though
certainly in no sense a disciple of him. Perhaps I
may venture to quote some sentences which I wrote
about him several years ago, certainly with no purpose of their serving any argumentative purpose :—
" It is an agreeable characteristic of Anselm's works
" that a very small portion of them indeed belong to
" controversy. There is one treatise, written at the
" instigation of the Pope, on the Greek doctrine of
" the procession of the Holy Ghost, and one against
" Roscellinus, on the Incarnation. With these excep-
" tions, meditations, prayers, letters, and books writ-
" ten for the solution of difficulties which had actu-
" ally occurred to some person who had consulted
" him, generally to some brother at Bec, form his
" contribution to Middle Age literature. Not more
" for the honour of Anselm himself than for the
" comprehension of his books, this last characteristic
" should be recollected. They were not hard dog-

" matical treatises written in cold blood, to build up a
" system or to vanquish opponents. They were actual
" guides to the doubter; attempts, often made with
" much reluctant modesty, to untie knots which worthy
" men found to be interfering with their peace and
" with their practice.

" The characteristic of Anselm as a man was, we
" think, a love of righteousness for its own sake.
" That noble habit of mind is illustrated in his con-
" versation respecting Alphege, scarcely less in a
" sentence of his, reported by Eadmer, which has
" given rise to some very uncharitable Protestant
" commentaries, that ' he would rather be in Hell if
" ' he were pure of sin, than possess the Kingdom
" ' of Heaven under the pollution of sin.' This too
" is the spirit of his writings. It is from this that
" they derive their substantial and permanent worth.
" Right there must be—that is the postulate of his
" mind. Then, partly for the sake of entering more
" deeply into the apprehension and possession of that
" which he inwardly acknowledged, partly for the
" sake of removing confusions from the minds of his
" brethren, he undertakes to establish his assumption
" by proof. Oftentimes we are compelled to doubt
" the success of these demonstrations. We have an
" uncomfortable feeling, that the principle which we
" are to arrive at by an elaborate process of reasoning
" has been taken for granted at the commencement
" of it; some of the arguments seem scarcely worthy

" of their object, some of them seem to interfere with
" it, by tempting us to accept one mode of contem-
" plating it instead of the object itself.   Theology has
" cause to complain of Anselm for having suggested
" theories and argumentations in connection with Ar-
" ticles of the Creed, which through their plausibility
" and through the excellency of the writer have gained
" currency in the Church, till they have been adopted
" as essential parts of that of which they were at best
" only defences and explanations.   But viewing him,
" as we are privileged to do, simply as philosophical
" students,—caring less about the results to which
" his treatises have led dogmatists, than about his
" principles and about his method of thought,—he
" offers us a very interesting subject of examination.
" In Johannes Scotus the metaphysical element was
" evidently predominant over the ethical; in Anselm
" the moral absorbs everything into itself.   Moral
" ends are first in his mind ; scientific truth he learns
" to love, because he is too honest a man not to feel
" that Goodness is a contradiction if it has not Truth
" for its support.   But the difference in the starting-
" point of these two writers affects all their intel-
" lectual habits.   Anselm is much more of a *formal*
" reasoner than Johannes ; amongst ordinary school-
" readers he would pass for a much more *accurate*
" reasoner.   He supplies many more producible ar-
" guments ; he meets the perplexities which the use
" of words occasions more promptly ; though far

" enough from a superficial thinker, he keeps much
" more the high-road of the intellect, and is not
" tempted to explore caverns. For such a person,
" Logic becomes an invaluable auxiliary; he has not
" the dread of its limiting the infinite which the
" other had ; he secures his moral truth from all
" verbal invasions; then he can let verbal refinements
" have their full swing in the discussion of objections
" and in the effort to remove them."

I believe this is a faithful description of the man.
It may explain to you the passages from the *Cur
Deus Homo* which Mr. Mansel has quoted. Anselm
was no doubt a Dogmatist. He received with the
simplest affection the creeds of his childhood, and not
only the creeds, but the ordinary mediæval system.
He was also, no doubt, a Rationalist. He tried to
meet difficulties, to account for facts, to establish
formulas, with what result I have tried to express.
But what saved him from being a mere Dogmatist
and a mere Rationalist? What gave his books a
beauty and worth which I am sure every earnest
student will find in them, now in this nineteenth
century, when all the forms and habits of the time
to which he belonged have passed away? It was
this, that God was to Anselm more than all systems ;
that he was sure God was a righteous Being,—that,
and only that; that he was sure God had revealed
His Righteousness to men, and meant that they
should know it. Caring then very little for his argu-

ments and proofs about the Atonement, I know of no truer witness for its essential character, no stronger witness against those who would bring back Paganism under the name of Christianity, and who suppose that the notions of men concerning an Atonement, instead of pointing to the one which God has made, are to be the measures and standards of its character or its method.

I will pass from the earliest instance in Mr. Mansel's Notes to the latest. I will venture, not without diffidence and hesitation, to speak of a passage he has quoted from his own learned and devout contemporary Professor Jowett. I have the misfortune to differ from that excellent man, not only in particulars of his interpretation of St. Paul, but in the fundamental maxim of it. Modern thought, it seems to me, has been approaching more and more near to a condition in which no teachers can meet it so directly as St. Paul and St. John, taken in their most literal sense. I could have recognized the chasm which he finds between their revelations and English thoughts and hopes in the *eighteenth* century. The nineteenth, I believe, as much by its doubts, perplexities, contradictions, as by what is noblest in it,—as much by its political as by its philosophical and theological movements,—has been brought into a state in which all glosses upon them will be cast to the winds; in which they will be received as the clearest, simplest messages to the scholar and to the wayfarer, capable of meeting what we sometimes fancy are the newest demands of humanity and Science. I differ from him therefore not as radically as I differ from Mr. Mansel, yet partly on the same ground. Nevertheless, I recognize in him one of the honestest and bravest of men,—honest and brave as few men are in this day,—in that he will not express more than he thinks, and that he will state what he thinks, without regarding consequences,—a quality all the more remarkable in one who evidently hesitates so much before he assumes a position. Such a habit of mind must, I should conceive, have a salutary effect upon us all, seeing that one of our great temptations is to use 'unreal words,' and to let our statements outstrip our convictions.

Having these feelings respecting this eminent Teacher, it is the greater duty as well as pleasure to express the most hearty concurrence in a sentiment which Mr. Mansel quotes from him for the purpose of fixing on him the charge of Rationalism on the subject of the Atonement. "In what did this "Satisfaction consist? Was it that God was angry, "and needed to be propitiated like some heathen "deity of old? Such a thought refutes itself by the "very indignation which it calls up in the human "bosom."—(*Jowett, Epistles of St. Paul,* vol. ii. p. 472.) Now mark for what purpose this passage is quoted. It is not to relieve St. Paul, or any writer of the Old or New Testament, from the possible imputation that he represented the God of Abraham, and Isaac, and Jacob, the God merciful and gracious, slow to anger, and of great mercy, forgiving iniquity and transgression and sin, but not clearing the guilty, the God who is just and without iniquity, as resembling 'a heathen deity of old.' It is not to show that the anger against sin which is attributed to the Lord God throughout the Bible is the most opposite thing possible to the anger against particular persons who had done them injury which is attributed to heathen deities. It is not to quote those long chapters of the Prophets in which God appeals to the conscience of His people against their revolts from Him, or in which He is contrasted with idols. It is not to urge that the declaration of our Lord, " *He that hath seen Me hath seen the Father,*" if it is taken as it stands, will at once settle all controversies respecting His character and Nature. No! but it is to say either that there is no moral indignation in the human bosom against the confusion of our God and Father with Moloch and Siva; or to say that that moral indignation is good for nothing. And this comes from a pupil of Butler, the great champion of the Conscience! And this comes from an Apologist for Prophets and Apostles, every one of whom would have died, many of whom did die, because they would not worship the gods of the nations! And this comes from the apologist of Apostles who said that in Jesus dwelt the fullness of the Godhead bodily! Mr. Mansel has put forth a defence of what is de-

nounced by some as anthropomorphic language. I
prize that language, little as I like his way of pleading for it. I hold, for instance, the name of 'jealous,'
which is so often given to God in Scripture,—to be
a true epithet for a holy and good Being. I believe God *is* jealous of His name and character,—
jealous of that confusion with wicked beings which
Mr. Mansel implicitly authorizes; which he pronounces it Rationalistic to abhor. Have not all dogmatists, when their schemes of accounting for the purposes of the Most High have been most gratuitous
and even most profane,—have not all Rationalists,
when their cries have had the most of an atheistical
form and character, been useful protestants against
this last, most hopeless, most horrible kind of orthodoxy? Can we dispense with their testimony while
this language is heard in high places, while it goes
forth from the central pulpits of the land? May we
not at least be sure that it will be listened to, and
that we shall have ourselves to blame for any consequences that may proceed from it?

I must repeat what I have said already in my Sermons. I do not impute to Mr. Mansel what his
language seems to convey. I fully believe he would
start with horror at the thought of identifying the
God in whom is light and no darkness at all, with
the dark beings whom men have made for themselves
to worship. But see what a Nemesis awaits those
who treat the most sacred portions of the Gospel—

those portions which speak most of union and reconciliation—chiefly as excuses for finding out how much
of wrong and unbelief there is in their fellow-men !
These doctrines lose their very nature.   They are to
be received at the point of the bayonet because they
are set down in a book.   *What* is set down there—
what we are asked to receive—*what* is involved in the
reception of them—there is not leisure to inquire.
The words are to be eaten; but it is the great business of those who enforce the eating, to prove that
we have no organs wherewith we can masticate or
digest them.

There is one eloquent passage in this Lecture
which, if I had read it without the context, I should
have claimed as a testimony on behalf of the truth
which Sir W. Hamilton, we have seen, was willing to
acknowledge, that man is made in the image of God,
and therefore that a participation of divinity is implied
in his constitution.   I should have supposed it was
meant to show philosophers that our assertion of the
union of the Godhead and Manhood in one Christ,
far from being the stumbling-block to the Reason
which they have taken it to be, is the one possible
reconciliation of that human belief which has pervaded the hearts of all human beings,—which has
been at the root of all mythologies,—with the protest
against it which their consciences have borne, and
which the Bible bears,—against the confusion of God
with the works of His hands.   Read it, and judge for
yourself.

"The origin of such theories is of course to be
"traced to that morbid horror of what they are
"pleased to call Anthropomorphism, which poisons
"the speculations of so many modern philosophers,
"when they attempt to be wise above what is writ-
"ten, and seek for a metaphysical exposition of
"God's nature and attributes. They may not, for-
"sooth, think of the unchangeable God as if He were
"their fellow-man, influenced by human motives, and
"moved by human supplications. They want a truer,
"a juster idea of the Deity as He is, than that under
"which He has been pleased to reveal Himself; and
"they call on their reason to furnish it. Fools, to
"dream that man can escape from himself, that hu-
"man reason can draw aught but a human portrait
"of God! They do but substitute a marred and
"mutilated humanity for one exalted and entire:
"they add nothing to their conception of God as He
"is, but only take away a part of their conception
"of man. Sympathy, and love, and fatherly kind-
"ness, and forgiving mercy, have evaporated in the
"crucible of their philosophy; and what is the *caput*
"*mortuum* that remains, but only the sterner features
"of humanity exhibited in repulsive nakedness? The
"God who listens to prayer, we are told, appears in
"the likeness of human mutability. Be it so. What
"is the God who does not listen, but the likeness of
"human obstinacy? Do we ascribe to Him a fixed
"purpose? our conception of a purpose is human.

" Do we speak of Him as continuing unchanged? our
" conception of continuance is human. Do we con-
" ceive Him as knowing and determining? What
" are knowledge and determination but modes of
" human consciousness? And what know we of con-
" sciousness itself, but as the contrast between suc-
" cessive mental states? But our rational philoso-
" pher stops short in the middle of his reasoning.
" He strips off from humanity just so much as suits
" his purpose ;—' and the residue thereof he maketh
" a god ;'—less pious in his idolatry than the carver
" of the graven image, in that he does not fall down
" unto it and pray unto it, but is content to stand
" afar off and reason concerning it. And why does
" he retain any conception of God at all, but that he
" retains some portions of an imperfect humanity?
" Man is still the residue that is left ; deprived in-
" deed of all that is amiable in humanity, but, in
" the darker features which remain, still man. Man
" in his purposes ; man in his inflexibility ; man in
" that relation to time from which no philosophy,
" whatever its pretensions, can wholly free itself ;
" pursuing with indomitable resolution a precon-
" ceived design ; deaf to the yearning instincts which
" compel his creatures to call upon him. Yet this,
" forsooth, is a philosophical conception of the Deity,
" more worthy of an enlightened reason than the
" human imagery of the Psalmist. ' The eyes of the
" ' Lord are over the righteous, and His ears are open
" ' unto their prayers.'

" Surely downright idolatry is better than this *ra-*
" *tional* worship of a fragment of humanity. Better
" is the superstition which sees the image of God in
" the wonderful whole which God has fashioned, than
" the philosophy which would carve for itself a Deity
" out of the remnant which man has mutilated.
" Better to realize the satire of the Eleatic philo-
" sopher, to make God in the likeness of man, even
" as the ox or the horse might conceive gods in the
" form of oxen or horses, than to adore some half-hewn
" Hermes, the head of a man joined to a misshapen
" block. Better to fall down before that marvellous
" compound of human consciousness whose elements
" God has joined together, and no man can put asun-
" der, than to strip reason of those cognate elements
" which together furnish all that we can conceive or
" imagine of conscious or personal existence, and to
" defy the emptiest of all abstractions, a something or
" a nothing, with just enough of its human original
" left to form a theme for the disputations of philoso-
" phy, but not enough to furnish a single ground of
" appeal to the human feelings of love, of reverence,
" and of fear. Unmixed idolatry is more religious
" than this. Undisguised atheism is more logical."
—(*Bampton Lectures,* 2nd ed., pp. 17–20.)

I cannot imagine a man writing such fervent sentences as these, denouncing men as 'fools' for fancying that God has not human qualities and sympathies—telling them that they had better worship the

most miserable idol, than hold what they hold,—assuring them that they would be wiser to be undisguised atheists—if he is not prepared to say, ' I can ' show you a more excellent way. I can tell you what ' God has done to satisfy " that marvellous compound ' " of human consciousness which He has joined toge- ' " ther, and which man cannot put asunder." I can ' show you how He has made Himself known to us ' in His only-begotten Son, so that we may not any ' longer confound Him with his feeble and sinful crea- ' tures, or yet divide Him from them as if His nature ' was not really the ground and archetype of theirs.' If this cannot be done, are we not bound, by the preacher's own showing, to take refuge in one or other of his terrible alternatives ?

How then does Mr. Mansel speak of the union of the Godhead and Manhood in Christ ? Thus: *"We " believe that Christ is both God and Man, for that is " revealed to us. We know not how He is so, for this " is not revealed, and we can learn it in no other way."* (pp. 14 and 15.) Now you will see at once that the revelation of this union is not presented here *in any sense whatever* as the interpretation of the doubt whether men are to worship God as one of His creatures, or whether they are to regard Him as separate from them all. It is an additional, a hard, an insoluble difficulty, which we must receive in addition to all other difficulties, because God commands us in His book to receive it. We are left by this amazing revelation—that He who was the express Image of the Father, was made man and dwelt among us—just where we were before. We are left just as much as ever to oscillate between unmixed idolatry and undisguised atheism, with only this additional comfort, that every attempt of a man to find a middle between them, makes him more irreligious than if he chose the first course, more illogical than if he chose the last.

To me this result is a very shocking one. Nor is the shock at all diminished as I trace the course of thought which justifies it to the mind of the Lecturer. A man whom many of us remember with gratitude and affection, who, we hope, is now in communion with those from whom on earth he thought it right to separate,—the late Mr. R. Wilberforce,—wrote a book, as you know, on the Incarnation. In that book he appears to ground the idea of the union of the Godhead and Manhood in Christ upon the assumption of a real Human Nature, distinct from the nature of each individual man. Mr. Mansel at once perceives that the writer has introduced into theology the realism of Duns Scotus and those schoolmen whom, as we commonly suppose, Occam confuted. Here, then, is a plausible excuse for warning his hearers that, if they receive the Incarnation as anything more than a tenet which is revealed in the Bible, they will certainly fall into all the mediæval confusions, will again blend Theology and Philosophy together, so destroying the simplicity of the one and the freedom of the other.

I have called this argument *plausible,* by which I mean that it is one which was quite sure to commend itself to a great majority of those who heard it. The word Realism would be just sufficiently understood by an Oxford congregation to cause a vague terror; the practical conscience of Englishmen would protest against the mixture of scholastic refinements with the faith of God; the events in the later life of the author who was criticized would be inevitably connected with the theses he had defended; that indolence which Butler considered so fatal to *his* course of inquiry, would make the moral palatable to all the no-thinkers among the crowd that listened to the Lectures; those whose minds had been exercised by the realistic and nominalistic questions, might eagerly welcome any promise of repose from them. I gave the argument no *better* name than plausible, because I regard it as the argument of an able rhetorician, not of an earnest philosopher or theologian who cares to explain what these mediæval strifes meant; to satisfy the honest conviction of the practical Englishman; to arouse the no-thinker out his slumbers; to show the perplexed thinker how he may find a way out of his perplexities without losing the great blessing of them.

It is the easiest thing in the world to talk as Mr. Mansel talks about " the forgotten follies of Scholas-

" tic Realism," and about " endangering the cause of
" Religion by seeking to explain its deepest mysteries
" by the lifeless forms of a worn-out controversy."
Many such things has one heard; there is always
a certain response to them in our minds. But they
help us exceedingly little. Why do these ' forgotten
follies' start up so often in connection with these
' deep mysteries' ? Why could not Realistic and Nominalistic controversies sever themselves from the
doctrines of the two Natures in Christ, and of the
Trinity ? Why have Divines and Philosophers both
been protesting for so many centuries against the
confusion of their provinces, while yet there is more
of it in our day than in any previous one ? Why
does Mr. Mansel protest against it, and yet put forth
a work which contains more appeals to the religious
feelings against Philosophers, and (as we shall see when
we come to his next Lecture) more of verbal subtleties that are likely to disturb simple faith, than almost
any book of the century? These facts are not to be
got rid of by loose declamation. They require the
most serious pondering. May I give you one or two
hints which will possibly assist your own reflections
upon them ?

If one considers the history of Mediæval Philosophy, not for the purpose of laughing at ' forgotten
follies,' but of understanding what a set of very earnest men were engaged in, and how God was leading them by a better way than they knew, this con-

clusion forces itself upon us. These men could not
be satisfied with regarding " the deepest mysteries of
our faith" as dogmas; if they were to be believed
at all, they must be more. They must be involved
in the very Constitution of things. They must be
at the very ground of it. The schoolmen were inclined enough to say, " We have received them as a
"tradition.   They are, *because* we have received
" them." But they could not. The tradition must
surely speak of that which is; if it did not, it was a
lying tradition, to be cast aside like those over which
the Gospel had triumphed.   Hence the vehement
protest on the part of the orthodox in the eleventh
century against Nominalism, because it seemed to
them that the deepest realities by this teaching were
changed into mere names; hence the fight, no less
honest, on the part of the Nominalists, to prevent a
confusion of notions in our minds with actual things.
Through this school conflict, I believe, if we use it
aright, we may discover true principles which do
not belong to the schools but to mankind have asserted themselves—we may discover what work the
schools can do and cannot do. As in the case of the
conflicts between the King and the Priest, between
the King and the Barons, between the King and the
Commons, it is not by ranging ourselves on either
side, least of all is it by despising both sides and
setting up ourselves as superior to both, that we
arrive at the right historical lesson. Rather should

we confess what a strong conviction was working in
the heart of each, and how that conviction proved its
worth and its stability in spite of all the dogmatical
vehemence and the dogmatical feebleness with which
it was accompanied.

The battle ceased for a time when the practical and
personal faith of the Reformers broke through the
webs of Scholasticism, and claimed a personal affiance
in the Son of God, who had taken our nature. Then
for awhile Theologians—Protestant at least—were
ready enough to take a position of their own, and to
let the Philosophers take theirs. But this assignment
of provinces was soon disturbed again; it was felt that
the personal faith could not determine that which it
believed; that into this determination, processes of the
understanding entered; the philosophers and logicians
must give their opinions about these processes. Theology became as dogmatic as it was in the Middle
Ages; *apparently* there was not the same conflict to
ascertain whether its dogmas pointed to realities or
were only notions of the understanding. But that controversy soon reappeared in another shape. Personal
faith again put in its vehement protest against dogmas; its claim to some actual living ground on which
it might rest: again it had to be asked, 'Can personal faith affirm *what* is to be believed?' The seventeenth century was full of these strifes. The eighteenth seemed to promise the subsidence of them.
Theology, it was hoped, might keep its own ground.

Philosophy might keep its ground. In no period did each more resolutely attack the province of the other. In no period were there more efforts, unsuccessful efforts, made for the adjustment of their respective claims. Meantime the strong convictions of men once more became violently impatient of religious dogmatism, as well as of mere moralities. The deep mysteries again were sought for, as realities to which the Conscience must betake itself as a refuge from its own torments. The *Cur Deus Homo* was a question debated in the hearts of peasants and miners with as much earnestness as it had been seven centuries before by the monks of Bec.

These miners and peasants cared little about philosophers or school Theologians; would have regarded them as profane men. But they affected, more than they knew, the speculations of both. It has been found impossible in our day for Theologians to shut themselves up in a set of opinions. They must answer, not to a demand of the schools, but to a demand of the people; ' Have those opinions any counterpart in Reality ? Do they mean anything ? You call them mysteries ; do you tell us, by using that word, that we have nothing to do with them,—that they stand in no relation to us? Speak ! for we will know.' On the other hand, it has been found absolutely impossible for Philosophers, from whatever point they might start, not to come into contact with the question of the union of Humanity with

Godhead.   Read Sir William Hamilton's discussions ; look through Mr. Mansel's Notes ; no further
evidence is necessary.   Warn philosophers off the
ground as you will ; call it a violation of neutrality,
a venturing into the Theological preserves.   Denounce it, laugh at it, persecute it ; you cannot
hinder it.   Remember, it has happened not only in
spite of Theological protests, but of Philosophical.
Numbers of Philosophers voted solemnly that they
would leave us to manage our own nonsense.   They
could not.   A necessity has urged them on.   Take the
extreme cases.   Choose them from whatever country
you please.   Shall it be Strauss? shall it be Feuerbach?
shall it be Comte ?   The question is still forced upon
us.   What is Humanity ?   Has it anything to do with
what has been called Divine ?   Yes, or No ?   What
if some answer, ' No—absolutely nothing' ?   What
if some answer, Yes, but on exactly the opposite principle to the one you set forth,—' Humanity is to make
itself divine.'   What if there are all degrees of opinion intermediate between these ?   Supposing we are
not asserting a truth ; supposing the Incarnation is *not*
a fact, but only a dogma ; supposing the union of the
Godhead and Manhood in a Person is *not* involved in
the very existence of man, in the very order of things
—all these contradictions, from the greatest to the
least, are very alarming.   No wonder that we quake at
them ; no wonder that we try by any means to stifle
them.   No wonder that we sometimes groan over the

paucity of the means which are left to us,—that the
sword and the fire, which, if they are used with a consistent, exterminating purpose, have done something,
should be exchanged for the paltry machinery of argument and ridicule. But what if that which we say is
even so? What if the Incarnation *is* a fact? What if
the union of the Godhead and Manhood in Christ is involved in the very existence of man, in the very order
of the Universe? Would it then be a cause of sorrow
that so much of questioning from all quarters should
be directed towards this point? Should we then shuf-
fle, and evade the conflict, saying that a mystery of
the faith could have no connection with the thoughts
that are working in the minds of philosophers?
Should we not rejoice and give thanks that it has so
much to do with them? Should we not tremble lest
any one of these inquiries should be hidden or sup-
pressed which indicate what men are needing,—which
compel us to offer them realities, and not opinions,
in exchange for the doubts and objections which they
offer to us?

I am as eager that Theology should hold its own
simple, positive ground as Mr. Mansel can be; I am
as eager that Philosophy should have its fullest range
and freedom. But I do not think that Theology
has any ground at all, if it merely accepts as a Tenet
what is revealed as a Truth; I do not think Philosophy has any freedom at all, if philosophers are
forbidden to learn anything but what Sir William

Hamilton teaches them. I admit that theologians may do more than mere philosophers, to mark out the respective spheres of Theology and Philosophy; by preserving their own simplicity they will best assert its liberty. But I am also convinced that theologians will not arrive at this result by falling back upon the maxims of the eighteenth century. They may arrive at it if they proceed in the course into which they have been led, as I think, by a higher wisdom than their own; if they sincerely ask themselves what has caused one and another to fail in that course.

What I mean by the course into which they have been led, is this. The Person of Christ, as distinguished from a mere doctrine about Christ, appears to have become more and more the absorbing subject among those divines who exercise any considerable influence over the thought either of England or of Germany. Even the growing Mariolatry of Romish countries, even the new Papal decree respecting the conception of the Virgin, points in this direction. That a 'Leben Jesu' should be the favourite work of each of the eminent theologians of Germany, is all the more remarkable from their specially abstract tendencies. That such a book as Mr. Wilberforce's on the Incarnation should have been written by one whose habits of thought inclined him to be peculiarly dogmatic, is also a very striking sign of the times. The study of Butler at Oxford must have affected the writer even more than he was aware of. He owns himself how much he had been led into that line of inquiry by finding the necessity of something to complete and sustain that personal faith, the all-importance of which he had learnt from the school in which he was educated. Other books, scarcely less significant, and pointing to a different kind of discipline, might be referred to; one of them, Mr. Young's 'Christ of History,' is quoted with qualified approbation by Mr. Mansel.

All these are attempts to escape from Dogmatism to a ground of reality. All of them, I think, may teach us much. All of them are open in some measure to the criticism which the Bampton Lecturer has directed against Mr. Wilberforce. They mix philosophy with revelation; at times you fancy they are forming a Christ out of their own thoughts,—at times, that they are recognizing a Christ such as is set forth by the Evangelists. The writers are perfectly innocent of any such confusion,—as innocent as I believe Mr. Wilberforce was of any wish to put a universal notion of Humanity between himself and Christ. They would gladly escape from notions. If they are hampered by them, it is from some defect of method. I suspect it is from their being too anxious to meet the thoughts of philosophers halfway; whereas if they had assumed a different standing-ground, they would have had a hope of meeting them altogether.

I will explain this statement to you. These writers

suppose that their opponents would never concede to them the *Divinity* of Christ; ' We will stand, there-'fore,' they say, ' on your own ground. We will talk 'to you about His Humanity. We will see if that 'does not command your affection and reverence. ' We will then inquire whether that affection and re-'verence must not ascend to a higher region still.' Mr. Wilberforce did not act on *this* maxim. He had discovered a deeper necessity than those who contemplate the life of Christ merely as the life of *a* man,— he had felt the force of the expression, *Son of Man,* which occurs so continually in the Gospels; of St. Paul's expression, *"He is the Head of every man;"* of that other, *" The Firstborn of every creature."* But with his method of ascending from the earthly to the heavenly, I do not see how he could give effect to this language, without falling into the Realism which Mr. Mansel objects to him. And I do not see how he could practically escape another danger to which his critic has not alluded. Duns Scotus, the great champion of Realism in its strongest sense, was also he who won laurels at Paris for defending the doctrine which Pius IX. has erected into an Article of Faith. The mere universal Humanity was an abstract notion, though he might invest it with reality ; its dreariness must be sustained by this worship of a concrete Humanity in the nature of the Virgin.

To that point I believe we shall tend,—Auguste Comte, as much as Pius IX., leading the way to it,—if

theologians are not willing to be theologians again,
and to proceed in directly the opposite method to that
which I have just been indicating,—the method which
the Church points out in the Epistle and Gospel for
Christmas Day,—the old method of the Creeds. Then
suppose we believe the Incarnation to be true, may
we not cry, must we not cry, to the cities of England, as the Prophet cried to the cities of Judah,
" *Behold your God?*" ' We declare how He has mani-
' fested Himself to us in that Son who is the bright-
' ness of His glory, the express image of His Person.
' This is the Being whom we praise and declare to be
' the Lord.   We say that Christ has come to make
' known the Father; we say that in Him all may
' know Him, because He has revealed Himself, fully
' revealed Himself, not in words and letters, but in a
' Man.'

Here, it seems to me, is the office of the theologian. He comes with this Gospel to mankind. So
far as he is asserting, he is a dogmatist. But he does
not rest his assertion upon his own judgment or upon
the judgment of ages; he addresses it to the conscience, heart, reason of mankind. He leaves God to
justify it in His own way, by the sorrows, needs, sins,
contradictions of men. He desires only that the news
should go forth with no force but its own. He can
trust it; for he can trust Him who has shown us in
His Son what He is, who has promised His Spirit of
Truth to guide us into all Truth. Dogmatism and Ra-

tionalism cannot be reconciled in words ; the verbal middle between them is feebler than either, destructive of what is good in both. Here is the living, real, uniting Mean between them. The verbal middle between the idolatry which is the worship of creatures, and the atheism which is the worship of nothing, is "less religious than the one, less logical than the other." God declaring Himself to His creatures in a Man, that the creature may rise to the full knowledge of Him,—here is that middle which you, if you are to be a clergyman of the Christian Church, must hold forth in the practical and living words of the Scripture, to the righteous and the sinful, to the wise and the unwise.

Very truly yours,

F. D. M.

LETTER V.

—◆—

MR. MANSEL'S SECOND LETTER.—RELIGIOUS PHI-
LOSOPHY. — MYSTICISM. — THE CRITERION OF
TRUTH.

MY DEAR SIR,

I did not enter upon the theological topics which
were considered in my last letter, because I was in a
hurry to introduce them before we had settled whether the maxim of Sir William Hamilton did or did
not prove that a knowledge of the Infinite or Eternal or Absolute is impossible for human beings. It
was Mr. Mansel who forced me into them. He could
not, apparently, lay the ground of his religious philosophy without referring to them. He could not
begin to build himself, till he had swept away certain thoughts about the Atonement and Incarnation
which had been put forth by divines or philosophers.
Being driven to this necessity, I have inquired what
those doctrines are which the Bampton Lecturer
complains of other men for not believing, or for
not fully believing. I have asked what is implied in

the *most* full belief of them, in the reception of them as an actual Gospel to be delivered to mankind. Clearly *this* was implied, that they were not mere doctrines or opinions contained in a book, or generalized by us from a book. If the doctrine of the Atonement was not false as a doctrine, as an opinion, there must have been an actual Reconciliation between God and His creatures in the person of His Son. If the doctrine of the Incarnation was not false as a doctrine, the Eternal Son must have actually come forth from the Eternal Father, and have taken human flesh, and have dwelt among men ; the nature and glory of the Eternal God must have come forth in the man, so that He could say, " *He that hath seen me hath seen the Father.*" You and I had to determine whether, *in this sense,* we could receive the Incarnation and Atonement,—whether, *in this sense,* we could proclaim them to men. For if we called on any human being to receive them as doctrines, and yet did not set them forth as facts, it seemed that we were committing a huge injustice to our fellows, deceiving our own selves, violating the trust we had received from God. But supposing we could do this,—supposing we believed that the word Gospel was not a treacherous sound, and that there is indeed a message from God to man,—then it seemed that we must rejoice in every indication which we found anywhere that men are seeking after the knowledge of God, and cannot be content without it. From whatever point such inquiries might start, whatever forms they might take, however they might be blended with confusion, contradiction, denial, there could be no doubt that they denoted a craving and a necessity which God Himself had awakened, and which He would satisfy. If they were attempts to solve by forms, phrases, and notions, that which demanded a real, not a verbal solution, the perplexity of those attempts which, of course, we had experienced ourselves and felt to be a human perplexity, would give them a deep interest for us; if they were attempts to break through all phrases, formulas, intellectual subtleties, and to reach that which lies behind them and beneath them,—then, however they might fail, they would be still more affecting proofs that God was inspiring men with a passion for that which they found was too large for them to grasp, and yet was altogether necessary to them. If, in the endeavour to get rid of their own partial conceits and notions, and to find a ground which was beneath all, they were often entangled in those conceits and notions, we should again recognize men struggling as we struggle,—we should again perceive how wide, human, universal, God's revelation must be.

For these reasons, I contended that the controversy which gave so much occupation to men's thoughts in the Middle Ages, the realistic and nominalistic controversy in its different stages, was a subject of profound interest and instruction to the modern theologian, inasmuch as it taught him how near words and things lie to each other,—what demands the Conscience and Reason of men make for Realities,—how they witness that the highest of all must be the most real, the ground of other reality,—how apt we are to confound notions and dogmas and conclusions of our intellect, with the truths to which they refer, and so to turn truths into mere names or mere opinions. I thought the rebellion against school logic just as full of meaning as the perplexities of that logic, and more consolatory,—because it is a deep, authentic testimony that human beings, the moment they are roused to the feeling that they are human, must look above and beyond themselves, must rise out of themselves, whether they can prove their right to do it logically or not. And for us even more interesting is that direction of men's minds which has been so manifest during the last hundred years, that direction which, as I said, made it impossible for us to adopt Butler's phrase of Natural and Revealed Religion,—though it made Butler's teaching respecting a revelation of God through the Constitution of Nature and through Man all the more precious.

I follow an excellent precedent, which Mr. Mansel has set us at the close of each of his Lectures, in thus recapitulating the lessons which we have been learning from his statements and from the facts which he has adduced. I am particularly anxious to do

so at the commencement of his second Lecture, because that is (1) the one in which he has formally announced what is the object and the character of his
" religious philosophy ;" (2) the one in which he has
applied himself most vigorously to the work of demolishing the dream of Mystics and Rationalists that
there is any criterion of truth in man ; (3) the one in
which he has exhibited most of his scholastical skill
in dealing with our notions of Cause, of the Absolute,
and the Infinite ; and in destroying Pantheism.   This
last portion of the Lecture I reserve for a separate
letter.   To the other two divisions I address myself
now.

(1.) I have used the phrase " Religious Philosophy."   It is Mr. Mansel's.   The following extract
will tell you what he does and does not mean by it.

" A philosophy of religion may be attempted from
" two opposite points of view, and by two opposite
" modes of development.   It may be conceived either
" as a Philosophy of the Object of Religion ; that
" is to say, as a scientific exposition of the nature of
" God ; or as a Philosophy of the Subject of Reli-
" gion ; that is to say, as a scientific inquiry into the
" constitution of the human mind, so far as it re-
" ceives and deals with religious ideas.   The former
" is that branch of Metaphysics which is commonly
" known by the name of Rational Theology.   Its
" general aim, in common with all metaphysical in-
" quiries, is to disengage the.real from the apparent,

" the true from the false: its special aim, as a The-
" ology, is to exhibit a true representation of the
" Nature and Attributes of God, purified from fo-
" reign accretions, and displaying the exact features
" of their Divine Original. The latter is a branch
" of Psychology, which, at its outset at least, con-
" tents itself with investigating the phenomena pre-
" sented to it, leaving their relation to further realities
" to be determined at a later stage of the inquiry.
" Its primary concern is with the operations and laws
" of the human mind; and its special purpose is to
" ascertain the nature, the origin, and the limits of
" the religious element in man; postponing, till after
" that question has been decided, the further inquiry
" into the absolute nature of God."—(*Bampton Lectures*, 2nd ed., pp. 34, 35.)

Though we are entering, you see, upon an inquiry
that is to be very accurate and scholastic, the two
principal words which are to engage our attention are
left undefined. We are not told what Religion is;
we are not told what Philosophy is. I have explained
already why I do not pretend to supply Mr. Mansel's
deficiencies with respect to the first word. I think it
is a peculiarly ambiguous one, and one that is likely
to continue ambiguous, because we connect it habitu-
ally with the study and treatment of the Bible, though
the Bible itself gives us no help in ascertaining the
force of the word, apparently sets no great store by it
or any similar one. So as far as I am able to make

out, it is best used to denote certain processes or habits or conditions of our own minds, so that, " the subject of religion," as opposed to the " object" of it, will be the subject of a subject, our thoughts about our thoughts—about what ?

Philosophy is a word which is much more easy to define. Sir William Hamilton has given it its natural, legitimate force, when he has called it a Search after Wisdom ; he has shown what is its relation to man, when he has adopted Plato's phrase, and described man as a Hunter after Truth. Supposing, as I have said already, there was a Truth to meet this search, a living Object to present itself to a creature who was made to pursue that object, we might have something to speak of which is not philosophy, whatever other name you give it. But with such an Object Mr. Mansel will have nothing to do. To begin from that, is to involve yourself in Mystical Theology ; to suppose we have any faculties for seeking that or testing it when it is presented to us, is to involve yourself in Rational Theology. The only escape from both is a philosophy of religion, *i.e.* if we add the definition we have now got to the previous one, a search after the way in which we should think about our thoughts— about what ? See whether the following passages do not bear out my statement.

" On the other hand, the second method of philo-
" sophical inquiry does not profess to furnish a direct
" criticism of Revelation, but only of the instruments

" by which Revelation is to be criticized. It looks to
" the human, not to the divine, and aspires to teach
" us no more than the limits of our own powers of
" thought, and the consequent distinction between
" what we may and what we may not seek to compre-
" hend. . . .

" Religious criticism is itself an act of thought;
" and its immediate instruments must, under any cir-
" cumstances, be thoughts also. We are thus com-
" pelled in the first instance to inquire into the origin
" and value of those thoughts themselves."—(*Bampton Lectures*, 2nd ed., pp. 36, 38.)

I wish to make one remark before I proceed. Mr.
Mansel has been celebrated by one of his reviewers as
a writer who appeals to the common sense of Englishmen against the wild and fantastic notions of the
Mediæval period, or of modern Germany and France.
Here, if anywhere, we are to look for the justification of that claim. The religious philosophy which is
announced in this programme, is expressly designed
to deliver us from the absurdities and ravings of Mystics and Rationalists. This is the sword which is to
lay low the Eckarts and Taulers of the fourteenth
century, the Hegels and Schellings of the nineteenth.
Now, I ask you to make this experiment with any
English gentleman you know. Set before him Mr.
Mansel's statement of his purpose, not in my words
but in his. You and I ought to make our message
intelligible to the uneducated as well as the educated :

it is meant for both. But you would not be dealing fairly with Mr. Mansel if you made that demand
upon him. He is a learned man, addressing a University audience. Choose then the most educated man
you can find, in the English sense of the word ' educated.' I mean, let him have had the full advantage
of our public school and university training, and have
profited by it. Let him then have had the discipline
of public life, all that discipline which goes to cultivate what we call our practical faculty, our common
sense. Let him be a man who has sounded the
meaning of words, but who loves things better than
words, and tests words by their relation to things.
Let him have, if you please (I should like that additional qualification), an excessive prejudice against
German philosophy. Try him with Mr. Mansel's account of *his* religious philosophy, and tell me if he
does not make some such observations as these upon
it. ' Why, my good Sir, you know that this is just
' what I abominate in those Teutonic doctors and di-
' vines. They seem to me to be always thinking about
' their own thoughts. I cannot open one of their
' books without finding something about the *Begriff*
' of this, or the *Begriff* of that ; most of all they tor-
' ment me with their *Begriff* of Religion. What do
' we want of any *Begriff* ? We who are tossed about
' in the world want a God. Tell us of Him if you
' can. If you cannot, hold your peace. The other thing
' or nothing we do not need at all.'

(2.) Mr. Mansel's purpose in submitting our thoughts about our thoughts about religion to a searching criticism, is that he may save Revelation from it. That is a delicate plant which the winds of heaven must not be permitted to visit too roughly. But the *word* Revelation surely is not exempted from criticism; we are not obliged to leave it in the vagueness which enwraps the word Religion. It must be the revelation of something to something. Is it the revelation of a religion? If it were, we should be able to know something of what that is; it would not be covered with the thick veil which Mr. Mansel allows to rest over it. Is it a revelation of God? So the Bible seems to say. That is its simple, obvious language. But if a revelation of Him, a revelation also to something. To what? Not to Angels, unless the Bible speaks falsely, but to Men. Not to the bodily eye of men, unless the Bible speaks falsely, for it says that the eye of the body has not seen God and cannot see Him. Then to some eye which is not in the body? So our Lord seems to say, for He speaks of a light that is in us which may become darkness. Here comes in Mr. Mansel's critical religious philosophy. He undertakes to show that there is no such eye in man which can receive a revelation of God. Thus he proceeds with his demonstration :—

" Such a conviction may be possible in two
" different ways. It may be the result of a direct

" intuition of the Divine Nature; or it may be
" gained by inference from certain attributes of
" human nature, which, though on a smaller scale,
" are known to be sufficiently representative of the
" corresponding properties of the Deity. We may
" suppose the existence in man of a special faculty
" of knowledge, of which God is the immediate ob-
" ject—a kind of religious sense or reason, by which
" the Divine attributes are apprehended in their own
" nature : or we may maintain that the attributes of
" God differ from those of man in degree only, not
" in kind; and hence that certain mental and moral
" qualities, of which we are immediately conscious
" in ourselves, furnish at the same time a true and
" adequate image of the infinite perfections of God.
" The first of these suppositions professes to convey
" a knowledge of God by direct apprehension, in a
" manner similar to the evidence of the senses : the
" second professes to convey the same knowledge by
" a logical process, similar to the demonstrations of
" science. The former is the method of Mysticism,
" and of that Rationalism which agrees with Mysti-
" cism, in referring the knowledge of divine things to
" an extraordinary and abnormal process of intuition
" or thought. The latter is the method of the vulgar
" Rationalism, which regards the reason of man, in
" its ordinary and normal operation, as the supreme
" criterion of religious truth.

" On the former supposition, a system of religious

" philosophy or criticism may be constructed by start-
" ing from the divine and reasoning down to the
" human : on the latter, by starting from the human
" and reasoning up to the divine. The first com-
" mences with a supposed immediate knowledge of
" God as He is in His absolute nature, and proceeds
" to exhibit the process by which that nature, acting
" according to its own laws, will manifest itself in
" operation, and become known to man. The second
" commences with an immediate knowledge of the
" mental and moral attributes of man, and proceeds
" to exhibit the manner in which those attributes will
" manifest themselves, when exalted to the degree
" in which they form part of the nature of God. If,
" for example, the two systems severally undertake
" to give a representation of the infinite power and
" wisdom of God, the former will profess to explain
" how the nature of the infinite manifests itself in the
" forms of power and wisdom ; while the latter will
" attempt to show how power and wisdom must mani-
" fest themselves when existing in an infinite degree.
" In their criticisms of Revelation, in like manner,
" the former will rather take as its standard that
" absolute and essential nature of God, which must
" remain unchanged in every manifestation ; the lat-
" ter will judge by reference to those intellectual and
" moral qualities, which must exist in all their essen-
" tial features in the divine nature 'as well as in the
" human."—(*Bampton Lectures*, 2nd ed., pp. 38–41.)

These, you perceive, are the two possible ways of arriving at any knowledge of God. Mr. Mansel has told us already that neither the Mystic nor the Rationalist necessarily rejects a Revelation. The principle of one or the other is just as absurd, according to him, with a Revelation as without it. All the attempts therefore which are made in this Lecture to enlist the sympathies of believers in the Bible on the side of his religious philosophy, by dwelling on the different objections to the Bible and the denials of the Bible which have proceeded form those who speak of a reason in man that can judge of a revelation, are rhetorical artifices, deserving of all commendation for their cleverness, but utterly worthless so far as the argument is concerned. What is said here against Mystics and Rationalists applies as directly, as sharply, to every person who believes as you and I believe, that we are bound in our sermons to set forth Christ as the Wisdom of God and the Power of God, and to take the words addressed to the Apostle Philip literally : *" Have I been so long a time with you, and yet hast thou not known me, Philip ? He that hath seen Me, hath seen the Father. How sayest thou then, Show us the Father ?"*

Do I then confess myself a Mystic or a Rationalist because I do not put in any plea for exemption from the charges of folly or of heresy which Mr. Mansel would fix upon them ? I have answered that question already as far as Rationalism is concerned.

I have confessed that I have in myself an evil Rationalism, and that there is also a Rationalism which
I desire to cultivate, which I believe it is killing
the spirit in us not to have. I make the same confession precisely about Mysticism. I find a number
of men, in all ages of the Christian Church, who have
been called Mystics; I find them amongst Germans,
Frenchmen, Englishmen, Italians,—amongst princes,
priests, scholars, shoemakers, women,—amongst Fran-
ciscans, Dominicans, Jansenists, Lutherans, Calvinists, English High Churchmen, Quakers; I find
among them those who have led the life of recluses,
those who have stood by dying beds in hospitals,
those who have preached to crowds and drawn crowds
after them, those who have produced a moral reformation in the most hardened and ignorant. I find
among them those who have been charged, perhaps
rightly charged, with affecting obscurity, and those
who have written the broadest, homeliest, most thoroughly idiomatic German or English. These men
have differed in all their opinions, feelings, habits
of mind. Even those who have stood to one another in the relation of pupil and teacher, like Eckart
and Tauler, have been markedly unlike each other.
Under the same name stand Sterry the chaplain of
Cromwell, and Law the Nonjuror. There must be
something which associates men so dissimilar together. In Mr. Mansel's eyes it is something altogether evil, something worthy of his profoundest con-

tempt. I cannot say so, seeing that I find every one
of them to be an immeasurably better and wiser man
than I am,—seeing there is not one of them, whose
writings I have read or into whose life I have had
any glimpse, that has not instructed me and done
me good; scarcely one from whom I have not learnt
increased reverence for the Scriptures and more distrust of my own judgment. Nevertheless I do think
I have seen a tendency in them which offers an excuse for the bad name they have earned; I should
not have understood it if I had not discovered it in
myself. Mr. Mansel has represented it harshly, but
perhaps not wrongly, when he speaks of the Mystics
referring "the knowledge of divine things to an ex-
"traordinary and abnormal process of intuition or
"thought." The description does not apply to any
one of those I have named, in his highest and best
moods. Some of them fought vehemently and almost to the death against it. Those who were followed in the fourteenth century by multitudes of
listening peasants, could scarcely have deemed that
they had some special "abnormal" insight. Still that
is unquestionably the mystical temptation. Out of
it have come a multitude of conceits respecting the
meaning of Scripture, a number of fantastical speculations respecting Nature, a number of harsh judgments respecting men of a different character from
their own, a number of sensual apparitions which
often contradict the principles they are most eager
to assert.

There is that in this habit which may ripen into a settled spiritual pride. Of that pride these men, so far as I can make out, gave few indications. But whence could the motive to it have arisen in minds like theirs? They had been dwelling, most of them, in a scholastical atmosphere, talking and thinking much about religion and religious motives, contemplating the world around them with some pity, speculating much on opinions right and wrong. At one crisis of their lives they were aroused to feel that they wanted something else than a religion, or a philosophy of religion. One whom they could not see, or who they thought was afar off, seemed to come very nigh to them, to question them about themselves, to bring not their acts and words merely, but *them*, the doers of the acts, the speakers of the words, into His clear and piercing light. The process was terrible. Out of it they emerged different men. The visible things with which they had conversed, looked shadowy and indistinct; that which was unseen had a fixedness, a certainty, which they could not express in words, which none who were about them appeared to recognize. 'We are out of the region of notions 'and appearances. We are in contact with Him who 'is.' For a time they were sure this was the sane, healthful condition of a man. 'In himself nothing, 'living by trust on One always near him, growing 'more and more into acquaintance with Him,—is 'not this what every one of us is meant to be? Is

'not being out of this condition the anomaly?' So
they felt, so in their practical discourses they spoke.
But yet, when they looked round upon the people
with whom they associated, the religious, the respectable, was not there an excuse for saying, 'These con-
' victions of ours are special, abnormal? They do not
' belong to our race; they belong to us, a certain fa-
' voured and select portion of the race. Are we not
' *new men, spiritual men, who can judge of all things,*
' *but can ourselves be judged of no man ?* Does not
' that text of St. Paul warrant us in vindicating to
' ourselves an intuition altogether unlike that which
' belongs to the herd of mere natural or *soullish*
' creatures.'*

Excuses for self-exaltation surely ! I have men-
tioned some of the antidotes to it ; the sympathy of
crowds, tendance on the sick. Insufficient, I should
think, without actual bodily sufferings, and the discovery of internal evils, which all the knowledge of
Good had not destroyed, perhaps had only brought
into stronger illumination.   But in the course of
history has there not also been a counteraction to
these dangers ? Mr. Mansel has pointed out one,
which in our day, I suspect, is working more effectually than we know, and which those who trace God's
hand in His Church and Universe will not fancy
has existed without His providence and appointment.
There are those *vulgar Rationalists,* so Mr. Mansel

* Ψυχικὸς δὲ ἄνθρωπος οὐ δέχεται τὰ τοῦ Πνεύματος τοῦ Θεοῦ.

calls them, " who regard the Reason of man in its " ordinary and normal operation as the criterion of " religious Truth."

It is not necessary that I should go over again the ground I travelled in my last letter. I tried then to show you that there is a *disorderly* operation of the Reason in us to which we are all prone, that which is busy in creating the object which it beholds, or else argues about it instead of contemplating it; —that there is a true and normal operation of the Reason, which we all recognize in reference to common things, an operation by means of which we discern that which is from that which merely seems or appears. Not to use this Reason in the daily pursuits of life, is to sink into the condition of an animal. One sees it in the liveliest exercise among those who are utterly incapable of drawing conclusions, who are not logicians, who can neither form dogmas nor understand them when they are formed. Among pure, true-hearted women, among honest mechanics, among those upon whose powers of sense and even of reflection death has laid his hand, this power of discerning the truth from the lie, the thing that is from that that is not, dwells often with enviable clearness. We turn to them as to oracles; does not the Statesman, with his hard experience, the Divine, with his well-learnt maxims and systems, find that they are seers while he is well-nigh blind?

Is this Reason critical only of low things? May it

not also exercise a discernment in the highest? That
is the question which has been especially raised in
our time; that is the one to which Mr. Mansel gives
his emphatic "No." To me it seems that in making
that denial, he is either forgetting what is the 'normal' use of the Reason in lower things, and speaking
merely of its irregular use; or that if he is saying
there is nothing in man which can distinguish between "*the thief who cometh to steal and destroy,
and the Shepherd who cometh that we might have life,
and have it more abundantly*"—he is simply setting
at nought the words of Christ, and overthrowing the
whole Bible. But I wish to show you how the assertion of this power by the Rationalist—whether he
exercises it legitimately or illegitimately—affects the
Mystic who is not only under Mr. Mansel's ban for
his abnormal intuitions, but is humbled in himself
by the recollection of having claimed them. Now he
begins to perceive that what he has to thank God for
with his whole heart, was not for giving him something which He has refused to the race generally, but
for opening in him that eye which belongs to us as
men, and which, through our desire to magnify our
own individual souls and to separate them from other
men's, we put out. So the words of St. Paul on
which he had been used to rest his case, assume an
entirely different aspect, and come forth to chastise
his vanity, as well as to nourish his hope. Is not the
spiritual man, as we are told in that very Epistle, the

man who will not divide himself from others, division being the sign of carnality,—who will not make his own notions or opinions the standards for men, or the measures of God's acts,—who will receive the things that are freely given him of God—who *therefore* has a faculty of discrimination, which does not suffer him to be deluded by impostors, or to confound the Devil with the true God?

In what I have said about the faculty of Reason, which one finds most alive in the simplest, truest, humblest people, often most dead in the clever and the learned,—in the writers of leading articles, and in doctors of divinity,—I may have seemed to take for granted a distinction of which Mr. Mansel has spoken in one of his notes thus :—

" If there is but one faculty of thought, that which
" Kant calls the Understanding, occupied with the
" finite only, there is an obvious end to be answered
" in making us aware of its limits, and warning us
" that the boundaries of thought are not those of
" existence. But if, with Kant, we distinguish the
" Understanding from the Reason, and attribute
" to the latter the delusions necessarily arising from
" the idea of the unconditioned, we must believe in
" the existence of a special FACULTY OF LIES created
" for the express purpose of deceiving those who trust
" to it."—(Note 24 to p. 127; p. 364.)

This sentence, you perceive, settles the whole question. That happy, courteous phrase, ' a faculty of

lies,' proceeding from an eminent philosopher, a great
enemy of Dogmatism, one who sets out from the
maxim, 'Know thyself,' ought to silence every objection and every argument. You will appreciate the
full force of it, even though you may not be a reader
of Kant, if you will turn back to that account of
him and his special objects which I have extracted
from Sir William Hamilton's discussion on the Unconditioned. You will see there that the tendency of
Kant's mind was destructive,—that he applied the severest logic to the overthrow of the metaphysical or
ontological notions of his predecessors,—that he did
effectually sweep away, so Sir W. Hamilton thinks,
all mere notions and conceptions about the Infinite. It was this man who, *because* he was a logician, could not bring himself to deny that there
is something in us which takes hold of fact, something which will not be circumscribed by notions
and conceptions, which confesses that which is. He
felt that if there is no such faculty in man as
this, there is not and cannot be any morality for
man, there is not and cannot be any truth for man.
It is because a stern necessity drove this philosopher to overleap the bounds of his own philosophy for the sake of reality, that Mr. Mansel says he
believed in a faculty of lies created for the especial
purpose of deceiving those who possess it. It is because he affirmed a principle so very like the principle of a conscience, for which Butler contends, that

every blow to the one is practically and effectually a
blow to the other, that a disciple of Butler, one who
desires to cultivate the study and spirit of Butler
in Oxford, uses language respecting Kant which is
scarcely paralleled in philosophical, even in theological controversy.

You and I, however, are not concerned with the
vindication of Kant. We *are* concerned in claiming
that great concession which Kant made to common
human beings, a concession of which the religious
philosophy of Mr. Mansel seeks to deprive us.

If there is nothing in the people to whom we
deliver our message but a faculty which forms notions, judges of opinions, criticizes documents, we
know that we have not a Gospel to the poor—it is
monstrous to pretend that we have. That faculty of
forming notions, judging opinions, criticizing documents, is a peculiar one; it requires a special cultivation; the degrees in which those possess it in
whom it has been cultivated, are more various than
it is possible to express. The difference between
Bentley and the most ignorant undergraduate who
answers a question at an Oxford or Cambridge examination, is an inadequate measure of the variety in
one direction. Those in whom the faculty exists in
the highest degree, are not always the persons to
whom one would appeal with confidence on a moral
question. And when one compares their different
exercises upon their own ground, *e.g.* the Discussion

on the Epistles of Phalaris with the Commentary
on Paradise Lost, one feels how a homely perception
of facts is needful even to a critic, how worthless
the merely critical power becomes without it. Even
therefore if one wanted to bring out this power in
its strength, one would have need to educate another
first, one which is not special, but human. In a
university, if that human faculty is denied or not appealed to, all special studies will be worthless,—yes,
mischievous and accursed. But for the Minister of
the Gospel, *that* is what he has to speak to: I had
nearly said *that* only. It is because the Bible addresses that human faculty and not some special
faculty, that it can bear to be translated into every
tongue of the earth, that it can speak to all tribes
and nations. For *us* to deny the existence of such a
faculty, is simply to deny our own work. Any one
who tells us that it does not exist, is bound also to
tell us that if we are honest men we must relinquish
that work.

'What,' you say, 'does it depend upon our accept-
'ance of a certain philosophy whether we shall do
'our work as Evangelists?' Not the least. You need
know nothing about philosophy. If you do not, you
will take for granted the existence of this faculty to
which you can speak. It is the ordinary postulate
of an Englishman's life that there is such a one.
That is what he means when he says, 'I do not
'care for your fine notions; I have something in me

'which tells me when a man is speaking truth or
'falsehood.' Of course, he may be very much deceived about his own preference for truth over falsehood in any particular case; he may be bribed to like
a lie better than the truth. But are you justified in
telling him that he has not that faculty? Are you
not destroying his soul if you do? Are you not sa-
ving his soul alive if you can persuade him to use
that faculty, if you can teach him how he may use
it,—who is helping him to use it,—who would deliver him from the falsehoods which are corrupting
and enchaining him? This, I say, is the ordinary
judgment of a practical man. And the part of Kant's
philosophy which Mr. Mansel rejects is the part
which owns that the philosopher *cannot* interfere with
this practical human faith,—that it is worth more
than all the notions of the understanding, because it
takes hold of that which is substantial,—worth more
than all the conclusions of the understanding, because it converses with premisses.

'Yes,' Mr. Mansel will say, 'but I acknowledge
'a faith which goes beyond these notions; I admit
'that the realm of existence is not bounded by the
'realm of thought. What I object to is your speak-
'ing of the Reason, as if that had anything to do
'with this faith, as if that were distinct from the
'Understanding.' Now observe; about nomenclature I care nothing, or next to nothing. Throw over
Kant's nomenclature if you dislike it. There is no

sacredness in the names of Understanding or of
Reason; one cannot be quite certain whether they
are respectively the best equivalents for the words
which Kant has used—supposing that were a point of
any importance. But we must not be cheated by
compliments to our faith, nor yet by the distinction
—all-important as it is when rightly apprehended—
between thought and existence. Does the faith you
speak of take hold of existence, or, as I should say,
—for I do not like school-terms when I can get
plain words,—of that which is? If not, it is not what
we mean by faith; it is not the faith which is the
substance of things hoped for, the evidence of things
not seen. It is an act of the mind; therefore I have
to ask, Of what mind? It is the belief in something; then I have to ask, What is that something?
The mind, according to Mr. Mansel, only gives out
thoughts, and thoughts are in no connection with existence or that which is. Whence then comes this
faith? Whither does it go? How should it be described? I know how it would be described by some
persons; they would call it a faculty or the exercise
of a faculty of lies. I do not like such language.
Mr. Mansel who does, must vindicate the Faith which
he speaks of from the imputation which he has bestowed upon Kant's Reason.

What concerns you and me is that faith should be
the act of the man himself, of that which is most
truly, radically human in him, call it by what name

NOT THE FAITH OF APOSTLES.

you please, and that it should be in direct contact
with that which is most living and most substantial.
Less than this we will not accept from any philosopher, religious or irreligious.   Any one who tells us
of another faith than this, must begin with erasing
the 11th chapter of the Epistle to the Hebrews out
of the Bible, must go on to destroy the whole Gospel
which the Bible contains.   Remember that that is
the issue.   We are not now talking about the Finite
or the Infinite, the Relative or the Absolute.   To
those words, and to Mr. Mansel's treatment of them,
I hope to come in due time; I have not the least
wish to avoid the fullest examination of what he says
about them.   But that is not our business now.   I
will repeat it even to weariness: the question is concerning that which *is* and that which is not; whethei
there is any faculty in man that can be brought to
perceive that which is, and to reject that which is
not, *in any matter whatsoever*; whether that faculty
is extinguished when we are called to pay the highest
reverence and worship to a certain object or objects;
or whether it is this to which God himself appeals.
For I must again beseech you not to be deceived by
Mr. Mansel's rhetoric into the supposition that what
he is saying only concerns those who reject the Bible,
or fancy that they are wiser than the writers of it.
It concerns quite as much every one who accepts the
Bible as God's speech to man; it concerns the humblest believer in every cottage, on every hospital pallet.

He himself has told us that he is equally at war with those who start from the Divine and reason down to the Human, as with those who start from the Human and reason up to the Divine. He *must* be equally at war with both. On the other hand, those who accept a revelation of God to man, *i.e.* of the Divine meeting the Human, must be very careful indeed how they trifle with any of those efforts, even if they have been failures, of the Human to meet the Divine, lest haply they should be fighting not merely with the spirit of man, but with the Spirit of God. Mr. Mansel has said himself:—" The Philosophy which " reasons downwards from the Infinite is but an ex- " aggeration (?) of the true conviction that God's " thoughts are not our thoughts, nor His ways our " ways : the philosophy which reasons upwards from " the human, bears witness, even in its perversion, " to the unextinguishable consciousness that man, " however fallen, was created in the image of God." (p. 43.)

Just so. It is the very point for which I am contending, and therefore it must be your business and mine to recognize the truth of both these opposing principles, quite indifferent who calls us Mystics and who calls us Rationalists, because it is our business to show that God's thoughts are not our thoughts, nor His ways our ways,—because it is our business to tell men that they are created in the image of God, and that Christ, the express Image of God, has come to raise them out of their fall, and to renew them after that image. Our preaching is continually encountered by the argument, 'We are fallen crea-'tures; what can we know of God? how can we 'ever rise to the perception of the Eternal Truth and 'Goodness?' Must we not answer that argument by appealing to every witness of the heart, the Conscience, the Reason,—if you will, to every contradiction of Philosophy,—that the spirit of man within us demands the knowledge of God, demands the perception of Eternal Truth and Goodness? If we can say also, 'What the spirit of man seeks, the Spirit of 'God will give,' may we not feel that we have indeed preached good news to our fellows?

Faithfully yours,

F. D. M.

LETTER VI.

———◆———

My dear Sir,

You are very much nearer to your undergraduate years than I am to mine. But they do rise
up at times vividly before me. Certainly nothing has
brought them back so vividly as reading the latter
part of Mr. Mansel's second Lecture. I listened to
many sermons in St. Mary's, when I was at Oxford,
which chilled my heart. I think, if I had heard that
one, it would have turned my brain. I do not think
it would have made me a sceptic, for I fancy I had
met with most of the statements about the Absolute,
the Infinite, and the Cause, in the pages of different
sophists, or that they had been presented to my own
mind. That which would have utterly bewildered me
would have been to hear them reproduced in a Christian pulpit as a defence of Christianity. I hope I
should have profited by the preacher's last words. I
hope I should have said, ' *Lord, to whom shall I go*

' when Thy servants consider it their business to up-
' hold Thy cause by proving to us that there is nothing
' around, beneath, above, but confusion and darkness?'
I hope I should have said, ' *Thou hast the words of*
' *Eternal Life*, though we are told that the Eternal
' lies at a hopeless distance from us, that we can have
' no fellowship with it. But I *might* have said, ' If
' that is true, what Lord is there to whom we can go?
' Where is He?   What have I to do with Him?'

   It is because I feel painfully convinced that many
who heard and who read Mr. Mansel's sermon *will*
say this;—that the argument which he looks upon
as so conclusive that it must shatter every form of
unbelief, is likely to shatter the feeble faith which it
finds, and to bewilder the more earnest faith;—it is
because everything in the circumstances and temptations of those who sat in the galleries when this
Lecture was delivered, is likely to make it more mischievous to them than it would be to those of any
other class or age,—it is therefore that I undertake
the task—which, when I am right-minded, is very
disagreeable, which I tremble at most when it becomes at all pleasant—of pointing out why I look
upon the whole course of his argument on this subject as worthless for its professed object of exposing
either Rationalists or Pantheists, and as utterly mischievous if it is supposed to be a mode of removing
objections to the Bible.   I will begin with quoting
the passage which introduces the subject :—

"There are three terms, familiar as household
"words in the vocabulary of Philosophy, which must
"be taken into account in every system of Meta-
"physical Theology. To conceive the Deity as He
"is, we must conceive Him as First Cause, as Ab-
"solute, and as Infinite. By the *First Cause*, is
"meant that which produces all things, and is itself
"produced of none. By the *Absolute*, is meant that
"which exists in and by itself, having no necessary
"relation to any other Being. By the *Infinite* is
"meant that which is free from all possible limita-
"tion; that than which a greater is inconceivable;
"and which consequently can receive no additional
"attribute or mode of existence, which it had not
"from all eternity."—(*Bampton Lectures*, 2nd ed.,
pp. 44, 45.)

Will you read over to yourself the first line of this
passage? "There are three *terms*, familiar as household words in the vocabulary of Philosophy." These
are key-words to the after discourse. It is with the
terms, First Cause, Absolute, and Infinite, that Mr.
Mansel deals here and throughout his volume. Terms
are all in all to him. To get beyond terms is with
him impossible. "Words, words, words" do not
drive him mad as they did poor Hamlet; they entirely satisfy him. He does not deny that there is
something lying beyond them, something which they
express. There is a region of mist and darkness,
what he considers the region of faith, which cannot

be put into formulas of logic, and therefore about which nothing can be known, which we have no criterion for judging of. But within this circle lies his world, and any one who tries to find a ground for his feet outside of that world, is for him a fool if he can reduce him under the notion of a Dogmatist, a dangerous disturber of men's serenity if he can bring him under the notion of a Rationalist. Once, with exceeding *naïveté*, he intimates that there must be reality, but that we are quite unable to conceive what it is, it cannot be brought under its proper notion. His book should be studied as the great apotheosis of Logic. Terrible as the name may sound to him, he actually becomes transcendental in his reverence for the formulas that are to exclude all transcendentalism.

You may remember that I noticed this tendency as characteristic of Sir William Hamilton. I spoke of him as emphatically a *notional* Philosopher. I believe that grand forehead of his showed that he was capable of being something immeasurably higher than this. If he had not been possessed by a love of fact, a reverence for fact, he could not have admired the phrase of Plato as he did; he could not have risen so far above his predecessors in the schools of Consciousness, whom he, somewhat haughtily, patronizes. He brought Scotch Philosophy to its climax. So now we know all about it, what it can and cannot do. He enables us to understand that fierce

reaction against it which one discovers in his countrymen. Evidently they must have been utterly
crushed under 'notions' and 'consciousnesses;' crushed
till all breath and life seemed to be impossible for
them. It has been nothing less than a question for
them whether the woods and fields in which Burns
grew up, and of which he sang, should be withered
by a school Sirocco; whether the life of those who
fought and bled on the soil should be turned into
mere moralities about life and fighting and bleed-
ing; whether the manhood of the present generation
should perish along with the manhood of their forefathers. Mr. Carlyle has been welcomed by Scotch-
men and Englishmen as the great protester against
notions, the witness for Fact ·and History. He has
avowed his indifference to anything else. He long
ago abjured metaphysics, German or Scotch. In his
latest work he has abjured poets as not sufficiently
savouring of the realty; he has complained of Shakespeare and Goethe for devoting their amazing powers
to dramas or novels, when they might have explained
what has been actually done in the world.*

A reaction against logical formulas, proceeding

* "It is frightful to see the *Gelehrte Dummkopf* (what we here
may translate 'Dryasdust') doing the function of History, and the
Shakespeare and the Goethe neglecting it."—*History of Frederick
the Great,* vol. i. p. 23.

Ante, pp. 21, 22 (speaking of a design of Schiller to write an
Epic poem on Frederick) :—" Happily Schiller did not do it. . . .
It is not the untrue, imaginary picture of a man and his life that

from an entirely different quarter, prompted by different feelings, and leading to quite different results, is more associated with English history than with Scotch, with Oxford than with Edinburgh. A young member of University College, who, while he was there, delighted, it is said, especially in the services of the chapel and in all the venerable traditions of the place, having been deprived of those opportunities of culture by the wisdom or unwisdom of the authorities of that time, b came the pantheistical poet of our land, the man who embodied in his verse and character the thoughts, dreams, aspirations, to which that name is most correctly affixed, those which were floating and are floating in the atmosphere of England as well as of France and Germany. In his ' Queen Mab,' his ' Alastor,' his ' Sensitive Plant,' his ' Skylark,' some only discover the denial of all which Christians believe; some have heard " the wailings of a child seeking for its Father." But one as much as the other must feel that that spirit could be circumscribed by no terms of logic. Sea, sky, air, birds, trees, flowers,—to these he fled from notions and formulas; with these he was certain he had a sympathy and a fellowship. They gave him his sense of the Infinite, the Absolute, the Eternal, by which he meant that which could not be put into the terms

I want from my Schiller, but the actual, natural likeness, true as the face itself, nay, *truer* in a sense, which the Artist might help to give, and the Botcher (*Pfuscher*) never can."

and forms of logic, that which a spirit within him was yearning after. If you could tell him how those yearnings might be satisfied without losing a personal God and his own personal being, you might reach his ear; if not, you would leave him a pantheist as you found him, exercising a charm over the freshest and noblest among the youth of his land, a charm which is most commonly broken by their sinking into the service of Mammon, now and then by their claiming their heritage as redeemed sons of God.

There is a third reaction against this tyranny of notions which I believe is beginning to be felt with particular strength in Oxford. It is what I would call the scientific reaction. I have hinted already, in my second Letter, at the strife between Sir William Hamilton and the mathematicians,—at his strong and apparently well-grounded conviction that he must destroy them before he could establish his own position securely. But is there not a science of Morals as well as of Physics? Aristotle has certainly led Oxford men to seek after one, to feel that they cannot dispense with one, whether he has himself discovered it to them or not. I think we have all been forced to feel that he is not the practical philosopher he wished to be, that he has not at all events given us the help we want for our lives, if—as some pretend, with whom I do not the least agree—he has merely taught us to look for a mean between two extremes. Our age has had plentiful experience of this seeking for a middle in Politics and Morals as well as in Theology. Something may perhaps come out of it hereafter. What has come out of it already has been described with considerable life and accuracy by the poet Cowper.

> " Some fretful tempers wince at every touch,
>   You always do too little or too much.
>   You speak with life, in hopes to entertain :
>   Your elevated voice goes through the brain.
>   You fall at once into a lower key :
>   That's worse, the drone-pipe of an humble-bee.
>   The southern sash admits too strong a light ;
>   You rise and drop the curtain : now 'tis night.
>   He shakes with cold ; you stir the fire and strive
>   To make a blaze : that 's roasting him alive.
>   .   .   .   .
>   Your hope to please him vain on every plan,
>   Himself should work that wonder if he can.
>   Alas ! his efforts double his distress ;
>   He likes yours little, and his own still less.
>   Thus, always teazing others, always teazed,
>   His only pleasure is to be displeased."

A moderation of this kind is scarcely satisfactory for those who have actually to fight their way through the world,—to choose a path for themselves, not merely to find fault with the extreme paths of every one else.

Butler too, I have contended already, has awakened in us the search after a scientific Morality, *i.e.* a Morality which has some ground in reality and not in notions. And Butler has certainly not satisfied the desire which he has kindled if, as some would tell us, he has only taught us that probability is the ground of all human actions. We have specimens enough among our statesmen, as well, I am afraid, as among our divines, of persons who have taken in that maxim in its fullness,—who think that the art of steering their life's vessel consists in following all chance currents, or in merely resisting them,—who have no principles to determine when they should yield or when they should resist,—who have a set of opinions to which they swore to adhere when they entered upon the business of the world, and from which they were forced to drift away when they become *actually* conversant with the business of it. These are not examples to encourage us in the worship of probability, but beacons to warn us from it. I am sure that Butler would have been more shocked than we can be at the results to which the supposed following of his precept is leading us. I am sure he would have told us, 'All probabilities and ' appearances will drag you into perdition, if there are ' not some fixed and unchangeable lights by which you ' are directing your course.'

Where then are these fixed and unchangeable lights to be found? Where is that immutable Morality which all earnest men have sought after? When Kant had discovered that no notions could possibly contain it or represent it, " he built again," Mr. Mansel indignantly exclaims, " the things which he destroyed, so making himself a transgressor ;" or, as I have stated the case somewhat differently in my last letter, he confessed that there was a witness in man for truths which he could not comprehend in notions, and that this witness had the closest connection with his practical morality. *What* connection it has is a subject of earnest interest to Englishmen and Germans. Each has discussed it in their own way. Each has felt that a morality which is not tied by our limitations, is at the root of that which is. Mr. Mansel tramples them all down in this triumphant style :—

" The Infinite, as contemplated by this philosophy,
" cannot be regarded as consisting of a limited num-
" ber of attributes, each unlimited in its kind. It
" cannot be conceived, for example, after the ana-
" logy of a line, infinite in length, but not in breadth;
" or of a surface, infinite in two dimensions of space,
" but bounded in the third; or of an intelligent
" being, possessing some one or more modes of con-
" sciousness in an infinite degree, but devoid of
" others. Even if it be granted, which is not the
" case, that such a partial infinite may without con-
" tradiction be conceived, still it will have a relative
" infinity only, and be altogether incompatible with
" the idea of the Absolute. The line limited in
" breadth is thereby necessarily related to the space
" that limits it; the intelligence endowed with a li-
" mited number of attributes, coexists with others
" which are thereby related to it, as cognate or oppo-

" site modes of consciousness. The metaphysical re-
" presentation of the Deity, as absolute and infinite,
" must necessarily, as the profoundest metaphysicians
" have acknowledged, amount to nothing less than
" the sum of all reality. ' What kind of an absolute
" ' Being is that,' says Hegel, ' which does not con-
" ' tain in itself all that is actual, even evil included ?'
" We may repudiate the conclusion with indignation ;
" but the reasoning is unassailable. If the Abso-
" lute and Infinite is an object of human conception
" at all, this, and none other, is the conception re-
" quired. That which is conceived as absolute and in-
" finite must be conceived as containing within itself
" the sum, not only of all actual, but of all possible
" modes of being. For if any actual mode can be
" denied of it, it is related to that mode, and limited
" by it; and if any possible mode can be denied of
" it, it is capable of becoming more than it now is,
" and such a capability is a limitation. Indeed it is
" obvious that the entire distinction between the pos-
" sible and the actual can have no existence as re-
" gards the absolutely infinite ; for an unrealized pos-
" sibility is necessarily a relation and a limit."—
(*Bampton Lectures*, 2nd ed., pp. 45–47.)

Again :—

" Not only is the Absolute, as conceived, incapable
" of a necessary relation to anything else, but it is
" also incapable of containing, by the constitution of
" its own nature, an essential relation within itself ; as

" a whole, for instance, composed of parts, or as a
" substance consisting of attributes, or as a conscious
" subject in antithesis to an object. For if there
" is in the absolute any principle of unity, distinct
" from the mere accumulation of parts or attributes,
" this principle alone is the true absolute. If, on
" the other hand, there is no such principle, then
" there is no absolute at all, but only a plurality
" of relatives. The almost unanimous voice of phi-
" losophy, in pronouncing that the absolute is both
" one and simple, must be accepted as the voice of
" reason also, so far as reason has any voice in the
" matter. But this absolute unity, as indifferent and
" containing no attributes, can neither be distin-
" guished from the multiplicity of finite beings by
" any characteristic feature, nor be identified with
" them in their multiplicity. Thus we are landed
" in an inextricable dilemma. The Absolute cannot
" be conceived as conscious, neither can it be con-
" ceived as unconscious: it cannot be conceived as
" complex, neither can it be conceived as simple: it
" cannot be conceived by difference, neither can it
" be conceived by the absence of difference: it can-
" not be identified with the universe, neither can it
" distinguished from it. The One and the Many,
" regarded as the beginning of existence, are thus
" alike incomprehensible."—(*Bampton Lectures*, 2nd
ed., pp. 49, 50.)

Or this :—

" Again, how can the Relative be conceived as
" coming into being ? If it is a distinct reality from
" the absolute, it must be conceived as passing from
" non-existence into existence. But to conceive an
" object as non-existent, is again a self-contradic-
" tion ; for that which is conceived exists, as an object
" of thought, in and by that conception. We may
" abstain from thinking of an object at all ; but, if
" we think of it, we cannot but think of it as exist-
" ing. It is possible at one time not to think of an
" object at all, and at another to think of it as already
" in being ; but to think of it in the act of becoming,
" in the progress from not being into being, is to
" think that which, in the very thought, annihilates
" itself. Here again the Pantheistic hypothesis seems
" forced upon us. We can think of creation only as
" a change in the condition of that which already ex-
" ists ; and thus the creature is conceivable only as a
" phenomenal mode of the being of the Creator."—
(*Bampton Lectures*, 2nd ed., pp. 53, 54.)

What greater proof do we need than these passages
furnish, that so long as we are busy with the terms
of logic, so long we shall never arrive at the truth of
things ? The acknowledgment of these contradictions
is common to Mr. Mansel with all the three classes
of which I have spoken. Those who seek for the
meaning of common facts, will joyfully refer to his
Lecture as a proof that you cannot leave that ground

and enter the logical ground without being involved
in a series of hopeless quibbles which no human
being ought to trouble himself with, unless he means
to abandon the business of existence, and to give
himself up to feats of jugglery. The Pantheist, in
one mood of his mind, will be strengthened by Mr.
Mansel's victorious analysis in his persuasion,

> " That nothing is, but all things seem,
> And we the shadows of the dream;"

in another, will exclaim triumphantly, ' Yes! now I
' know that I must fly to Nature and lose myself in
' the great Universe, and seek a God there, since you
' show me so clearly that He is not to be found in
' any of your notions and dogmas.' And what will
he who is at the most opposite point to Pantheism,
who longs to escape from vagueness, and to find some
safe foundation for his own thoughts and acts—for
his own self—say to these elaborate logical confu-
tations of his right to engage in any such pursuit?
What can he say but this?—' After working dili-
' gently through Aldrich, reading Whately, studying
' Mill, I did not require to be told that the terms
' Finite and Infinite, Absolute and Relative, exclude
' each other,—that you cannot comprehend the Many
' under the One, or the One under the Many,—
' that the intellect unawares assumes a beginning
' for that which it calls First Cause. I thought
' these were nuts for children to crack, conundrums
' for breakfast-parties; if introduced into the solemn

' lecture-room, to be noticed there only for the pur-
' pose of explaining how dishonest men had turned
' them to vile services—how verbal contradictions had
' been used by Athenian rhetoricians as a plea for
' atrocious deeds—or for the purpose of illustrating
' the method by which Socrates cut these webs and
' brought his disciples back through converse with
' homely life and actual things into a perception of
' their deepest necessities, into a conviction that for
' them they must seek a real, not a nominal satisfac-
' tion.   I never dreamed that these riddles were to be
' Church entertainments, that the Christian teacher
' inherited the functions of Protagoras and Prodicus.
' But if that is settled,—if Christianity does wrap her-
' self in these conceits, and pronounce herself incapa-
' ble of meeting those demands which remain just as
' deep, just as practical, after these demonstrations as
' before,—what have we to do ?   The term Finite, in
' the schools, does, we know, exclude the term Infinite.
' The actual finite in ourselves, the partial good we
' perceive in ourselves and in those about us, compels
' us to ask if there is not that which is good in itself,
' which is not partial.   The term Relative excludes
' the term Absolute.   But since my brother is a being
' in himself, and not only a brother, since every father
' is a being in himself, and not only a father,—the
' actual relation, the living relation, drives us to seek
' for an Absolute, which lies beyond and behind the
' Relation.   Of course we entangle ourselves in con-

' tradictions every time we try to think of a Cause.
' It is that very entanglement which drives us to ask
' for some ground beneath our thoughts, not included
' in them, but the only explanation of them. I know
' that the One and the Many negative each other.
' But I know that amidst a world of pluralities, I
' must seek Unity. What then does your arguing re-
' prove ? What effect has it but to force us beyond
' the confines of your Logic, and therefore, as it
' seems from your statement, beyond the confines of
' what you call your Revelation?'

Alas! alas! for those critics of human doubts and
questionings who, like the critic in Sterne, never look
at the living countenance of him on whom they are
commenting, but only at their stop-watches ! They
never find out what the opponent means, what he
wants; they only find out what he does not mean
and does not want ! What they suppose are green
withs, fresh cut, that will be sure to bind Samson,
especially when he is asleep—are in truth very dry
withs, not green at all, which he has broken from off
his limbs a hundred times, and which he will arouse
himself in a moment to break again. But may you
not be doing a worse thing ? May you not have
found the secret of his strength, the lock that has
not yet been severed from the head? May you not
be robbing him of that ? May you not, with your
fine logic, have been scattering that belief in an Eternal Goodness and Truth which has been the treasure,

if as yet the unrealized treasure, of his life? May you not have been convincing him that what has come to him continually a thousand times as the dawn of a distant hope,—what has sometimes come very nigh to him as a word in his heart,—is a delusion after all? Oh, what have you done for his present life, for his future life, when you have done this?

There is an awful passage in Milton's letter to Mr. Hartlib, which I used to hope had scarcely any application to the Oxford of the present day. Read it,—I doubt not you know it already,—in connection with the passages I have quoted from the Bampton Lecturer, and judge.

" And for the usual method of teaching Arts, I
" deem it to be an old error of Universities not yet
" well recovered from the Scholastic grossness of bar-
" barous ages, that instead of beginning with Arts
" most easie, and those be such as are most obvious
" to the sence, they present their young unmatricu-
" culated Novices at first comming with the most
" intellective abstractions of Logick and Metaphy-
" sicks: So that they, having but newly left those
" grammatick flats and shallows where they stuck
" unreasonably to learn a few words with lamentable
" construction, and now on the sudden transported
" under another climate to be tost and turmoil'd
" with their unballasted wits in fadomless and un-
" quiet deeps of controversie, do for the most part

" grow into hatred and contempt of Learning, mockt
" and deluded all this while with ragged Notions and
" Babblements, while they expected worthy and de-
" lightful knowledge; till poverty or youthful years
" call them importunately their several wayes, and
" hasten them with the sway of friends either to an
" ambitious and mercenary, or ignorantly zealous Di-
" vinity; Some allur'd to the trade of Law, ground-
" ing their purposes not on the prudent and heavenly
" contemplation of justice and equity, which was
" never taught them, but on the promising and pleas-
" ing thoughts of litigious terms, fat contentions,
" and flowing fees; others betake them to State af-
" fairs, with souls so unprincipl'd in vertue, and true
" generous breeding, that flattery, and Court shifts
" and tyrannous Aphorisms appear to them the
" highest points of wisdom; instilling their barren
" hearts with a conscientious slavery, if, as I rather
" think, it be not fein'd.   Others, lastly, of a more
" delicious and airie spirit, retire themselves, know-
" ing no better, to the enjoyments of ease and luxury,
" living out their daies in feast and jollity; which
" indeed is the wisest and the safest course of all
" these, unless they were with more integrity under-
" taken.   And these are the errours, and these are
" the fruits of misspending our prime youth at the
" Schools and Universities as we do, either in learn-
" ing meer words or such things chiefly, as were
" better unlearnt."

These are fearful considerations—all of them. But
oh, I beseech you, dwell most upon that which concerns you most! Consider whether ' these intellective
abstractions' can ever be the ground for your Gospel,
ever the defence of your Bible? Is not your Gospel
a message concerning the Infinite, the Absolute, the
Eternal? Is not your Bible a book of Facts by which
men are led gradually on to know what the ground is
at their feet; to feel, through the actual finite, for the
Infinite,—through the actual temporal, for the Eternal?
If it is, as Mr. Mansel delights to tell us, *unsystema-
tical*, is not that because it is in the highest sense
methodical? Does it not begin with the facts of
family life, discovering a God of Abraham and Isaac
and Jacob at work in them? Does it not go on to
the facts of National life, discovering an I AM, an
unchangeable Lawgiver and King and Judge in the
midst of them? Does it not explain at last the facts
of Human or universal Life, the mystery of a Father,
a Son, and a Spirit, being discovered through these?
If you speak out of this Bible, will you not have
something else to tell the student of Facts than that
he cannot reconcile opposing Notions,—the seeker of
a divine Morality, than that he cannot bring his finite
notions into fellowship with the Infinite,—the yearner
after the sympathy of the Universe, than that he cannot prove his right to it in the schools? May you not
bid the first rejoice and give thanks that the Highest
of All has explained His government over His crea-

tures through facts, and not through notions? May we not say to the second, that the whole Law and Gospel is a discovery of that Absolute Goodness and Truth which lie at the foundation of all Goodness and Truth in us? May we not ask the Pantheist if the revelation of a God in Whom we are living and moving and having our being, the Life-giver to all creatures,—of One who is above all and through all and in us all,—will not satisfy the cravings of his spirit, without compelling him to forget the eternal boundaries of Right and Wrong?

Ever yours faithfully,

F. D. M.

LETTER VII.

—◆—

MR. MANSEL'S THIRD AND FOURTH LECTURES.—
PHILOSOPHY OF CONSCIOUSNESS.—THE SCOTCH.
— SCHLEIERMACHER. — MR. MANSEL'S OWN
TREATMENT OF THE SUBJECT.—PRAYER.

My DEAR SIR,

At the close of Mr. Mansel's second Lecture, he
states his reasons for using the philosophical terms
Infinite, Absolute, Cause, in their dry formality, instead of introducing the awful name of God, and
making that the theme of such tormenting subtleties. I appreciate the reverence which led him to
adopt that course. Yet I cannot help thinking that if
he reconsiders it, he may be led to detect a practical
sophism in his argument. I grant it is a fearful
thing to connect plays upon words with awful realities. But can he avoid the connection? Is he not answerable for bringing them together?   At all events,
the summary of his conclusions, with which he commences his third Lecture, must help to break down
the distinction which he tried to establish in the previous one.   Read, and consider it.

" My last Lecture was chiefly occupied with an
" examination of the ideas of the Absolute and the
" Infinite,—ideas which are indispensable to the foun-
" dation of a Metaphysical Theology, and of which a
" clear and distinct consciousness must be acquired,
" if such a Theology is to exist at all. I attempted
" to show the inadequacy of these ideas for such a pur-
" pose, by reason of the contradictions which to our
" apprehension they necessarily involve from every
" point of view. The result of that attempt may be
" briefly summed up as follows. We are compelled,
" by the constitution of our minds, to believe in the
" existence of an Absolute and Infinite Being,—a
" belief which appears forced upon us, as the comple-
" ment of our consciousness of the relative and the
" finite. But the instant we attempt to analyze the
" ideas thus suggested to us, in the hope of attaining
" to an intelligible conception of them, we are on
" every side involved in inextricable confusion and
" contradiction. It is no matter from what point of
" view we commence our examination;—whether,
" with the Theist, we admit the co-existence of the
" Infinite and the Finite, as distinct realities; or,
" with the Pantheist, deny the real existence of the
" Finite; or, with the Atheist, deny the real exist-
" ence of the Infinite;—on each of these suppositions
" alike, our reason appears divided against itself,
" compelled to admit the truth of one hypothesis, and
" yet unable to overcome the apparent impossibilities

" of each. *The philosophy of Rationalism, thus traced*
" *upwards to its highest principles, finds no legitimate*
" *resting-place, from which to commence its deduction*
" *of religious consequences."*—(*Bampton Lectures*, 2nd
ed., pp. 67, 68.)

I have put the last sentence in italics, that I may
make a remark which is not more important for this
passage than for the whole volume. You and I are
very little concerned in ascertaining whether " the
philosophy of Rationalism," or any other philosophy,
religious or irreligious, has " a legitimate resting-
place." But if it is true that " *our* reason is divided
against itself,"—if that division has reference to the
question whether Theism, *i. e.* the doctrine that there
is a God; Pantheism, *i. e.* the doctrine that everything
is God; Atheism, *i. e.* the doctrine that there is no
God, is the right doctrine,—this is a point of all importance to us,—this is a matter of life and death.
That division must in some way be brought to an
end; for what does it mean? That *we* have no legitimate resting-place; that there is no foundation for
our being.

One more remark before I proceed to the business
of the Lecture. Mr. Mansel hopes to deliver us from
Hegel and the modern Germans. Have you considered to what point he takes us back, that he may
effect that deliverance? Need I remind you that
there was a Hume before there was a Hegel; that the
utter incapacity of deciding between Theism, Pan-

theism, Atheism—of deciding any question whatever
concerning the Nature of God—was precisely the
point from which he " commenced his deduction of
religious consequences." I am far indeed from saying that Mr. Mansel's religious consequences are the
same as Hume's. I know that they are not. But will
you allow me to remark that he does not differ from
Hume *in this respect,* that he recommends general
acquiescence in the established religion of the day.
Hume would have recommended the same acquiescence. He hated the Puritans as cordially as he
could hate anything, because they were not acquies-
cent, but had wild dreams of knowing something of
the Infinite and Eternal. He reverenced the Stuart
policy as much as he could reverence anything, because he thought it the best check upon this extrava-
gance. He cared for no institution more than for
what he called a State Establishment of Religion, because he supposed that it restrained men from any
excess of thinking respecting subjects upon which
people will think, though their thinking can bring
them to no result. I frankly tell you that in my
judgment the latter opinion was not only the proper
sequel of the first, but that it has produced immensely
more mischief to English morality and English faith.
According to a tradition which Sir James Mackin-
tosh believed, Butler rather advised than discouraged
the publication of one of the books on which Hume's
infidel reputation rests; so confident was he that

the truth would bear discussion, and would rise more strongly out of it. But the doctrine that the Church, of which he was a Bishop, existed to keep alive the kind of indifference which he longed to disturb, would, I think, have been extremely shocking to him. Hume's Scepticism was followed by an almost immediate reaction; the notion of him as a Defender of Ecclesiastical and Tory faith has not forsaken the minds of many clergymen, even after a century· of revolutions.

This is no digression. It is the proper introduction to the subject of the coming Lecture, which is to develope the Philosophy of Consciousness as opposed to the Philosophy of Rationalism. Now I am bound to own—and I do it with great pleasure—that if we find ourselves shut in by Hume's contradictions, this may be the best process for escaping from them. Supposing it is needful—and perhaps it may be— to travel again over that ground which our fathers in the last century travelled, that is, I conceive, the proper route. In England and in Scotland, even in France and Germany, men appear to have been led along it, if they were not able ultimately to find their ' resting-place' in it. I spoke of a great impatience and weariness of this ' Consciousness,' and, above all, of a ' Philosophy of Consciousness,' which has manifested itself in our time, and which I thought had much justification. I am therefore the more anxious to show what service those who spoke of Consciousness in the last age were rendering to mankind, and how much we may lose if we despise the lessons which they left us.

Hume's favourite word was *Experience*. How can we know anything to be true except by experience? What experience can we have about those facts and doctrines of which the believers in a Revelation talk to us? Do not they in their very nature and statement transcend Experience? Theological Apologists nibbled at this net, and tried to make or find holes in it. Actual sufferers, Christian men and women who had never heard Hume's name, cut through it. Those who are far less familiar than you are with the phraseology of the religious men of the last generation, cannot be ignorant that Hume's watchword was also theirs. He said there could be no experience save that which reached us through the senses, or was derived from impressions on the senses. They spoke of spiritual experiences which were not only most precious and sacred to them, but the absence of which left them bare of all motives to right and kindly actions. Were they self-deceivers, or bent upon deceiving others?—fanatics, or hypocrites? These solutions were evidently the easiest; the majority of their opponents, wits and doctors, resorted to one or the other. There were those who could not,—who had known enough of such feelings themselves, to believe that some which they had not known might be genuine. These mental operations, to whatever source they might be attributed, were surely worthy of investigation. If they could be fairly investigated according to some legitimate method already recognized, might not those which seemed 'abnormal' be reduced into order? might not enthusiasm be checked? might not the limits of experience be stretched at least some way beyond the point which Hume had fixed for them?

Good and evil, I conceive, were mixed in this experiment as in most others. It was good to defend the worth and verity of experiences which concern the invisible as well as the visible world; it was good to show that all human experiences have some relation to each other, and, if possible, to trace out the relation. On the other hand, there was great danger that the investigator would 'murder to dissect;' that he would kill the experience, of whatever kind it was, in order to examine its nature; and would discourse about Experiences which, for him, were no Experiences at all. There was fear that the student would become a contemplator of actual mental operations till they ceased to be actual, or that he would merely conceive of them, and affix certain labels to them, as if they were lying outside of him, and were not in any sense his.

But these mischievous results might perhaps be avoided. The honey might be extracted from the hives without the destruction—without more, at most, than the temporary stupefaction—of the bees that had

gathered it. And there was something to encourage
hope—if there was also something to make the alarm
look all too reasonable—in the proceedings of those
who engaged in this branch of the philosophical business.

The phrase which they adopted,—in some degree
superseding that of the sceptical philosopher and of
the unphilosophical believers,—was, it seems to me, a
specially happy one. All words like those into which
the proposition *cum* enters,—Conviction, Conception,
Conversion, Consciousness,—are worthy of the closest
study and examination; hardly any are so sugges-
tive; hardly any contain so much light respecting
our processes of thought, respecting our human nature. No one of them has more of this value than
the word Consciousness; that it should have been accepted in an age by no means philological, and by
men who were rather the reverse of philologers,* is
one of those indications of a Providence that shapes
our ends which ought not to be overlooked. The
word 'Experience' might be limited to that which
passed in the subject of the experience; the word
'Consciousness'. at once hinted by its formation,—
showed by every one of its simplest applications,—
that there is a fellowship and participation between
the conscious man and something else. '*To be conscious*,' says Mr. Mansel, '*we must be conscious of*

* I allude to Reid and Dugald Stewart ; not, of course, to Sir William Hamilton, who was a philologer.

something.' Or, as he says afterwards, in rather
grander, but not better language:—*' There must be
a Subject, or person conscious, and an Object or thing
of which he is conscious.   There can be no Consciousness without the union of these two factors.'* Exactly;
and therefore my Consciousness must of necessity
carry me beyond myself. If it is the lowest consciousness of mere physical pain or physical pleasure, it
carries me to something which is the source of that
pain or that pleasure. If it is the consciousness of
regard or affection, it carries me to the person who
awakens that regard or affection. If it is a consciousness of dependence, it carries me to that thing or
that person on whom I am dependent; if it is a consciousness of wrong, it carries me to that which I
have wronged, or to him I have wronged. What a
deliverance then may this word be from those perils
which I have hinted at as likely to beset those who
philosophize on our mental operations !   How it will
remind them, at every step, of the direct relation between us and facts, between us and persons !   How
they will tremble if they discover that they are inter-
posing any mere nominal or formal barriers between
the conscious man and that whereof he is conscious !
How anxious they will be to look at those other
words to which I have alluded, in the spirit and according to the maxims which they have already
brought to bear upon this one !   The word ' Conception,' for instance,—how gladly they will avail them-

selves of the physical mystery which it denotes as an analogy to the mental mystery! How many confusions they will see might have been averted in the use of that word, how many hard judgments respecting other men's use of it, if it had been recollected that every act of ours which seems most internal, most our own, implies co-operation, implies something which is not our own!

I do not complain of the Scotch philosophers for not dwelling as much as they might have done upon these truths which are latent in their own chosen phrase. They were too obvious; they lay too much on the common high-road of life to attract much of their attention. They were working out a great book-system; one ought to be thankful for every homage which they paid to ordinary facts whilst they were engaged in such a task; to have stooped too often to them would have destroyed their school reputation. We Englishmen can afford to join the late Professor Blunt in admiring Paley because he illustrated some part of his doctrine of adaptations by speaking of the great difficulty he experienced in procuring a wig which exactly fitted his head; but we cannot require other people to feel that admiration, seeing that it arises from our stupid attachment to the concrete and the practical.

There is, however, a country which is supposed to be as much addicted to abstractions as Scotland. The Philosophy of Consciousness, in Germany, as it pre-

sents itself in Schleiermacher, was a rebellion against
the abstract tendency. Trained in Moravian habits of
reverence and affection for the Person of Christ, feeling in his manhood the full attraction of that Pantheistic movement which is, as I said in my last Letter, a vehement effort to escape from formulas into
sympathy with the living Universe,—taught by his
country's sufferings the need it had of a ground for
personal life and morality which neither formulas
nor Pantheism could give,—instructed by his earnest
study of the Socratic method in the Platonic Dia-
logues that the truest Philosophy does not consist in
pursuing Notions, but in rising out of them—finding
the orthodox defenders of Scripture, as well as the
Naturalists who sought to reduce it according to their
maxims, equally averse from this method, equally determined to bring the most earnest thoughts and questionings of his countrymen within their narrow rules,
equally indifferent to the deepest necessities of the
human soul,—perceiving in the New Testament much
which met his cravings, which presented itself to him
as the divine satisfaction of his wants, much that
for him lay in shadow,—and being almost entirely out
of sympathy with the lessons of the Old Testament,—
he became the most thorough, devout, accomplished
defender of Consciousness as the instrument, to some
extent the measure, of belief whom the world has seen
or is likely to see. Mr. Mansel has testified (Lecture IV., p. 113) that Schleiermacher's *writings have*

had, perhaps, more influence than those of any other man, in forming the modern religious Philosophy of his own country. He adds, that his *' views, in all ' their essential features, have been ably maintained, ' and widely diffused among ourselves.'* Those of Schleiermacher's countrymen whom I have known, and who have described to me the influence he has exerted over them, have not spoken so much of 'his forming their religious philosophy,' as of his leading them to think what Philosophy was, and what Religion was. He found his disciples, they said, eager for a set of conclusions well packed and ticketed as religious or philosophical. He withdrew them from that ambition ; he led them to feel for themselves after that which was needful for their own being. His teaching or method, they said, encouraged the activity and earnestness of their minds; but it forbade, by its very nature, the acceptance of the decrees or dogmas of the teacher. If, therefore, it is true, as Mr. Mansel affirms, that some are wishing to establish a Schleiermacher school among us, the best way of defeating their purpose would be, not to display Schleiermacher's weakness, but to exhibit him in his full strength. If he was the man which his countrymen say that he was, which his Scotch or English admirers think that he was, he must be shrivelled, distorted, changed into the thing that he was not, when he becomes the representative of a certain bundle of opinions. Those who would maintain

" his views in all their essential features," will commit
a practical solecism, of which that slipslop phrase is
a tolerably faithful exponent.

I should grieve much for the sake of Schleiermacher's own character, still more for the sake of
our English faith and honesty, if there was this attempt to copy, or rather to caricature, him in England. But Mr. Mansel certainly has done nothing
to avert the danger by describing Schleiermacher
" as the chief modern representative of Eclectical
Christianity." Such language will at once be felt
by those who know the facts to be coarse and unjust,
merely adapted to the prejudices of English hearers.
A man who seeks that which he needs for his moral
life is the very reverse of an eclectic, who takes that
which will fit into his system, and leaves out that
which disturbs it. Nor will the far more sympathizing criticism on Schleiermacher, part of which Mr.
Mansel quotes (Note, p. 419) from Mr. Vaughan's
' Remains,' have much effect on those who have felt
his power. That accomplished writer made a clever
point when he demanded that the man who built so
much on religious consciousness, should have had a
religious consciousness of the fidelity of all the statements in the Old and New Testament. But Mr.
Vaughan, with his knowledge of the processes of
German thought, must have felt that this statement
was *only* a clever point, and must have lamented
it as one of the *dulcia vitia* into which reviewers

are apt to be betrayed. He was perfectly aware that
Schleiermacher's effort to realize facts as his own was
avowedly a protest against the opinion that they were
to be received merely on the authority of the Scriptural documents. To ask him to receive that authority as part of his consciousness, was simply asking
him to contemplate the subject from another point
of view, to assume another ground. I do not think
that a pious demand, any more than a consistent or a
wise one. If there was in the German divines, when
Schleiermacher appeared, an inclination to mere opinions about Scripture, either positive or negative, it
is not too great an exercise of faith in God to suppose
that He may have led a student into a course of inquiry which at least made portions of Scripture very
dear to him. And if this is so, the study of his course
of thought, as it was, must be more profitable to us
than a remonstrance against the direction which was
imparted to it. I believe that study may be very useful indeed. An ordinary English reader of Mr. Mansel's book might easily suppose that Schleiermacher
and Hegel exhibited the same habit of mind in different measures. He could scarcely conjecture that
they were direct opponents; that Hegelism is fled to
by numbers just because the Consciousness of Schleiermacher is felt to be unsatisfactory, because it is
thought to make Truth dependent upon our feelings
instead of being fixed and eternal; that Schleiermacher is fled to by numbers because Hegel's abso-

lute teaching appears to be so hard and inhuman. A fair examination of *this* conflict might surely avail more to make us feel what is weak and wanting in each, and to prevent us from accepting the dogmas of either, than a denunciation of both. Such an examination would, I believe, prepare us for appreciating the deep worth and reality of those parts of our creed which Schleiermacher rejected, would prepare us also to feel the unspeakable worth of that Evangelical movement in favour of conscious faith to which we owe what is most vital in our English Christianity,— to which we owe it that the notion of Christianity has not extinguished the belief in a personal Christ. Mr. Mansel, the common foe of Schleiermacher and Hegel, is also, it seems to me, the foe of all that conscious faith " in the finite and relative" which characterized our Evangelical teachers, of that Revelation of the Eternal which " complements it." I proceed to illustrate this assertion from the third and fourth Lectures.

I have pointed out already the valuable hints which Mr. Mansel has given us for the study of Consciousness, in the two propositions that we must be *conscious of something*, and that all consciousness *supposes relation between a subject and an object*. Equally promising is the assurance that he will speak of "human " consciousness in general before he speaks of the " religious consciousness in particular." No method could be so desirable. If those principles are ad-

hered to,—if this method is followed,—we must receive the greatest help from the discussion. For
before any attempt is made to tell us what consciousness is not, we shall of course be led, by a gradual
inductive method, such as Reid and Stewart professed, to discover what it is; we shall hear nothing
of the Infinite, with which Consciousness is said not
to be concerned, till we have been shown how it is
concerned with the Finite; the domain of the relative will be thoroughly explored, if it be only in order
that we may not presume to approach the Absolute.
Hear how these obvious conditions of such an investigation are complied with. Thus it is that Mr. Mansel
commences his whole argument.

" To be conscious, we must be conscious of some-
" thing; and that something can only be known,
" as that which it is, by being distinguished from
" that which it is not. But distinction is necessarily
" limitation; for, if one object is to be distinguished
" from another, it must possess some form of exis-
" tence which the other has not, or it must not pos-
" sess some form which the other has. But it is
" obvious that the Infinite cannot be distinguished,
" as such, from the Finite, by the absence of any
" quality which the Finite possesses; for such ab-
" sence would be a limitation. Nor yet can it be
" distinguished by the presence of an attribute which
" the Finite has not; for, as no finite part can be a
" constituent of an infinite whole, this differential

" characteristic must itself be infinite; and must at
" the same time have nothing in common with the
" finite. We are thus thrown back upon our former
" impossibility; for this second infinite will be dis-
" tinguished from the finite by the absence of qua-
" lities which the latter possesses. A consciousness
" of the Infinite as such thus necessarily involves a
" self-contradiction; for it implies the recognition,
" by limitation and difference, of that which can only
" be given as unlimited and indifferent.

" That man can be conscious of the Infinite, is
" thus a supposition which, in the very terms in
" which it is expressed, annihilates itself. Conscious-
" ness is essentially a limitation; for it is the deter-
" mination of the mind to one actual out of many
" possible modifications. But the Infinite, if it is to
" be conceived at all, must be conceived as poten-
" tially everything and actually nothing; for if there
" is anything in general which it cannot become,
" it is thereby limited; and if there is anything in
" particular which it actually is, it is thereby ex-
" cluded from being any other thing. But again, it
" must also be conceived as actually everything and
" potentially nothing; for an unrealized potentiality
" is likewise a limitation. If the infinite can be that
" which it is not, it is by that very possibility marked
" out as incomplete, and capable of a higher perfec-
" tion. If it is actually everything, it possesses no
" characteristic feature, by which it can be distin-

" guished from anything else, and discerned as an
" object of consciousness.

" This contradiction, which is utterly inexplicable
" on the supposition that the infinite is a positive
" object of human thought, is at once accounted for,
" when it is regarded as the mere negation of thought.
" If all thought is limitation ;—if whatever we con-
" ceive is, by the very act of conception, regarded as
" finite,—*the infinite*, from a human point of view, is
" merely a name for the absence of those conditions
" under which thought is possible. To speak of a
" *Conception of the Infinite* is, therefore, at once to
" affirm those conditions and to deny them. The
" contradiction, which we discover in such a concep-
" tion, is only that which we have ourselves placed
" there, by tacitly assuming the conceivability of the
" inconceivable. The condition of consciousness is
" distinction; and the condition of distinction is li-
" mitation. We can have no consciousness of Being
" in general which is not some Being in particular :
" a *thing*, in consciousness, is one thing out of many.
" In assuming the possibility of an infinite object of
" consciousness, I assume, therefore, that it is at the
" same time limited and unlimited ;—actually some-
" thing, without which it could not be an object of
" consciousness, and actually nothing, without which
" it could not be infinite."—(*Bampton Lectures,* 2nd
ed., pp. 70–73.)

What is this ? An account of the facts of human

Consciousness generally as distinguished from the facts of Religious Consciousness specially? I ask you to read over the passage which I have extracted, and the rest of the Lecture, down to the beginning of the ninety-sixth page, in which the author announces that he has concluded this first portion of the argument, and is ready to enter upon the second, and to say whether I am or am not justified in making these assertions. (1.) That instead of examining any single instance of Consciousness as applied to some finite thing which he admits to be a legitimate and possible object of it, he at once plunges into the question of the Infinite, and the impossibility of exercising consciousness upon that. (2.) That, so far from holding himself aloof from questions concerning the religious Consciousness in this part of his inquiry, all the most awful subjects with which, rightly or wrongly, religious Consciousness has been assumed to have some connection—the Consciousness, Personality, Nature of God—come into the discussion, and the settlement of them is taken for granted. (3.) That this violation, not of some other method, but of that which Mr. Mansel has chosen for himself, enables him to introduce a number of topics for censure and condemnation, which serve admirably the purpose of a rhetorician who wishes to prepossess his hearers with a horror of any opinion but his own, but which either Sir William Hamilton, Bishop Butler, or any person whose judgment is entitled to respect, would have pronounced worthless for the purposes of the argument.*

But this is a small part of my complaint. I could have forgiven Mr. Mansel for anticipating what was to come hereafter, if he had done the very smallest justice to the subject which lay before him. But when he enters the region of Consciousness he is so far from forsaking the dry terminology with which we found him exclusively occupied in the last Lecture, that we have here a mere repetition of that terminology. His whole argument turns not on my consciousness of finite *things*, and my incapacity for being conscious of infinite *things*; but upon my consciousness of the *term* finite, and the *term* infinite. I could not convince myself for some time, that a man of Mr. Mansel's clearness of mind had fallen into so monstrous a confusion as this. I looked again and again at passages which proved that he knew as well

---

* Thus, for instance, one may join with him in denouncin Fichte's conclusion respecting moral order (see the 74th page), but I solemnly protest against the introduction of it into a discourse to a mixed audience, who could know nothing of the writer's general purpose, or the real meaning of a doctrine which is embodied in a single sentence. Such a course may please religious critics, but it is immoral, and furnishes a precedent which might be applied with tremendous force to Mr. Mansel himself. So also I can have no objection to the exposure of "the dreams of a godless philosophy" (*e. g.* of that Hume philosophy which leaves us utterly in doubt whether Theism, Pantheism, Atheism, is most true or most false), but what has it to do with that division of the Lecture which excludes religious questions?

as any one that terms are no objects of thought, nay,
in which he denounced other philosophers for making
them so. I gave all weight to these remarks and denunciations. I confessed that they were in the strictest accordance with his own primary maxim; and yet,
when I considered the passage which I am about to
quote, I could not but fall back upon the conviction
that Terms and Realities are hopelessly mingled in
his intellect, nay even in his conscience.

" This contradiction, again, admits of the same
" explanation as the former. Our whole notion of
" existence is necessarily relative ; for it is existence
" as conceived by us. But *Existence,* as we conceive
" it, is but a name for the several ways in which ob-
" jects are presented to our consciousness,—a general
" term, embracing a variety of relations. *The Abso-*
" *lute,* on the other hand, is a term expressing no ob-
" ject of thought, but only a denial of the relation
" by which thought is constituted. To assume ab-
" solute existence as an object of thought, is thus to
" suppose a relation existing when the related terms
" exist no longer. An object of thought exists, as
" such, in and through its relation to a thinker ;
" while the Absolute, as such, is independent of all
" relation. *The Conception of the Absolute* thus im-
" plies at the same time the presence and the ab-
" sence of the relation by which thought is consti-
" tuted ; and our various endeavours to represent it
" are only so many modified forms of the contradic-

" tion involved in our original assumption. Here, too,
" the contradiction is one which we ourselves have
" made.   It does not imply that the Absolute cannot
" exist; but it implies, most certainly, that we can-
" not conceive it as existing."—(*Bampton Lectures*,
2nd ed., pp. 75, 76.)

What deep truth is contained in the last part of
this extract !   *Here is a contradiction which we ourselves have made.*   Assuredly it is.   I make the term
Existence, and use that *term* to denote a variety of
objects which are presented to my consciousness ; I
make the term Absolute, to denote something that
is not relative.   I make the term Infinite to denote
that which is not finite.   None of these terms can
possibly have anything to do with my consciousness.
For never let us forget ' I am conscious of *something.*'
But the *term* finite is just as much nothing as the
term infinite, the term relative as the term absolute.

If we are thus defeated of all the help and guidance we were promised respecting the ordinary human
consciousnesses,—if we can hear nothing of them except what they are not,—it is not to be expected that
the special religious consciousness should be treated
more satisfactorily.   This beginning does not seem to
me very hopeful.

" Taking, then, as the basis of our inquiry, the
" admission that the whole consciousness of man,
" whether in thought, or in feeling, or in volition, is
" limited in the manner of its operation and in the

" objects to which it is related, let us endeavour,
" with regard to the religious consciousness in parti-
" cular, to separate from each other the complicated
" threads which, in their united web, constitute the
" conviction of man's relation to a Supreme Being.
" In distinguishing, however, one portion of these as
" forming the origin of this conviction, and another
" portion as contributing rather to its further deve-
" lopment and direction, I must not be understood
" to maintain or imply that the former could have
" existed and been recognized, prior to and indepen-
" dently of the co-operation of the latter. Conscious-
" ness, in its earliest discernible form, is only possible
" as the result of a union of the reflective with the
" intuitive faculties. A state of mind, to be known
" at all as existing, must be distinguished from other
" states ; and, to make this distinction, we must
" think of it, as well experience it. Without thought
" as well as sensation, there could be no conscious-
" ness of the existence of an external world : with-
" out thought as well as emotion and volition, there
" could be no consciousness of the moral nature of
" man. Sensation without thought would at most
" amount to no more than an indefinite sense of un-
" easiness or momentary irritation, without any power
" of discerning in what manner we are affected, or of
" distinguishing our successive affections from each
" other. To distinguish, for example, in the visible
" world, any one object from any other, to know the

" house as a house, or the tree as a tree, we must be
" able to refer them to distinct notions; and such
" reference is an act of thought. The same condition
" holds good of the religious consciousness also. In
" whatever mental affection we become conscious of
" our relation to a Supreme Being, we can discern
" that consciousness, as such, only by reflecting upon
" it as conceived under its proper notion. Without
" this, we could not know our religious conscious-
" ness to be what it is: and, as the knowledge of a
" fact of consciousness is identical with its existence,
" —without this, the religious consciousness, as such,
" could not exist."—(*Bampton Lectures*, 2nd edit.,
pp. 105–107.)

To ascertain, then, what Religious Consciousness
is, we begin with laying down what the whole Consciousness of man is *not*. But have we even that
starting-point? Have we found even the *limits* to
this general Consciousness? We have found that
there are *terms* or limits which no doubt have their
meaning and use. But apparently they are verbal
limits merely; therefore limits which do not apply,
and cannot apply, to that which is a vital act, or
nothing. The effect of the confusion in the first
stage of the inquiry becomes sadly evident in this.
The Religious Consciousness, just like the general
Consciousness, perishes in the statement of it. "*In
whatever affection we become conscious of our relation
to a Supreme Being, we can discern that Conscious-*

ness as such only by reflecting on it under its proper notion." Read over these words four or five times. Examine them word by word. Weigh them in your mind. And then ask yourself whether you ever met with language which so entirely bewildered and extinguished (I can use no other word) the feeling which it professes to set forth. What becomes of the actual Consciousness thus " reflected upon as conceived under its proper notion "?

But let us hope for some path through this wilderness of words; for some heavenly manna to drop on us when we are quite faint with travelling through it. We now approach the positive part of the Lecture.

" Religious thought, if it is to exist at all, can only
" exist as representative of some fact of religious
" intuition,—of some individual state of mind, in
" which is presented, as an immediate fact, that re-
" lation of man to God, of which man, by reflection,
" may become distinctly and definitely conscious.

" Two such states may be specified, as dividing be-
" tween them the rude materials out of which Reflec-
" tion builds up the edifice of Religious Conscious-
" ness. These are the *Feeling of Dependence* and the
" *Conviction of Moral Obligation.* To these two facts
" of the inner consciousness may be traced, as to
" their sources, the two great outward acts by which
" religion in various forms has been manifested among
" men;—*Prayer,* by which they seek to win God's
" blessing upon the future, and *Expiation,* by which

" they strive to atone for the offences of the past.
" The Feeling of Dependence is the instinct which
" urges us to pray. It is the feeling that our exis-
" tence and welfare are in the hands of a superior
" Power;—not of an inexorable Fate or immutable
" Law; but of a Being having at least so far the
" attributes of Personality, that He can show favour
" or severity to those dependent upon Him, and can
" be regarded by them with the feelings of hope,
" and fear, and reverence, and gratitude. It is a
" feeling similar in kind, though higher in degree,
" to that which is awakened in the mind of the
" child toward his parent, who is first manifested to
" him as the giver of such things as are needful,
" and to whom the first language he addresses is
" that of entreaty. It is the feeling so fully and
" intensely expressed in the language of the Psalmist:
" ' Thou art he that took me out of my mother's
" ' womb: thou wast my hope, when I hanged yet
" ' upon my mother's breasts. I have been left unto
" ' thee ever since I was born : thou art my God
" ' even from my mother's womb. Be not thou far
" ' from me, O Lord : thou art my succour, haste
" ' thee to help me. I will declare thy Name unto
" ' my brethren : in the midst of the congregation
" ' will I praise thee.' With the first development
" of consciousness, there grows up, as a part of it,
" the innate feeling that our life, natural and spiri-
" tual, is not in our power to sustain or to prolong;

" that there is One above us, on whom we are de-
" pendent, whose existence we learn, and whose pre-
" sence we realize, by the sure instinct of Prayer.
" We have thus, in the Sense of Dependence, the
" foundation of one great element of Religion,—the
" Fear of God.

   " But the mere consciousness of dependence does
" not of itself exhibit the character of the Being on
" whom we depend. It is as consistent with super-
" stition as with religion;—with the belief in a ma-
" levolent, as in a benevolent Deity : it is as much
" called into existence by the severities, as by the mer-
" cies of God ; by the sufferings which we are unable to
" avert, as by the benefits which we did not ourselves
" procure. The Being on whom we depend is, in
" that single relation, manifested in the infliction of
" pain, as well as in the bestowal of happiness. But
" in order to make suffering, as well as enjoyment,
" contribute to the religious education of man, it is
" necessary that he should be conscious, not merely
" of *suffering*, but of *sin ;*—that he should look upon
" pain not merely as *inflicted*, but as *deserved ;* and
" should recognize in its Author the justice that
" punishes, not merely the anger that harms. In
" the feeling of dependence, we are conscious of the
" Power of God, but not necessarily of His Good-
" ness. This deficiency, however, is supplied by the
" other element of religion,—the Consciousness of
" Moral Obligation, carrying with it, as it necessarily

" does, the Conviction of Sin."—(*Bampton Lectures,*
2nd ed., pp. 108–110.)

The reader will ask why I stop at these words,
'Conviction of Sin.' Do they not point to the most
awful fact of human experience? Ought I not, in
all justice, to let the writer show, by his interpretation
of them, that he does mean Consciousness by Consciousness, Conviction by Conviction,—that he does
not, after all, merely put them at a distance from himself, and range them under " their proper notion " ?
I would gladly have continued the quotation, if it
had thrown any light—even the faintest—upon those
fearful struggles in the human spirit which this
scriptural phrase so wonderfully expresses. But the
moment it has been uttered, Mr. Mansel proceeds to
refute Kant's doctrine of an ' Autonomy of the Will;'
as well as to attack the " the fiction of an absolute
law binding on all rational beings." I may venture to meet him again, some time or other, on that
last question ; but I will not be diverted by it from
the one that is now in hand.

We are speaking of Religious Consciousness ; let
us confine ourselves to that. It is said to be " an
edifice built up" " of the rude materials" formed out
of " two states of mind." The first rude material is
the feeling of Dependence. Surely a most deep and
wonderful feeling or state of mind ! But is it not
itself a Consciousness ? Am I not conscious of actual dependence on something or some Person ? The

Child is so, from whom Mr. Mansel draws the best,
because the simplest, of all illustrations and proofs.
David is so, in that Psalm which he quotes. Neither
the child nor the king builds up a Consciousness out
of one or two states of mind. Each has a deep want
and is drawn by it to a Person who meets the want,
to a Person who has been the awakener of it. Is
it not a grievous thing to put a multitude of phrases
between this fact and ourselves? Do not David's
words take us into the very heart of the Consciousness? If it is anything but a school phrase, is it
not this? And what do we gain by reducing it into
this school jargon, but the destruction of the thing
which that jargon endeavours to explain? The words
of the Psalmist tell us of an act of direct trust in a
Person, in whom for some reason or other he *can*
trust, whose character (or Name) is worthy of his
trust, and worthy of other men's trust too, seeing
that he says he will proclaim it to his brethren and to
the Congregation. And am I the better for being
told that this is the ' foundation—of one great element—of Religion.' It is impossible that an accomplished scholar could have spoken of the foundation
of an element, if he had not been busy in leading us
further and further from the real and the actual into
vagueness and emptiness.

Mr. Mansel speaks next of another of these elements of Religion,—the Consciousness of Moral Obligation. Here, again, one is pained by finding how

the near is explained by the distant, the known by
the unknown, the undoubted fact by the logical
term. That the Consciousness of Sin in us involves
the Consciousness of God's Goodness, is a remark as
practical as it is profound ; if Mr. Mansel would have
dwelt upon it, he would have seen, I fancy, the necessity of altering many of the moral statements which
occur in the latter part of his book ; he would have
made this part of it far clearer and simpler. But to
do so, he must have faced those actual experiences
of sin which devout men have recorded. He must
have asked himself whether they were deceived in supposing that Sin meant an alienation from a Being
with whom they were meant to be united,—an opposition between their character and His who has
made them to be like Him. No doubt, they would
one and all have entirely acquiesced in his statement that this Consciousness of evil had been a part,
a necessary and wonderful part, of their "religious
education." They would have testified, more strongly
than he does, to the connection between the Consciousness of Suffering and of Sin in this Education. They would have said that they regarded all
the bodily or outward sufferings they had undergone,
as of unspeakable worth, because they had been instruments by which the Spirit of God had awakened
in them the Conviction of Sin, that so He might
lead them on to the Conviction of Righteousness.
But if, after all, these Experiences were resolved into

the 'Consciousness of Moral Obligation,' I think
they would have exclaimed that a tame, respectable,
presentable school-formula was substituted for living
facts; that the facts were required to give the formula a meaning; that they had always recognized
'moral obligation,' without attaching a very distinct
signification to either the adjective or the substan-
tive; that they had learnt, by their Experience, who
obliged them, and what was obliged; how a moral
obligation differs from the force which acts upon the
mere brute nature. Such persons would, unless I am
greatly mistaken, read such a passage as the following with something more than a chill. They would
feel that it carries them round in a weary circle of
words and notions, each returning into the other, till
all reality is lost, all practical guidance for life becomes hopeless, all personal consciousness is extinguished.

" We are thus compelled, by the consciousness of
" a moral obligation, to assume the existence of a
" moral Deity, and to regard the absolute standard
" of right and wrong as constituted by the nature of
" that Deity. The conception of this standard, in
" the human mind, may indeed be faint and fluctuat-
" ing, and must be imperfect: it may vary with the
" intellectual and moral culture of the nation or the
" individual: and in its highest human representa-
" tion, it must fall far short of the reality. But it is
" present to all mankind, as a basis of moral obli-

" gation and an inducement to moral progress : it is
" present in the universal consciousness of sin; in
" the conviction that we are offenders against God;
" in the expiatory rites by which, whether inspired
" by some natural instinct, or inherited from some
" primeval tradition, divers nations have, in their
" various modes, striven to atone for their transgres-
" sions, and to satisfy the wrath of their righteous
" Judge. However erroneously the particular acts
" of religious service may have been understood by
" men ; yet, in the universal consciousness of inno-
" cence and guilt, of duty and disobedience, of an
" appeased and offended God, there is exhibited the
" instinctive confession of all mankind, that the mo-
" ral nature of man, as subject to a law of obligation,
" reflects and represents, in some degree, the moral
" nature of a Deity by whom that obligation is im-
" posed."—(*Bampton Lectures*, 2nd ed., pp. 112, 113.)

" *We are compelled*"—by what ? "*by the consciousness of moral obligation*,"—*i. e.* of moral compulsion,
" *to assume the existence of a moral Deity.*" But what
is moral? Do I derive my knowledge of its meaning from this compulsion which has not been explained, or from something else ? I am further compelled to regard "*the absolute standard of right and
wrong as constituted by the Nature of that Deity.*"
Now we begin to see light. Now we can know what
morality is; now we can know what a moral compulsion is. Ah, no ! Read the next passage. In place

of the standard itself, we have a "*conception of this standard in the human mind,*" which may "*vary with the intellectual and moral culture of the individual and the nation;*" which in fact therefore is no standard at all. But there is this consolation. This varying conception is "*present to all mankind as a basis of moral obligation and an inducement to moral progress.*" We started from the consciousness of moral obligation. We have had the glimpse of a standard which would tell us what that is. We have lost that glimpse, and now we have the conception of this standard, *i. e.* (if it is anything) the consciousness of moral obligation, as a basis of moral obligation! And all we can find out about this basis of moral obligation is, that "*there are expiatory rites by which divers nations have in their various modes striven to atone for their transgressions and to satisfy the wrath of their righteous Judge;*" *e. g.* the offerings to Moloch and to the Queen of Heaven, which the God of Abraham pronounced to be abomination in His sight. 'Moral obligation' has certainly a very firm 'basis'! And this is the lore which our sons are to hear from a University pulpit!

A portion of the Lecture is devoted to the subject of Prayer. One might have hoped that while speaking of it, Mr. Mansel would have cared more to express his own convictions, than to prove how absurd are the convictions of other men. But it would seem that to confute is the one "moral obligation" of a Preacher. When he refers to Communion with

God, it is that he may denounce a theory of Schleiermacher, which has been adopted, he says, by Mr.
Morell. This theory is described in the following
language.

" According to Schleiermacher, the essence of Re-
" ligion is to be found in a feeling of absolute and
" entire dependence, in which the mutual action and
" reaction of subject and object upon each other,
" which constitutes the ordinary consciousness of
" mankind, gives way to a sense of utter, passive
" helplessness,—to a consciousness that our entire
" personal agency is annihilated in the presence of
" the infinite energy of the Godhead. In our inter-
" course with the world, he tells us, whether in re-
" lation to nature or to human society, the feeling of
" freedom and that of dependence are always present
" in mutual operation upon each other; sometimes
" in equilibrium; sometimes with a vast preponder-
" ance of the one or the other feeling; but never to
" the entire exclusion of either. But in our com-
" munion with God, there is always an accompanying
" consciousness that the whole activity is absolutely
" and entirely dependent upon Him; that, whatever
" amount of freedom may be apparent in the indi-
" vidual moments of life, these are but detached and
" isolated portions of a passively dependent whole."
—(*Bampton Lectures*, 2nd ed., p. 114.)

Now I think any one who will be at the pains to refer
to the 'Christliche Glaube,' of Schleiermacher, will

discover that he certainly was not putting forth a theory
on the subject of Religion* or of Prayer. Rightly or
wrongly, he had evidently a dread of theories in this
region. He was disposed, his opponents always say,
to exaggerate the feeling above the intellect. " Piety
" in itself," he says, in one of his fundamental axioms,
" is neither a knowing nor a doing (*weder ein Wissen*
" *noch ein Thun*), but an inclination and determina-
" tion of the Feeling (*eine Neigung und Bestimmtheit*
" *des Gefühls*)." Evidently he desired to describe
what he regarded as a fact, or rather as the central
fact of his own being, that in which he could not be
singular or different from other men, but in which he
most realized what was common to him with them
all. There was a consciousness, it seemed, which lay
beneath all others : it expressed the deepest necessity
of the creatures in whom the other Consciousnesses
dwelt,—it was the want of his own very self. He
confessed a Being not imperfect and limited, like
himself, apart from whom he could not be, in whom
he could lose himself and find rest. Such a statement as this has surely nothing in it of the arro-
gance and self-sufficiency of the Philosopher. It may

* *Frömmigkeit* is his word, which I submit ought not to be translated Religion. My edition is probably not the same as Mr. Mansel's ; but the ninth Proposition of the Introduction may be taken
as a specimen. " Das Gemeinsame aller frommen Erregungen, also
das Wesen der *Frömmigkeit*, ist dieses, das wir uns selbst als
schlechthin abhängig bewusst sind, das heisse, das wir uns abhängig
fühlen von Gott."

be inadequate; no one probably would have felt the inadequacy of words to represent the profoundest reality more than its author. But something like it, I think, all persons who have ever prayed, or tried to pray, have coveted and adopted as the expression of their own impotency, of their surrender to the Almighty and the All-good.

Mr. Mansel makes the following comments upon it:—

" Of this theory it may be observed, in the first " place, that it contemplates God chiefly in the cha- " racter of an *object of infinite magnitude.* The rela- " tions of the object to the subject, in our conscious- " ness of the world, and in that of God, differ from " each other in degree rather than in kind. The " Deity is manifested with no attribute of persona- " lity; He is merely the world magnified to infinity: " and the feeling of absolute dependence is in fact " that of the annihilation of our personal existence in " the Infinite Being of the Universe. Of this feeling, " the intellectual exponent is pure Pantheism; and " the infinite object is but the indefinite abstraction " of Being in general, with no distinguishing cha- " racteristic to constitute a Deity. For the distinct- " ness of an object of consciousness is in the inverse " ratio to the intensity of the passive affection. As " the feeling of dependence becomes more powerful, " the knowledge of the character of the object on " which we depend, must necessarily become less and

" less; for the discernment of any object as such, is
" a state of mental energy and reaction of thought
" upon that object. Hence the feeling of absolute
" dependence, supposing it possible, could convey no
" consciousness of God as God, but merely an inde-
" finite impression of dependence upon something.
" Towards an object so vague and meaningless, no
" real religious relation is possible.

   " In the second place, the consciousness of an ab-.
" solute dependence in which our activity is annihi-
" lated, is a contradiction in terms; for conscious-
" ness itself is an activity. We can be conscious of
" a state of mind as such, only by attending to it;
" and attention is in all cases a mode of our active
" energy. Thus the state of absolute dependence,
" supposing it to exist at all, could not be distin-
" guished from other states; and, as all conscious-
" ness is distinction, it could not, by any mode of con-
" sciousness, be known to exist."—(*Bampton Lectures,*
" 2nd ed., pp. 115–117.)

   The remark that one who prays thus must contemplate God " as an infinite magnitude," is the
most astounding I ever met with. How can any
human being feel that an infinite magnitude over-
powers his will, subjects his restlessness, leads him
captive? And what a strange fancy that this is the
meaning and attraction of Pantheism! Doubtless,
Scheiermacher had heard, as most earnest men, at
some time or other, have heard, the singing of the

Mermaid who would draw down the fisherman into the deep; doubtless the charm of sinking all personal existence in the vast whole had once seemed to him irresistible. But never, we may be sure, for a single moment did the hope of being crushed under an infinite magnitude dawn upon him as a vision of delight. He must have known even then too much of the nature of self, and of the burden of self, to think of bulk as having anything to do with the power that extinguished it. As he grew better to understand what that Self is which is identical with Sin,—what that independence is which is only another name for slavery,—he will have known that no infinite WORLD could receive the sacrifice, that nothing can claim the subjection of the spirit, but an infinite Love.

The second objection is curiously in accordance with Mr. Mansel's treatment of the whole subject. " *An absolute dependence in which our activity is annihilated, is a contradiction in terms.*" Of course it is; but is it a contradiction in fact? It is a *paradox* certainly. All Consciousness is a paradox on this very ground, that it is an activity in us, and yet that it is always passing out of us into that of which we are conscious. Every feeling of child, friend, lover, is tending towards this consummation. When the activity is highest, it becomes self-forgetfulness. And what is "*putting our trust in the Lord, believing in Him, casting our burden upon Him,*" but the full realization of this self-oblivion? Can Prayer, if it be communion with God, be anything but that? And if we believe, as the Scripture teaches us, that all **Prayer** is but our response to God's voice in us—if it is the Spirit who maketh intercession for us with groanings that cannot be uttered—is not Schleiermacher's language something more in accordance with the Spirit of Psalmists, Prophets, Evangelists, and Apostles, than the following passage, though it appeals so confidently to their authority?

" In the third place, the theory is inconsistent with " the duty of Prayer. Prayer is essentially a state " in which man is in active relation towards God; in " which he is intensely conscious of his personal ex-" istence and its wants; in which he endeavours, by " entreaty, to prevail with God. Let any one con-" sider for a moment the strong energy of the lan-" guage of the Apostle; 'Now I beseech you, bre-" ' thren, for the Lord Jesus Christ's sake, and for the " ' love of the Spirit, that ye strive together with me " ' in your prayers to God for me:' or the conscious-" ness of a personal need, which pervades that Psalm " in which David so emphatically declares his depen-" dence upon God. 'My God, my God, look upon " ' me; why hast thou forsaken me, and art so far " ' from my health, and from the words of my com-" ' plaint? O my God, I cry in the day-time, but " ' thou hearest not; and in the night season also I " ' take no rest:'—let him ponder the words of our " Lord himself,—' Shall not God avenge his own " ' elect, which cry day and night unto him?'—and " then let him say if such language is compatible

" with the theory which asserts that man's persona-
" lity is annihilated in his communion with God.

" But, lastly, there is another fatal objection to
" the above theory. It makes our moral and reli-
" gious consciousness subversive of each other, and
" reduces us to the dilemma, that either our faith or
" our practice must be founded on a delusion. The
" actual relation of man to God is the same, in what-
" ever degree man may be conscious of it. If man's
" dependence on God is not really destructive of his
" personal freedom, the religious consciousness, in
" denying that freedom, is a false consciousness. If,
" on the contrary, man is in reality passively depend-
" ent upon God, the consciousness of moral responsi-
" bility, which bears witness to his free agency, is a
" lying witness. Actually, in the sight of God, we
" are either totally dependent, or, partially at least,
" free. And as this condition must be always the
" same, whether we are conscious of it or not, it fol-
" lows, that, in proportion as one of these modes of
" consciousness reveals to us the truth, the other
" must be regarded as testifying to a falsehood."—
(*Bampton Lectures*, 2nd ed., pp. 117, 118.)

To the argument from the Psalms I have replied
already. That they express the utmost energy of
the human spirit is admitted at once. But is not
that energy put forth in acts of dependence and
trust? Is not its regular expression : "Thy will be
done on earth, as it is in heaven"? Does it not

reach its highest power and agony in the words of the only-begotten Son : " Not my will, but thine be done" ?

A note, which is subjoined to this passage, is necessary for the full illustration of it.

"Schleiermacher himself admits (' Christliche Glau- " be,' § 33) that the theory of absolute dependence is " incompatible with the belief that God can be moved " by any human action. He endeavours, however, " to reconcile this admission with the duty of prayer " by maintaining (§ 147) that the true Christian will " pray for nothing but that which it comes within God's " absolute purpose to grant. *This implies something* " *like omniscience in the true Christian, and something* " *like hypocrisy in every act of prayer.*"*—(*Bampton Lectures,* 2nd ed., Note 16, p. 360.)

Is not this a direct answer—not to Schleiermacher, but—to the Apostle John ? ' If omniscience in the act of prayer,'—if ' something like hypocrisy in every act of prayer,' is chargeable on the writer of the

---

* The proposition which I find in § 33, in my edition of the ' Christliche Glaube,' is this. I do not quote it because I suppose it is that to which Mr. Mansel refers, but because it illustrates the purpose of the author, and removes, I think, some of the charges which Mr. Mansel brings against him. " Da die christliche Fröm- " migkeit beruht auf den gefühlten Gegensaz zwischen der eignen " Unfähigkeit und der durch die Erlösung mitgetheilten Fähig- " keit das fromme Bewusstsein zu verwirklichen, dieser Gegensaz " aber nur ein relativer ist ; so werden wir den Umfang der christ- " lichen Lehre erschöpfen, wenn wir das fromme Gefühl betrachten " sowohl in den Aeusserungen, worin der Gegensaz am stärksten,

' Christliche Glaube,' is not the writer of an Epistle
which contains these wonderful words still more
open to that blame?—" *And this is the confidence
that we have in Him, that if we ask anything according to His Will, He heareth us.   And if we know
that He heareth us, we know that we have the peti-
tion that we desired of Him.*" Another deep paradox,
surely! Infidels have again and again applied to it
the very language which Mr. Mansel applies to the
German author. To me it seems that the whole paradox of our Consciousness, as well as all the paradox
of Christ's Gospel, is hidden here. To me it seems,
that for the prayer which is not this—for that
prayer which answers to Mr. Mansel's idea of conscious activity in beseeching a Being of whose will
we know nothing—we must seek our precedent, not
in the New Testament, not in the Book of Psalms,
but in that memorable passage of the Book of Kings:
" *And they took the bullock which was given them,
and they dressed it, and called on the name of Baal
from morning even until noon, saying, ' O Baal, hear
us !' but there was no voice nor any that regarded.*"

Surely it is not to such prayers as these that

" als in denen worin er am schwachsten ist ; und wir theilen daher
" die gesammte christiche Lehre in die Betrachtung des frommen
" Gefühls abgesehen von dem Gegensaz und in der Betrachtung
" desselben unter dem Gegensaz."   I do not pretend that this
method of treating ' Christian Doctrine' would be satisfactory to
me ; but it shows, at least, the importance which Schleiermacher
attached to Redemption, and it exhibits very strikingly his sense of
the impotency of the will when left to itself.

an Oxford Teacher in the nineteenth century of the
Christian era would bring us back. It is clear, from
the concluding passage of his Lecture, that a very
different idea of Prayer is present to his inner mind,
than that which his religious Philosophy builds up by
Reflection out of Consciousness. He speaks of our
drawing nigh to God as sinners, and as sharers in a
common Redemption. If we will but ask ourselves
how our sin has separated us from God, what He. is
from whom it has separated us, out of what slavery
He has redeemed us, to what freedom He has brought
us;—if we will but consider what answers the Bible
gives us to these questions, what answers we receive
to them as we kneel,—our ardour to refute ' opposing
theories' will be less, our desire to receive any light
which comes from any one who has himself prayed
and suffered greater ; we shall feel that dependence on
an *Unknown* Being who is very near us, and in whom
we are living, becomes impossible through the restless eagerness of our intellect to conceive and create
objects for itself out of the things which we see;
that utter dependence upon that Being when He
has made Himself known,—when He has revealed
Himself to us in His Son as the Absolute, Infinite,
Eternal Good, who has called us to be His children,
—*is* possible,—is the highest realization of all that
the spirit within us craves for,—since it craves to
be lost in itself, to be found in Him.

Faithfully yours,

F. D. M.

LETTER VIII.

———◆——

My dear Sir,

Mr. Mansel commences his fifth Lecture with
an allusion to the well-known chapter on Necessity,
in Butler's ' Analogy.' He could not have referred
to a passage in that book which illustrates better the
assertion I made in my Third Letter, that Butler is
pre-eminently a student of facts, and is indifferent,
even to a fault, about the notions with which Sir
William Hamilton and his Oxford disciple are chiefly
conversant. The whole of that chapter might be
summed up in some such language as this :—' Esta-
' blish your Notion of Necessity as satisfactorily as
' you please. I shall not dispute with you about it.
' That is no business of mine. I want to know what
' the facts of life are. This is one. *I am treated and
' dealt with as if I were free.* By that I stand.'

But though Butler was so heedless of *notions*, he was profoundly solicitous about *principles*. For these he was always seeking. These he found lying in the facts and under the facts. The carelessness of men in inquiring after these principles—their readiness to substitute for them merely fancies and speculations as to what might be—provoked him far more than any contradiction of his own conclusions. So little did he desire any one to take them for granted, that he would have liked people to write books without even enunciating their conclusions, leaving their readers to work them out for themselves.

It is Mr. Mansel's misfortune that he cannot distinguish between a Principle and a Notion. He is therefore obliged to misrepresent—actually to invert —Butler's lessons, whenever he comes in contact with them. So it is in this instance. He remarks, with self-evident truth, that Butler's " observation has not " settled the speculative difficulties involved in the " problem of Liberty and Necessity." He might have gone much further. He might have said, that it does not *by itself* settle the *practical* difficulties which are involved in that problem. It merely puts us in a method by which those practical difficulties may be removed, viz. by facing them, and not evading them; by meeting them, on whatever side they present themselves to us in action, and by believing that we may find a principle which will enable us to act rightly, be the notional perplexity ever so great.

More than two centuries before Butler, Martin Luther
had seen these difficulties from the other side. He had
as deep a conviction that his will was enslaved, and
that he was 'treated and dealt with' on that supposition, as Butler had that he was treated and dealt with
on what seems to be the contrary supposition. He
manfully cut through all scholastical webs which set
at nought this great experience of his life; he proclaimed that he was a bondsman till God made him
free. He would not have understood Butler; Butler
would have utterly misunderstood him. But we cannot dispense with either; the facts of Luther are as
much facts for us as the facts of Butler. We cannot
seesaw between them, or complain of the vehemence
with which either maintained his own position as one
which it was life to hold, death to abandon. They
might have been—at least we may be—less of deniers. God forbid that they should have been less
of asserters! God forbid that any one should have
persuaded them that what they asserted might not be
true because there was so much to say on the other
side! That they resisted all such arguments, was the
sign that they were God's heroes,—that they had
renounced the world and the devil. And I am sure
that we shall not do any work for Him, that we
shall not maintain the vow of our baptism, if we
listen to such language as the following, which is
put forth under Butler's authority,—which no one
would more indignantly have repudiated than Butler.

" In Religion, in Morals, in our daily business, in
" the care of our lives, in the exercise of our senses,
" the rules which guide our practice cannot be reduced
" to principles which satisfy our reason." (Page
135.) To which proposition I would oppose another.
In Religion, in Morals, in our daily business, in the
care of our lives, in the exercise of our senses, all
rules will be unpractical, insincere, deceitful, promising much, performing nothing, unless they can
be referred to some principle which our conscience,
heart, reason, confess as fixed, unchangeable, eternal.

You will remember, surely, the opening chapter of
the Analogy, concerning the imperishable *I*, who uses
all senses, exerts all energies, puts forth all thoughts.
See how Mr. Mansel introduces the same awful subject into his Lecture :—

" The very first Law of Thought, and through
" Thought, of all Consciousness, by which alone we
" are able to discern objects as such, or to distin-
" guish them from one another, involves in its con-
" stitution a mystery and a doubt, which no effort of
" Philosophy has been able to penetrate :—How can
" the One be many, or the Many one ? We are com-
" pelled to regard ourselves and our fellow-men as
" *persons,* and the visible world around us as made
" up of *things :* but what is *personality,* and what is
" *reality,* are questions which the wisest have tried to
" answer, and have tried in vain. Man, as a Person,
" is one, yet composed of many elements ;—not iden-

" tical with any one of them, nor yet with the aggre-
" gate of them all; and yet not separable from them
" by any effort of abstraction. Man is one in his
" thoughts, in his actions, and in the responsibilities
" which these involve. It is *I* who think, *I* who act,
" *I* who feel; yet I am not thought, nor action, nor
" feeling, nor a combination of thoughts and actions
" and feelings heaped together. Extension, and resist-
" ance, and shape, and the various sensible qualities,
" make up my conception of each individual body as
" such; yet *the body* is not its extension, nor its shape,
" nor its hardness, nor its colour, nor its smell, nor
" its taste; nor yet is it a mere aggregate of all these
" with no principle of unity among them. If these
" several parts constitute a single whole, the unity,
" as well as the plurality, must depend upon some
" principle which that whole contains: if they do not
" constitute a whole, the difficulty is removed but a
" single step; for the same question,—what consti-
" tutes individuality?—must be asked in relation to
" each separate part. The actual conception of every
" object, as such, involves the combination of the
" One and the Many; and that combination is prac-
" tically made every time we think at all. But at
" the same time, no effort of reason is able to explain
" how such a relation is possible; or to satisfy the
" intellectual doubt which necessarily arises on the
" contemplation of it."—(*Bampton Lectures*, 2nd ed.,
pp. 135, 136.)

The former part of this passage contains that marvellous sentence about Reality to which I referred in a former letter. *What is reality, is a question which the wisest have tried to answer, and tried in vain.* So one would imagine! They have tried to reduce that which is, into a name, and they have not succeeded! With Reality, *Personality* is joined,—a melancholy fact, because all that is most powerful and effective in these Lectures has turned upon a denunciation of the Germans for losing sight of Personality either in themselves or in the Divine Being. And now we hear that what it is the wisest have tried in vain to ascertain. But the sentence I especially wish to notice is that concerning the *I*. Mr. Mansel perceives that it is *I* who think, *I* who act, and then proceeds to remark " that I am not thought, nor " action, nor feelings, nor a combination of thoughts " and actions and feelings heaped together." Oh, if he had paused there one instant!—if he had allowed Butler to lead him into a solemn consideration of what is involved in that personality of mine, whether the wise can define it or not!—if he had not rushed into a wilderness of words about the combination of the One and the Many !—if he could have held fast to the One when he had found it!

For what is all this leading to? Is he trying to awaken in his Undergraduate hearers some sense of the mystery of that *I* which each one of them is and must be through ages upon ages? Is he bidding

him ask himself, *What* am I? *what* shall I be? whence
have I come? with whom have I to do? Is he thus
cultivating the spirit of Butler, and teaching them
how to profit by the study of him in their lecture-
rooms and in their chambers? Is he thus leading them
to a Book which teaches us more of divine analogies,
more of the way in which God awakens and meets
these questionings, than Butler's book ever can?

No! it is precisely to *prevent* all inquiries of this
kind; precisely to show these young men that they
must not trouble themselves about that which is;
that they can have no acquaintance except with
phenomena or appearances;—it is for this end that
the Bampton Lectures were delivered; this is the
moral which has been unfolding itself through all
that have preceded, and which is now to burst upon
us in its full magnificence. In the following passage
we may be said to have reached the kernel of these
discourses :—

   "The conclusion which this condition of human
"consciousness almost irresistibly forces upon us, is
"one which equally exhibits the strength and the
"weakness of the human intellect. We are com-
"pelled to admit that the mind, in its contemplation
"of objects, is not the mere passive recipient of the
"things presented to it; but has an activity and a
"law of its own, by virtue of which it reacts upon
"the materials existing without, and' moulds them
"into that form in which consciousness is capable of

" apprehending them. The existence of modes of
" thought, which we are compelled to accept as at
" the same time relatively ultimate and absolutely
" derived,—as limits beyond which we cannot pene-
" trate, yet which themselves proclaim that there is a
" further truth behind and above them,—suggests, as
" its obvious explanation, the hypothesis of a mind
" cramped by its own laws, and bewildered in the
" contemplation of its own forms. If the mind, in
" the act of consciousness, were merely blank and
" inert;—if the entire object of its contemplation
" came from without, and nothing from within;—no
" fact of consciousness would be inexplicable; for
" everything would present itself as it is. No reality
" would be suggested, beyond what is actually given:
" no question would be asked which is not already
" answered. For how can doubt arise, where there is
" no innate power in the mind to think beyond what
" is placed before it,—to react upon that which acts
" upon it? But upon the contrary supposition, all is
" regular, and the result such as might naturally be
" expected. If thought has laws of its own, it cannot
" by its own act go beyond them; yet the recogni-
" tion of law, as a restraint, implies the existence of a
" sphere of liberty beyond. If the mind contributes
" its own element to the objects of consciousness, it
" must, in its first recognition of those objects, ne-
" cessarily regard them as something complex, some-
" thing generated partly from without and partly from

" within. Yet in that very recognition of the com-
" plex, as such, is implied an impossibility of attain-
" ing to the simple; for to resolve the composition
" is to destroy the very act of knowledge, and the
" relation by which consciousness is constituted. The
" object of which we are conscious is thus, to adopt
" the well-known language of the Kantian philosophy,
" a *phenomenon*, not a *thing in itself;*—a product, re-
" sulting from the twofold action of the thing ap-
" prehended, on the one side, and the faculties appre-
" hending it, on the other. The perceiving subject
" alone, and the perceived object alone, are two un-
" meaning elements, which first acquire a significance
" in and by the act of their conjunction.

" It is thus strictly in analogy with the method of
" God's Providence in the constitution of man's men-
" tal faculties, if we believe that, in Religion also, He
" has given us truths which are designed to be re-
" gulative, rather than speculative; intended, not to
" satisfy our reason, but to guide our practice; not
" to tell us what God is in His absolute nature, but
" how He wills that we should think of Him in our
" present finite state."—(*Bampton Lectures*, 2nd ed.,
pp. 141–143.)

I do not know why Mr. Mansel attributes the distinction between a *phenomenon* and a *thing in itself*
to the Kantian philosophy. It has been a recognized distinction in every philosophy of the East or
West for at least two thousand years; it has been

felt to be the critical distinction in most. That we can *only* know Phenomena, was a dogma among the Greeks before the time of Socrates; that we *cannot* know Phenomena,—that only Being is the object of knowledge,—was the assertion of the most eminent thinkers of the opposing school. To ascertain what there is in us which takes account of Phenomena, what there is which demands the truth which is behind them and which they misrepresent, was the great enterprise of Plato, who cheerfully confessed that his practical master had preceded him in the inquiry, and that the best hope for any scientific result was to follow in his steps. Kant's connection with the distinction, I have spoken of already. He had asserted, with more emphasis than all his predecessors, that the mere understanding in man converses only with phenomena; he felt himself compelled to assert also, with equal emphasis, that there must be an organ in man which converses with the thing itself, and that without this organ moral principle would be impossible for man. I am sorry to repeat myself so often upon this point, but I only do so when Mr. Mansel obliges me by repeating himself, or when, as in this case, he unintentionally misleads his readers by imputing to Kant specially what he has in common with half the world.

I use that last phrase deliberately, intending you to understand that this is a question which concerns the world just as much as the schools. The doctrine which Mr. Mansel has enunciated, that we must in all cases be contented with rules of conduct and must dispense with 'any principles that satisfy the reason,' is merely, as he confesses, the doctrine, in another form, that we have nothing to do except with phenomena. He has himself given us an admirable series of tests for trying that doctrine by. I proceed to apply them one by one, in his own order. What I propose to show is—(1.) That all the experience of the most earnestly religious men in this country, those who have had the least to do with German Philosophy, who have hated it most, is against him. (2.) That the experience of all who are forming the minds of their children and pupils to practical morality is against him. (3.) That the experience of men occupied in common business is against him. (4.) That the experience respecting the care of our lives is against him. (5.) That the experience respecting the exercise of the senses is against him.

1. I begin, since Mr. Mansel begins, with the highest subject of all. I have spoken of the strong tendency, in the last age, among those in whose minds any thought had been awakened respecting the unseen world, to dwell upon their experiences and consciousnesses. That tendency was a protest and reaction against the prevalent habits of the eighteenth century; habits which were characteristic of its divines, and which found their full justification in a part of its philosophy. The evangelical teachers bore

a clear and strong witness that the man must have that within him which the doctors only presented to him in formal lessons. Those who bore this witness spoke of themselves as asserters of 'experimental' or 'vital' religion.

But there was again a protest and reaction against *this* tendency. I mean, one proceeding not from those who undervalued it, but from those who had felt in themselves the full force of it. I mean one which did not merely aim at the hypocritical affectation of it, but which pointed out the dangers into which those were likely to fall who had passed through the spiritual processes which they recorded. For instance, the ablest of all the religious philosophers of the Calvinistical school, Jonathan Edwards, the writer who had attempted to expound most accurately the nature of the religious affections, was the man who most strongly asserted that consciousness never can be an ultimate end to the religious thinker. Nothing will satisfy him but *being*. He must rest in One who is; in One who is deeper than his consciousness; if he does not, that will only deceive him.

I refer to Edwards lest I should seem to be selecting a writer with whom I have any special sympathy. If he is too much of a formal philosopher for the illustration of my position, I could refer to a class of divines who had no pretensions of that kind, and yet who were continually warning their disciples not to trust 'in their frames and feelings,'—to rest only in

that which was fixed, settled, eternal, dependent on
nothing in them, the only ground of all that they
found in themselves. Any one the least conversant
with religious literature will be familiar with such
admonitions as these. I allude to them in those
from whom they might least be expected, to show
how impossible it has been for any serious man who
has known most of *phenomena*, of the phenomena
of his own mind, to be content with them; how all
demands for action and suffering have driven him
beyond these,—to seek a permanent rock and basis
for his own being, even if he has not been forced by
the reelings and convulsions of society to seek for one
which should sustain all human beings. And this
—not because he has sought any help from a ' godless philosophy'—but because he has meditated on
the Bible day and night. He has read in Psalm after
Psalm how men in a horrible pit, or with the water-
floods going over them, found at last a ground beneath all their feelings, thoughts, consciousnesses. He
has heard the voice which cried once in a poor sinful
mortal, which sounded again from the Cross of the
sinless One, " *My God, my God, why hast thou forsaken me?*" still able to say, " *Thou continuest holy,
O thou worship of Israel.*" He has read in the New
Testament of a peace which we do not keep in our
Consciousness, but which keeps us in the knowledge
and love of God and of His Son Jesus Christ; he has
found the beloved Disciple describing this as the pri-

z

vilege of the adult Christians, *the fathers—that they knew Him who was from the beginning.* And these are not only the discoveries of individuals. The whole course of religious thought for many years has been setting in this direction. Mr. Mansel may persuade some, that by the laws which God has imposed upon them, they cannot pass beyond the limits of their own consciousness,—they cannot know anything but phenomena. Those who understand what he means —who do not receive his decrees merely as an abracadabra which they may interpret as they like—will abandon their deepest consciousness, that they may not transcend it; will give up the faith which has sustained their souls, that they may not become infidels.

2. Some of the lessons which I have got from this religious history bear very clearly upon the next subject; but I will keep them apart so far as I can, that I may do justice to Mr. Mansel's division. What has been the most practical teaching of morals in our time? What efforts have been made to deliver it from the formal, unpractical teaching of the last century? I should not scruple to draw my examples from any school. Take the writings of the most accomplished women of this age, who have given us the most valuable hints respecting the moral training of their own sex or of ours. Take the prudential lessons of Miss Edgeworth, the lessons on individual piety by Miss Hannah More, the lessons of Christian wisdom in social life by Miss Sewell or Miss Young.

In this quality they are alike. Their practical sense, their experience of actual men and women, leads them all to neglect mere rules of conduct, for the sake of discovering principles which mould and govern the character. They are always disobeying Mr. Mansel. Each, according to her own light, is seeking for that which is beneath appearances; each sees no way of delivering our sons and daughters from mere conventions that fail in every hour of trial, but by showing them that they must *be* in order to *do*.

3. *Our daily business.* Let us be as literal as possible in construing all these expressions. Can I be more so than if I take our daily business to be our *trade?* Then I say, that from Adam Smith downwards thoughtful men have been trying to cast off rules—most plausible rules, deduced from obvious phenomena—which had been wont to govern the operations of trade, and the conduct of statesmen respecting it, and to seek for principles deduced from the nature of things, 'satisfying to the Reason.'

4. *The care of our lives.* This is a very general phrase. It means, I suppose, the health of our bodies. If that is so, it may point either to the care of our individual health, so suggesting the functions of the domestic physician, or the sanitary discipline of the country at large. Every step, I affirm, from barber-surgery to the period of Sir Benjamin Brodie and Mr. Lawrence, has been a step out of rules deduced from the phenomena of diseases into anatomical

and physiological principles; these being discovered
by the study of the actual human body, first in its
healthy normal state, then under its morbid conditions.   In like manner, every movement towards the
improvement of dwellings, the removal of nuisances
that have caused disease, the prevention of accidents, has been a step from rules grounded on the
observation of phenomena into principles satisfactory
to the reason.   So much is this fact acknowledged
by those who have the practical administration of
affairs, that in case of any explosion in a mine, some
scientific chemist, or geologist, is always sent down
to examine and expound what principles have been
neglected through the adherence to rules generalized
from experience.

5. *The exercise of the senses.*   Such exercises, I
presume, as the observation of forms, which leads to
the art of drawing, painting, sculpture; the observation of sounds, which leads to the art of music.
Other exercises of the senses may be intended, but
I choose these because they do not involve us in
a cross division; we are less in danger of mixing
this head with the second, which concerned morals.
Then I affirm here also, that just as these exercises have
become more orderly, more beneficial, more general,
just in proportion as they have been taken more out
of the dominion of artificial rules, and have been
more connected with principles.   I am not speaking
of Germans who have elaborated a doctrine of Æsthe-

tics, and have sought to discover the laws which our
senses follow in their workings; I am not speaking
of Winckelmann, or Lessing, or Goethe. Our own
Burke,—who knew nothing of them, who was the
great enemy of mere speculation, the laborious student of facts,—set the example, in his ' Essay on the
Sublime and Beautiful,' of a search for grounds that
would satisfy the reason in a subject which had been
given up to the caprices of taste, or to traditional
maxims.

Englishmen and Englishwomen have thus, in every
department of thought to which Mr. Mansel has referred, been transgressing his canons, and moving in
the line in which he would forbid them to move. And
this, precisely because they have been sternly practical, because they could not be hindered from doing
the thing that was to be done by any precepts of Philosophy.

The inhabitants of other lands have felt the same
impulse, the same necessity. But as they have not
our enviable faculty of speaking prose for a whole life
without being aware of it, they have tried to investigate the seeming contradiction that while our direct
consciousness is of that which presents itself to us,
i. e. of appearances, all Science is and must be conversant with things in themselves, or (generally) with
that which is. They have not indeed sought "to
solve the mystery of knowing and being;" they have
been at least as well aware as Mr. Mansel that it is a

mystery. But they have said to themselves, 'Since
'*truth* is involved in this question; since, if we are
'the victims of appearances, there can be no truth,
'or we are not to be hunters after it as Plato, Les-
'sing, and Sir William Hamilton say we are, it is
'worthy of all investigation what this connection of
'Science and Being involves; what those eternal ne-
'cessary laws and principles are which we must con-
'fess, though we cannot arrive at them through our
'consciousness, and though that cannot be the crite-
'rion of them.' Out of this examination numerous
results have followed. It led Schelling, in his later
days, to a recognition of the Christian revelation and
the Christian mysteries. Hegel is represented by his
opponents and by one class of his followers, as having been led by it into pure Negation. Some of his
disciples, on the other hand, maintain that they can
accept just those assertions of our creed which
Schleiermacher cast aside because they did not meet
his consciousness; these commending themselves to
the Reason which asks for that which is in itself, not
merely for that which is relative to us.

Whether Hegel's Logic must stop at the discovery
of a void of Nothingness,—whether it only leaves a
blank, which a Revelation of God would fill, whether
it offers excuses for rejecting the actual appearance
of the Son of God in the likeness of sinful flesh,
or only declares that that likeness cannot be an adaptation to certain notions and conceptions of ours,

—must have been a manifestation of the Eternal and Infinite Being as He is,—are questions which I am quite incompetent to settle, and which I do not think concern us greatly. I am quite sure that Mr. Mansel has not settled them in his Lectures. I am quite sure that he has done nothing to assist his hearers in settling them. He has taken a course which combines, it seems to me, the greatest possible amount of injustice to the persons he was attacking, with the greatest possible mischief to those who were hearing him. He has extracted passages from Hegel; from an orthodox representative of his school, Marheinecke; from that disciple of his who is notorious for his negative criticisms on the Gospels, Strauss. He knew that no one of these passages would convey any meaning to ninety-nine out of a hundred of the assembly which was gathered around him. He knew that some would be exceedingly pleased with themselves at their own freedom from such incomprehensible wickedness; that a great number would only be restrained by the decorum of a church from bursting into laughter. And this appeal to the very vulgarest feelings of young men is the Lecturer's method of leading them to think with reverence of our Lord's Incarnation—for that is the subject to which these extracts refer! If a similar experiment was made before a German audience,—I do not say upon any nonsense of mine, which would be at once dismissed as ignorant John-Bullism, but

upon Mr. Mansel himself, with his great metaphysical
acumen and undoubted knowledge,—if a body of students at Berlin or Heidelberg were entertained with
excerpta from the Bampton Lectures, the Professor
interspersing them with witticisms of his own about
'profound riddles,' 'grandiloquent obscurity,' 'a literal translation being too ludicrous for the occasion'
—might the result have been altogether different?
And would not Mr. Mansel anticipate, as some compensation for the ill-bred contempt of the class generally, that a few of the more earnest might be driven,
by the manifest injustice of that mode of exhibiting
him, to an actual study of his work? I may doubt
whether the addiction of a German student to Mr.
Mansel would profit him much more than an addiction of English students to Hegel, Marheinecke, or
Strauss. But I hint at the probable consequences of
an unfair mode of treating one or the other.

I have said, however, and I repeat it, I do not feel
myself in the least competent to pronounce between
the Christian and the Atheistic Hegelians. For those
who have leisure to investigate the subject it may
have much interest. Our business is to take care
that we are not cheated of what is necessary to our
English faith and English practice, either by Germans or by the impugners of Germans. If what I
have said in this Letter is true, Mr. Mansel is striking
through them at us. He is robbing us of principles
which we have found necessary for honest action,

that he may throw us back upon rules which we have
found utterly ineffectual. He wishes to shut us up in
Consciousnesses, in which those who have had most
of them have discovered that they cannot be shut up.
In the following sentence we reach the climax of his
doctrine.

" Action, and not knowledge, is man's destiny and
" duty in this life; and his highest principles, both
" in philosophy and in religion, have reference to
" this end. But it does not follow, on that account,
" that our representations are untrue, because they
" are imperfect. To assert that a representation is
" *untrue*, because it is relative to the mind of the re-
" ceiver, is to overlook the fact that truth itself is
" nothing more than a relation. *Truth and false-*
" *hood are not properties of things in themselves, but*
" *of our conceptions, and are tested, not by the com-*
" *parison of conceptions with things in themselves,*
" *but with things as they are given in some other*
" *relation.* My conception of an object of sense is
" *true*, when it corresponds to the characteristics of
" the object as I perceive it; but the perception it-
" self is equally a relation, and equally implies the
" co-operation of human faculties. Truth in relation
" to no intelligence is a contradiction in terms: our
" highest conception of absolute truth is that of truth
" in relation to all intelligences. But of the con-
" sciousness of intelligences different from our own we
" have no knowledge, and can make no application."
—(*Bampton Lectures*, 2nd ed., p. 149.)

What does this mean? 'Action is man's duty and destiny in this life.' Granted at once, 'in this life,' and, if Scripture is to be believed, in the life to come. 'And his highest principles have reference to this end.' Certainly ; he must act : therefore he wants principles to determine how he shall act; true principles, that his actions may not be false. "But it does not follow on that account, that our representations are untrue because they are imperfect." Who could have imagined that it followed, from action being our duty and destiny, 'that our representations were untrue'? What has been said about representations? Of what are they representations? But they must be imperfect because action is our duty and destiny? Why must they be imperfect, and *what* must be imperfect? Here is a labyrinth of words leading apparently to no issue. Alas ! it *is* leading to an issue. What is to be solved no one may be able to tell. But the solution is a solemn and tremendous one. '*Truth itself is nothing more than a Relation. Truth and Falsehood are properties of our Conceptions.*' These are axioms ; they do not require to be demonstrated ; we are simply to receive them. May we at least consider them? Truth is a relation. To what? Between what or whom? Or is a Relation an ultimate Fact? Is a relation that which is? For this is what Englishmen have been wont to understand by Truth. They have supposed Truth to be the thing that is; Falsehood to be the thing that is not. They have be-

lieved that each one of us stands in a relation to the
thing that is; that to break that relation is to speak
or act a lie; that to break this relation is the sin of
all sins, the misery of all miseries. This may be
what Mr. Mansel intends, when he says, Truth and
Falsehood are properties of our conceptions. I do not
say that it is not. I am utterly in the dark. But I
do say, with all emphasis, that if this is *not* what he
intends; if he takes Truth to be *not* the end for which
all other ends are to be sacrificed, and for which we
are to live and die,—Falsehood *not* to be the curse
and horror from which we are to fly at any risk to
body or soul,—he is not in sympathy with whatever
is sound in the heart of Englishmen; he is not teaching the lessons which the best English fathers demand that their children should be taught; he is not
teaching them how they are to overcome the temptations of jobbers and gamblers; he is not teaching
them how they may save their country from sinking
into the most insincere and false of all countries on
God's earth, because the one which has most sense
of the wickedness of insincerity and falsehood. A
flatterer has said that an Englishman cannot frame
his lips to a falsehood. If we believed the compliment, we should instantly prove its emptiness. The
security for speaking truth or acting truth is the
knowledge that the Spirit of Lies is at every moment
seeking to make us forswear it; though what we forswear, or what we adhere to, if Truth and Falsehood

are properties of our conceptions, I leave those who hold that opinion to explain.

This at least I am sure of; the most simple and earnest believers among our countrymen, while they will easily admit, on Mr. Mansel's authority, that Hegel and the Germans are in some terrible manner undermining it, will say that *this* language respecting Truth at once lays the axe to the Gospel which they have received from our Lord's Apostles, and which has been confirmed to them by their own experience. They have been used to take our Lord's words literally, " *I am the Truth;*" and they have not learnt to consider Him a relation, or a property of their conceptions. They have believed that when He described the Comforter whom He would send from the Father, as the Spirit of Truth, He was not speaking of a relation, or of a property of their conceptions, but of a living and personal Teacher and Guide. They have believed that when He promised that that Spirit should guide them into all Truth, and when He afterwards interpreted those words by saying, " He shall take of mine, and show it to you, because all that the Father hath is mine," He did not wish them to contemplate the Father and the Son as properties of their conceptions.

Nor can this be the faith which Mr. Mansel cherishes in his inmost heart. He has condemned other men for worshipping Abstractions. He has exclaimed with passion and vehemence, 'These are thy gods, O Philosophy; these are the Metaphysics of Salvation.' He set forth the personal life of Christ as opposed to these gods and these metaphysics in a passage of great rhetorical power.

"It is for this that we are to obliterate from our " faith that touching picture of the pure and holy " Jesus, to which mankind for eighteen centuries has " ever turned, with the devotion of man to God " rendered only more heartfelt by the sympathy of " love between man and man: which from genera- " tion to generation has nurtured the first seeds of " religion in the opening mind of childhood, by the " image of that Divine Child who was cradled in the " manger of Bethlehem, and was subject to His pa- " rents at Nazareth: which has checked the fiery " temptations of youth, by the thought of Him who " 'was in all points tempted like as we are, yet " 'without sin:' which has consoled the man strug- " gling with poverty and sorrow, by the pathetic " remembrance of Him who on earth had not where " to lay His head: which has blended into one bro- " therhood the rich and the poor, the mighty and " the mean among mankind, by the example of Him " who, though He was rich, yet for our sakes became " poor; though He was equal with God, yet took " upon Him the form of a servant: which has given " to the highest and purest precepts of morality an " additional weight and sanction, by the records of " that life in which the marvellous and the familiar

"are so strangely yet so perfectly united;—that life
"so natural in its human virtue, so supernatural in
"its divine power: which has robbed death of its
"sting, and the grave of its victory, by faith in Him
"who 'was delivered for our offences, and was raised
"again for our justification:' which has ennobled and
"sanctified even the wants and weaknesses of our
"mortal nature, by the memory of Him who was
"an hungered in the wilderness and athirst upon the
"cross; who mourned over the destruction of Jeru-
"salem, and wept at the grave of Lazarus."

Yes, the personal life of Jesus has, no doubt, been
this to Christendom; is this, and far more than this,
to hundreds of thousands who would not be able to
speak of it in such words, or perhaps in any words
at all. But what interpretation has Christendom
given of the exceeding worth and preciousness of this
life to us? It has said that He of whom we read in
the Gospels is the Head of a body, of which we are
members; that this Life is that from which our life
is derived. It has said that this is the life which was
with the Father, and has been manifested to us. The
humble Christian who has accepted the doctrine of
the God-Manhood of Christ, as our creeds set it forth,
has not been careful to prove how many men were
not blessed by that Life, how many men were not
within the scope of that divine fullness. He has been
sure that he was not worthy to partake of it. He
has been sure only that to know the God in whom

this Life dwells is to have Eternal Life. He has
said in his weakness and nothingness, when the wickedness of his heels was compassing him about,—
'When I wake up, I shall find that this is the God
'I have waited for; I shall behold Him, and not
another. I believe that He who is Truth and no
'Lie, has revealed Himself to me in the Person of
'His only-begotten Son,—not some poor imperfect
'representation of Himself, such as He pleases I
'should think to be like Him. Therefore I can trust
'Him, knowing what He is; therefore I can keep
'myself from idols, and can learn to hate all false
'ways as He hates them.'

Let us consider then what we have been learning
from this Lecture.

(1.) It has been a great point with Mr. Mansel to
maintain that the laws which regulate religious
thought, must be the same with those which regulate
our thoughts on all other subjects. The point is established. In all other subjects the most serious and
practical people have discovered a necessity for transgressing the limits which he would impose upon
thought. From no ambition of being sublime; from
no admiration of foreigners; from the obligation to
act; from the determination not to let theory interfere with action, the necessity has arisen. (2) He
has taken great pains to show us that our finite intellects can never be the measure of the Infinite. The
maxim is established; it is one to start from. And

because the finite cannot be the measure of the infinite,—because our conceptions can never be the measure of that which is,—because those conceptions will lead us only to the apparent, therefore we need that which shall be the measure of our finite thought, which shall lift us above our conceptions, which shall bring us into contact with that which our conceptions are feeling after, but cannot reach. (3) He has shown us that a mere negation, such as is expressed by the word Infinite, can never content a creature who needs what is positive, living, personal, to rest upon. We heartily sympathize with the observation. For Infinite, let us substitute the word which is so dear to St. Paul and St John. Let us speak of the Eternal. Let us distinguish, with St. Paul, between the things that are seen, which are temporal, and the things that are not seen, which are eternal. Let us speak not of knowing the Infinite, but of knowing Him who is from the beginning, Him who was and is and is to come. So we shall be in exact harmony with the teaching of Scripture; so shall we avoid mere speculations about that which is at a distance from us; so we shall be brought to ask for that which is the ground of our own being; for that Rock on which we and the Universe and resting. (4) Mr. Mansel quotes a beautiful passage from Hooker in this Lecture, one from Augustine in the next, both of which indicate what deep awe they had of the Being in whom they were living and moving and having their being; how, as one worthy to stand beside them, our holy and admirable Leighton, expresses it, 'The posts of the door of the spiritual temple moved at the voice of Him that cried.' Such passages might have been multiplied indefinitely; none would have been more to the purpose than the well-known soliloquy in the fifth book of Hooker respecting the Eucharist. They should be read and re-read, that we may feel how true the saying is, that ' those who know most of God, and trust most in His love, will fear Him most;' how impossible it is to cultivate the fear of God in any sense in which the Scriptures speak of it, if we regard Him as a distant, unknown Being whose Nature and Character we cannot enter into, or partake of; how certainly, if we entertain that opinion, our fear will be taught us by the precepts of men; how certainly it will alternate between the sentiment of slaves towards a cruel Taskmaster, and that of idolaters who have made their own Gods, and therefore feel—as the Greeks did about their heroes, as the Italians do about their saints—that they have a right to scold them and scoff at them ; how truly the words of Job express the whole difference between the mere traditional homage, and that which comes from actual discovery. *" I have heard of Thee by the hearing of the ear, but now my eye seeth Thee.* WHEREFORE *I abhor myself, and repent in dust and ashes."* (5) Mr. Mansel offers many admonitions to his youthful auditors, concern-

ing the dangers to which they are exposed from the
assaults of false Philosophy. The warnings are worthy
of all heed. You and I have need to lay them deeply
to heart. Leighton, in more than one passage of his
lectures to the Edinburgh students, warns them that
the philosophers, though they occasionally use phrases
which point to something higher, would, in general,
make them content with their own narrow and limited
thoughts, would hinder them from thirsting for the
Eternal Good which alone can satisfy them. I am
convinced that this is the danger of which young
men most need to be warned. While they are seeking for *the* good,—for the Eternal Truth,—they may
commit thousands of mistakes; their mistakes will
become part of their discipline. When they suppose
it is impossible for man to rise above himself, they
inevitably become poor and grovelling in their aims,
self-conceited, contemptuous. (6) In one passage,
Mr. Mansel speaks of young students parting 'with
their wedding-garment of Faith.' Of course he does
not use such language lightly, or merely as a phrase
of rhetoric. The wedding-garment in Scripture describes what is most deep and real—our union to
Christ, our adoption to be members of His body.
Surely a young man who has been told when he was
a child, that this is his state, cannot be too earnestly
exhorted not to deem lightly of it. To preserve his
wedding-garment, he need not shut himself out from
the world, or any of its thoughts, experiences, tempta-

tions; it will preserve him amidst them. But if he forgets that he is united to Christ in order that he may seek the things that are above, where Christ sitteth at the right-hand of God—the 'eternal things,' 'the knowledge of Him who has called him to glory and virtue,'—is not the garment cast off? is not the marriage-vow broken?

Faithfully yours,

F. D. M.

P. S. One of the passages in Leighton to which I referred occurs in Prælection xvii., p. 121 (Scholefield): "Eatenus quidem probandi sunt (philosophi), quod ab externis animum ad se revocant; sed in hoc deficiunt, quod intro ad se reversum altius non dirigunt nec *ut supra se ascendat*, docent."

LETTER IX.

———◆———

THE SIXTH LECTURE.—CHRISTIAN MYSTERIES.— THE TRINITY.—NATURE OF THE APOLOGY.—EFFECTS OF IT.—THE APPROACHING CRISIS.—THE TWO NATURES.—MIRACLES.

My dear Sir,

The sixth Lecture of Mr. Mansel is occupied (1) with a discussion of the Christian Mysteries, the Trinity, and the Union of two Natures in Christ; (2) with the questions of a Special Providence and of Miracles. The following passage will explain to you the method of the whole Lecture.

"The Principle of Causality, the father, as it has "been called, of metaphysical science, is to the philo- "sopher what the belief in the existence of God is "to the theologian. Both are principles inherent "in our nature, exhibiting, whatever may be their "origin, those characteristics of universality and cer- "tainty which mark them as part of the inalienable "inheritance of the human mind. Neither can be "reduced to a mere logical inference from the facts

" of a limited and contingent experience. Both are
" equally indispensable to their respective sciences :
" without Causation, there can be no Philosophy ;
" as without God there can be no Theology. Yet to
" this day, while enunciating now, as ever, the funda-
" mental axiom, that for every event there must be
" a *Cause*, Philosophy has never been able to deter-
" mine what Causation is ; to analyze the elements
" which the causal nexus involves ; or to show by
" what law she is justified in assuming the universal
" postulate upon which all her reasonings depend.
" The Principle of Causality has ever been, and pro-
" bably ever will be, the battle-ground on which, from
" generation to generation, Philosophy has struggled
" for her very existence in the death-gripe of Scepti-
" cism ; and at every pause in the contest, the answer
" has been still the same : ' We *cannot* explain it, but
" we *must* believe it.' Causation is not the mere
" invariable association of antecedent and consequent :
" we feel that it implies something more than this
" Yet, beyond the little sphere of our own volitions,
" what more can we discover ? and within that sphere,
" what do we discover that we can explain ? The
" unknown something, call it by what name you will,
" —power, effort, tendency,—still remains absolutely
" concealed, yet is still conceived as absolutely indis-
" pensable. Of Causality, as of Deity, we may almost
" say, in the emphatic language of Augustine, ' Cujus
" nulla scientia est in anima, nisi scire quomodo eum

" nesciat.' "—(*Bampton Lectures,* 2nd ed., pp. 172, 173.)

Thus, you see, these awful subjects are to be treated as questions between the Philosopher on the one side, and the Christian Theologian on the other. Mr. Mansel holds a brief for the latter. If any objection is alleged by the Philosopher against any doctrine of our Creeds, it is to be answered by saying, " There is " a similar objection which applies just as strongly " against you." Mr. Mansel does not shrink from the most startling statement of his design. " The " belief in the existence of God is to the Theologian " what the belief in the existence of Causality is to " the Philosopher." Each demands the respective belief for his respective science; each—this is the inference—is equally baffled when he pretends to know anything of that which he demands. It is well to understand and remember that the question of the Being of God is thus treated, because we shall be better prepared for that which follows.

The controversy respecting the Many and the One, I need not tell you, has been a wearisome enough controversy in the Schools. But need I tell you also that these words express a profound difficulty to the wayfarer? Every man who finds himself the member of a family must grapple with it. He must speak of his family as One; he must feel it to be One; you contradict his conscience and his reason if you tell him that it is not one; you make him do unloving and lying acts if you persuade him to act as if it were not one. Yet he knows and feels continually that he is a distinct man, that he has a life of his own, a responsibility of his own; you contradict his reason and conscience if you tell him that his personal existence is swallowed up in the existence of his family, or that his brother's is, or his sister's, or his father's, or his mother's. You lead him into vile acts if you tempt him to act upon this maxim, or if you sanction him in requiring the other members of his family to act upon it. Here is the problem of the One and the Many thrust upon every man, woman, and child. The more we know of families, the more we know of ourselves, the more we know what a problem it is; what the effort of solving it is; how it springs up afresh at every turn and corner of our history; how little it has to do with distinctions of wealth and poverty, of learning or ignorance. Moral evils mingle with this problem, and add fresh complications to it. But no mere denunciation of those evils in others can settle this question; the triumph over them in ourselves only contributes to that result by making us less rash and impatient in assuming our first conclusions to be right, more willing to await the discoveries that may scatter them and satisfy us.

This problem of the Many and the One, which is thus forced upon us by our earliest domestic experience, becomes again the problem of our life as citizens of a State. Mr. Mansel and the Logicians have

a short and easy way of settling it in this form, by
assuring us *ex cathedrâ* that the State or the Nation is merely a conception of ours; it is not a reality at all. When they have settled what reality is
—when they have put it "under its proper notion,"
—we may be glad of their help. At present we must
be content to believe, as our fathers believed before
us, as those men who are called patriots believed,
that a Country, or Nation, or State, is something,
which it is worth while to live for and suffer for.
And if that is so, if the Unity of the Nation is not
a fiction, but the very reverse of a fiction,—then to
know how that Unity may co-exist with the distinctions of the different persons of whom the Nation consists,—rather, to find how it comes to pass that one is
essential to the other, that without a set of distinct
persons, there is not and cannot be a living united
Nation, while yet that distinctness, that personality,
seems always threatening to break up the Unity,—this
must be the great practical problem, not only for the
Statesman, not only for the Historian, but for the
inhabitant of every land such as ours professes to be.

Most especially does the problem of the One and
the Many appear in all its fearful significance, in all
its fullness of promise and hope, to the Churchman,
to him who has to deal with the Unity of Human
Society, as composed of different tribes, and tongues,
and nations. The problem meets us in the upper
room of the Temple on the day of Pentecost; it

pursues us though the Apostolical History and the
Apostolical Epistles ; it starts forth full-armed in the
Apocalypse ; it is the problem which the Roman Eagle
and the Cross discussed in words and at stakes in the
first ages; it is that which the armies of the Cross
and the Crescent debated through the mediæval period; it has been the question of Imperial and Papal
rulers; of both with the Protestant nations. Papists,
Imperialists, dogmatic Protestants, are wrestling about
it now with those who speak of a Humanity that is to
supersede Families, Nations, Churches, and to create
a God out of itself; and with those who say that the
Union of the Father and the Son, in One Spirit, is
the foundation of Families, Nations, Churches.

There having been in all ages, there being pre-eminently in our own, this profound meaning in that
question of the Many and the One for human creatures, any indication on the part of Philosophers, that
they are occupied with it, that they cannot evade it,
should be welcomed as a proof that they are coming
into contact with our actual necessities, and that they
cannot merely think and speak as Schoolmen. And
if they not only give this promising sign, but confess
that they cannot find the solution which they want
of the human problem, without venturing into the
region of the divine,—that there must be a passage
from one to the other,—surely this should be hailed
as one of the proofs that the occupation of the Theologian is not gone; that those who have affirmed such

a connection, have not followed a cunningly devised fable. And might not the Theologian himself gain something from the discovery that he is not engaged with phrases and formulas; that he also stands in a direct relation with the life and needs of man? If he perceives that the Philosopher is trying again to find a mere formal explanation of a real perplexity, he will be right to point out the vanity of that experiment; that so he may explain more clearly how the divine principle which he is maintaining, is the substitute for that explanation.

Read over and consider the following passage :—

" From the fundamental doctrine of Religion in
" general, let us pass on to that of Christianity in
" particular. ' The Catholic Faith is this : that we
" worship one God in Trinity, and Trinity in Unity.'
" How, asks the objector, can the One be Many, or
" the Many one? or how is a distinction of Persons
" compatible with their perfect equality ? It is not
" a contradiction to say, that we are compelled by
" the Christian Verity to acknowledge every Person
" by Himself to be God and Lord ; and yet are for-
" bidden by the Catholic Religion to say, There be
" three Gods, or three Lords.

" To exhibit the philosophical value of this ob-
" jection, we need only make a slight change in the
" language of the doctrine criticized. Instead of a
" Plurality of Persons in the Divine Unity, we have
" only to speak of a Plurality of Attributes in the

" Divine Essence. How can there be a variety of At-
" tributes, each infinite in its kind, and yet altoge-
" ther constituting but one Infinite? or how, on the
" other hand, can the Infinite be conceived as ex-
" isting without diversity at all? We know, indeed,
" that various attributes exist in man, constituting
" in their plurality one and the same conscious self.
" Even here, there is a mystery which we cannot ex-
" plain; but the fact is one which we are compelled,
" by the direct testimony of consciousness, to accept
" without explanation. But in admitting, as we are
" compelled to do, the coexistence of many attributes
" in one person, we can conceive those attributes only
" as distinct from each other, and as limiting each
" other. Each mental attribute is manifested as a
" separate and determinate mode of consciousness,
" marked off and limited, by the very fact of its ma-
" nifestation as such. Each is developed in activi-
" ties and operations from which the others are ex-
" cluded. But this type of conscious existence fails
" us altogether, when we attempt to transfer it to
" the region of the Infinite. That there can be but
" one Infinite, appears to be a necessary conclusion
" of reason; for diversity is itself a limitation: yet
" here we have many Infinites, each distinct from the
" other, yet all constituting one Infinite, which is nei-
" ther identical with them nor distinguishable from
" them. If Reason, thus baffled, falls back on the
" conception of a simple Infinite Nature, composed

" of no attributes, her case is still more hopeless.
" That which has no attributes is nothing conceiv-
" able; for things are conceived by their attributes.
" Strip the Infinite of the Attributes by which it is
" distinguished as infinite, and the Finite of those
" by which it is distinguished as finite; and the re-
" sidue is neither the Infinite as such, nor the Finite
" as such, nor any one being as distinguished from
" any other being. It is the vague and empty con-
" ception of Being in general, which is no being in
" particular :—a shape,

> " If Shape it might be called, that shape had none
> Distinguishable in member, joint, or limb,
> Or Substance might be called, that Shadow seemed,
> For each seemed either."

" The objection, ' How can the One be many, or
" the Many One?' is thus so far from telling with
" peculiar force against the Catholic doctrine of the
" Holy Trinity, that it has precisely the same power,
" or want of power, and may be urged with precisely
" the same effect, or want of effect, against any con-
" ception, theological or philosophical, in which we
" may attempt to represent the Divine Nature and
" Attributes as infinite, or, indeed, to exhibit the In-
" finite at all. The same argument applies with equal
" force to the conception of the Absolute. If the
" Divine Nature is conceived as being nothing more
" than the sum of the Divine Attributes, it is not
" Absolute; for the existence of the whole will be

" dependent on the existence of its several parts. If,
" on the other hand, it is something distinct from
" the Attributes, and capable of existing without
" them, it becomes, in its absolute essence, an abso-
" lute void,—an existence manifested by no charac-
" teristic features,—a conception constituted by no-
" thing conceivable.

" The same principle may also be applied to ano-
" ther portion of this great fundamental truth. The
" doctrine of the Son of God, begotten of the Father,
" and yet coeternal with the Father, is in no wise
" more or less comprehensible by human reason, than
" the relation between the Divine Essence and its
" Attributes. In the order of Thought, or of Na-
" ture, the substance to which attributes belong has
" a logical priority to the attributes which exist in
" relation to it. The Attributes are attributes *of a*
" *Substance.* The former are conceived as the de-
" pendent and derived; the latter as the independent
" and original existence. Yet in the order of Time,
" (and to the order of Time all human thought is
" limited,) it is as impossible to conceive the Sub-
" stance existing before its Attributes, as the Attri-
" butes before the Substance. We cannot conceive
" a being originally simple, developing itself in the
" course of time into a complexity of attributes;
" for absolute simplicity cannot be conceived as con-
" taining within itself a principle of development,
" nor as differently related to different periods of

"time, so as to commence its development at any
"particular moment. Nor yet can we conceive the
"attributes as existing prior to the substance; for
"the very conception of an attribute implies rela-
"tion to a substance. Yet the third hypothesis, that
"of their coexistence in all time, is equally incom-
"prehensible; for this is to merge the Absolute and
"Infinite in an eternal relation and difference. We
"cannot conceive God as first existing, and then as
"creating His own attributes; for the creative power
"must then itself be created. Nor yet can we con-
"ceive the Divine Essence as constituted by the eter-
"nal coexistence of attributes; for then we have
"many Infinities, with no bond of unity between
"them. The Mystery of the Many and the One,
"which has baffled philosophy ever since philosophy
"began, meets it here, as everywhere, with its eter-
"nal riddle. Reason gains nothing by repudiating
"Revelation; for the mystery of Revelation is the
"mystery of Reason also."—(*Bampton Lectures,* 2nd
ed., pp. 174–178.)

I have not curtailed this extract, long as it is,
because I would not have you, or any reader, derive
your notion of the course of argument from my statement. The remarks I have to make upon it are very
obvious; after what has been said on the former
Lectures, they will occur to you at once. But I must
set them forth fully, that you may not accuse me of
being merely an objector.

Consider then that the Name of the Father, the Son, and the Spirit, is the Name into which an immense majority of all the children in Christendom, for at least fourteen centuries, have been baptized. Consider how it has entered into all the thought, the speech, the laws, of the most civilized nations. Consider how it was debated for centuries, and how the debates about it affected the condition of the whole Roman Empire, in the West and in the East. Consider the facts which illustrate this conflict, as they are set forth to us, not by some ecclesiastical historian, but by Gibbon. Consider how the belief in the Trinity affected and determined the whole life and thought of the centuries which compose what we call the Middle Ages. Consider how it became the subject of debate after the Reformation as it had been before, in Geneva as it was at Rome. Consider what questions it has engendered in our own land; how, in spite of the forms of our Church—which are constructed upon the acknowledgment of it, which connect it with every old psalm and modern prayer,—it almost ceased to be believed in the last century, both among Churchmen and Dissenters. Consider how that great revival of conscious faith to which I have alluded before, brought back this belief with it, and changed the character of religious feeling in England. Consider how that conscious faith nevertheless was always apt to regard this theological principle chiefly in relation to its own movements, so that it seemed as if the Divine Being were living to accomplish certain blessings for certain of His creatures. Consider what a reaction there has been against this anti-theological temper, not in Germany more than in England, not among Rationalists more than among ecclesiastical Dogmatists. Consider how, after all this conflict for sixteen or seventeen centuries, the most accomplished advocate for orthodoxy in Oxford stands forth to plead that this doctrine has not left the problem of the Many and the One in greater perplexity than former ages have left it; that if the theologian compels us to receive it, the philosopher may compel us to receive something quite as strange and monstrous! Is it really come to this? Is this the best hope that is left for those who have to fight their way through the world,—for those who had believed that there was an everlasting Name in which they could rest when they could fight no longer?

Surely the disbelievers in the doctrine of the Trinity never can have felt as much satisfaction in any of their own arguments as in this elaborate refutation of them! When they have spoken scornfully of battles about an iota,—when they have affirmed that we have substituted an unintelligible formula for great moral principles, and have forced men's assent to it, by the sacrifice of them,—when they have appealed to all the bitter persecutions that in different ages have been waged by Athanasians against Arians, by Arians against Athanasians, as evidence that

the Gospel of Peace and Goodwill has suffered from
our Creed, and that mankind would have been better
without it,—they have had a secret misgiving that
there was something behind of which they had not
taken account, some other facts besides these which
are quite as pregnant of meaning. They have been
forced to say to themselves, 'Yes! but how has the
' faith stood *in spite of* the formalism of doctors,
' the fury of persecutors, the apparent interest of
' nations, the obvious inclination of many Protestant
' Churches,—for a long time of the English,—to throw
' it overboard as a troublesome badge which might
' be exchanged for some other much less perplexing?
' Why have experiments for this purpose not been
' successful? Why was Unitarianism more popular
' and triumphant in the last century than in this?
' Why has it been shaken not merely by a more fer-
' vid belief, but by the great political and philoso-
' phical movements which seemed likely to establish
' its ascendency? Why are we less satisfied with our
' own traditions now, when the general dislike of dog-
' matism might seem to promise them a reception,—
' more uncertain about the solidity of our own nega-
' tive reasonings when they can be propounded with-
' out peril, and when there are so many discontented
' hearts ripe for shaking? May there not be some
' moral principle, may there not be some social prin-
' ciple involved in what has seemed to us a mere
' logical contradiction? Is there not a region above

2 B

'logic,—a region not of shadows but of realities,—a
'region where all these relations which exist among
'us in imperfect forms have their archetypes; where
'the full meaning of them is satisfied? Might not a
'Revelation of God be the discovery of them to us?
'May not that which we have deemed an exclusive
'opinion reconcile actual beliefs that have been pos-
'sessing men in all ages? May it not point to a
'Unity deeper than the one which we have made
'our watchword?'

Such questions do present themselves to serious
men whose education and habits of mind put them
most out of sympathy with our confessions. Amidst
the hot and cold fits which alternate in the experience of every man who is occupied by them, how
certainly will these Bampton Lectures be received by
him as a great witness in favour of his early conclusions, as a peremptory check upon all the doubts that
had been awakened in him as to their possible soundness! 'Here is *the* orthodox authority, the latest
'Apologist—charged with a weight of Oxford and
'Edinburgh learning,—bringing us the last result of
'of both. He has put forth a defence of the Trinity,
'which satisfies equally the doctors of the English
'Sorbonne and the representatives of public opinion
'in the religious newspapers and magazines. And
'how does he contemplate the doctrine? Not the
'least as involving any great moral principles; prin-
'ciples that satisfy the reason, he says we must dis-

' pense with. Not the least as connected with the
' life or history of Mankind. Simply as an opinion;
' very startling and puzzling, no doubt, but not more
' startling and puzzling than certain opinions of phi-
' losophers. Our fathers at least taught us to believe
' in a God, and to call him Father. This Oxford
' schoolman appears to cut the ground even for that
' faith from under our feet; but he urges us to accept
' a certain theological tenet respecting the Being we
' worship, because we really can know nothing of
' Him; because as He is infinite, and we finite, it is
' impossible for us to say that this representation of
' Him may not be as near the truth as any other.
' Certainly there was need of persecution or bribes to
' persuade people of the duty of accepting a doctrine
' which by the showing of its defender could attach
' itself to no deep or inward conviction! If bribes
' and persecution should both fail, what will become
' of it?'

Perhaps this is a result which Mr. Mansel may
contemplate with more philosophical indifference than
I can. Is he prepared also for another? Has he
reflected on the kind of feelings with which the young
Churchmen he was addressing would henceforth be
tempted to regard the Name with which they were
sealed in their infancy, in which they have declared
their belief day after day? Can one imagine anything
sadder than the dreariness of heart which will come
to some devout student, who has thought that the

Creed must be everything or nothing, that it must declare what are the pillars of his own being and of the Universe, or else be a mere school quibble, when he finds that it is to be maintained and held fast precisely because by the constitution of our minds we are incapable of refuting it? Yes, I can imagine something sadder still. Jeremy Taylor says, after his wonderful catalogue of the ills that flesh is heir to, " But a careless, merry sinner is worse than all that." I believe that among Mr. Mansel's auditors there will have been not a few on whom his words will have acted as a most soothing lullaby; who will have wrapped themselves in comfortable thankfulness that they were not Rationalists, Spiritualists, or even as that German; who will have rejoiced to think that they did not trouble themselves about eternal things which are out of men's reach, like Puritans and Methodists; who will proclaim that they accept Christianity in the lump, and so are not impeded by any of its little details in thinking and doing what they list. Such men, I believe, do more to lower the moral tone and moral practice of England than all sceptics and infidels together. As far as they themselves are concerned, I should think their self-contentment was worse than all that pain and restlessness which some of their companions will have experienced as they listened to these logical demonstrations.

But the more gloomy these consequences appear to me, the more certain I feel that they will only be temporary, and that good, even the highest good, is to come out of a course of reasoning which in itself I regard as pernicious. If there has been, as nearly all of us feel that there has been, a fearful amount of hardness and cruelty in the methods by which Churchmen in all ages have pleaded for their Creeds; if this hardness and cruelty seem to have been always closely connected with the feeling that they were *their* Creeds, the utterance of *their* opinions, which were therefore to be defended by such weapons as they could call into play, swords when they could be had, the bitterness of words when these were wanting; if one finds—mixed with this belief that no schemes for vindicating the doctrines of the Creed were too savage—a belief that the Name which the Creed uttered was the expression of the Perfect All-embracing Charity; if with that zeal for *our* opinion has been combined a rooted conviction that it was not an opinion at all for which we are fighting, but for Him before whom the angels veil their faces, for Him who knoweth our thoughts long before, for Him whom we are permitted to know because He has Himself removed the veil which conceals Himself from us, and has met us in that Son, by whom He created the world, in whom all things consist, who is the Light of every man; if there have been these anomalies, practical not logical anomalies, in the life of Christendom, in the life of each one of us,—must there not come a time of sifting and separation, a

time when God will burn up our chaff with unquench-
able fire, that he may gather His wheat into the gar-
ner? Mr. Mansel is the last, the ablest, the most
ultra defender of the Trinitarian dogma simply as a
dogma. No one before him has so completely exhausted the air about it; no one has so completely
reduced it to a formula. Unless some one had appeared to do that, some one to startle us with the
question, '*Is that what you mean? Is that what you
believe in?*' we might have gone on for some time
longer halting between the most opposite feelings and
convictions. Now—thanks be to God!—we shall be
obliged to speak. I say for one, ' I am certain Atha-
' nasius did not fight against the world for a Dogma;
' I am certain I was not baptized into a Dogma. I
' am certain that Christ did not send forth His dis-
' ciples to baptize all nations into a Dogma. Atha-
' nasius said that he wrestled for the Name of the
' Living God, which the Logicians would contract into
' a notion, robbing the poor and needy of that which
' had been revealed to them. The minister said that
' he baptized me into that Name. Our Lord bade
' His Apostles baptize all Nations into that Name.
' I believe it to be the Name on which I stand as a
' Member of the Universal Family in Heaven and
' Earth. I believe it is the Name which sustains that
' Universal Family. I thank Him in whom I believe
' that He has given different ages such a sense of the
' sacredness and importance of that Name. I thank

' Him that He has allowed it to be a subject of such
' infinite controversies, since so it has seemed good
' in His sight. I am sure they have all contributed
' to the discovery of His truth and the exposure of
' our falsehood and ignorance. I confess to Him that
' as the Israelites sinned against that name of the
' God of Abraham, and that name of the I AM, which
' was revealed to *them*, not owning Him to be the
' ground and ruler of their Family and their Nation,
' not obeying His laws and being the instruments of
' His purposes, but setting up gods of their own, gods
' after their own likeness, and making them their lords
' —afterwards, when this sin had been grievously pu-
' nished, using his own Holy Name and the covenant
' that they were to be a blessing to all the families of
' the earth as an excuse for self-exaltation, and for
' contempt of all families of the earth but their own,
' —so have we, the members of the Universal Church,
' sinned more grievously, first, in setting up creatures
' of our own race and visible things as objects of the
' reverence and honour which are owing to Him in
' whom we live and move and are ; then turning His
' all-uniting, all-loving Name, which we were to pro-
' claim to all people, into an excuse for the glorifica-
' tion of our own opinion. Which evil if He winked
' at in the ages that are past, I am sure He is now
' calling us all everywhere to repent of, because He is
' giving clear tokens that He will judge us by that
' Son of Man whom He has set over us ; that He will

' call us to account for the knowledge we have pos-
' sessed and the privileges we have abused; and that
' if we have been found unfaithful stewards of His
' mysteries, He will discover them to other tribes of
' the earth, who cry for that revelation of the Unseen
' and Eternal which we have made light of, and at last
' have denied that we possess.'

To this issue, I believe, Mr. Mansel's apologies
are helping to bring us, and therefore I cannot but
trust they will do an important service for the Church,
though not, perhaps, exactly what their author or his
admirers have looked for. I am less anxious to follow him into the second topic of the sixth Lecture,—
the Union of the two Natures in Christ,—because I
have spoken so much on the subject already, directly
in my fourth Letter, incidentally in every other. But
I have a special reason for quoting the following passage, which I am sure is a favourite one with Mr.
Mansel's disciples.

" Let Religion begin where it will, it must begin
" with that which is above Reason. What then do
" we gain by that parsimony of belief, which strives
" to deal out the Infinite in infinitesimal fragments,
" and to erect the largest possible superstructure of
" deduction upon the smallest possible foundation of
" faith? We gain just this; that we forsake an in-
" comprehensible doctrine, which rests upon the word
" of God, for one equally incomprehensible, which
" rests upon the word of a man. Religion, to be a

" relation between God and man at all, must rest on
" a belief in the Infinite, and also on a belief in the
" Finite; for if we deny the first, there is no God;
" and if we deny the second, there is no Man. But
" the coexistence of the Infinite and the Finite, in
" any manner whatever, is inconceivable by reason;
" and the only ground that can be taken for accept-
" ing one representation of it, rather than another, is
" that one is revealed, and another is not revealed.
" We may seek as we will for a ' Religion within the
" limits of the bare Reason;' and we shall not find
" it; simply because no such thing exists; and if we
" dream for a moment that it does exist, it is only
" because we are unable or unwilling to pursue rea-
" son to its final consequences. But if we do not,
" others will; and the system which we have raised
" on the shifting basis of our arbitrary resting-place,
" waits only till the wind of controversy blows against
" it, and the flood of unbelief descends upon it, to
" manifest itself as the work of the ' foolish man
" which built his house upon the sand.'"—(*Bampton
Lectures*, 2nd ed., pp. 182, 183.)

This passage is a reply to a treatise of Kant, or
rather to the title of a treatise of Kant, ' *Religion,
within the bounds of mere Reason.*' I need hardly
say, that the ordinary Englishman would attach very
little sense to this title. He would not know what
Kant intended by the pure reason. He would only
have a vague, hazy impression of what Kant intended

by Religion, possibly of what he intends by it him-self. But he would have little doubt that he under-stood Mr. Mansel's first sentence perfectly. If he were an earnest, devout man, a man with a strong "re-ligious consciousness," he would probably exclaim, 'I am sure the Lecturer is right. I am sure that 'when I believe in Christ, I rise above my reason, 'my thoughts, myself. I leave the appearances and 'fantasies which have deluded me in the world; I 'enter into converse with divine realities; my faith 'brings me directly into contact with them. Does 'the German philosopher deny this? How little he 'can have known of the Scriptures, or of the powers 'of the unseen world!' Such a person, you see, this religious Englishman, will admire Mr. Mansel's lan-guage, and sympathize with it, because he gives it that sense which the Bampton Lectures are written to prove is an untenable and impossible sense. Our old English poet says,—

> " Except he can
> Above himself erect himself, how poor a thing is man !"

The moral of the Bampton Lectures is, 'If he tries by one means or another above himself to erect him-self, what a fool is man !' I am not now arguing the point, Which is right? I am merely showing that Daniel expressed what is the ordinary conviction among pious people who are not philosophers; I am showing how much Mr. Mansel will owe the charac-ter which he obtains among English believers, as a defender of the Faith against Germans, to an entire misapprehension of his object; how far more they would disagree with him than with Kant, if they understood the purpose of either.

So the same Englishman would respond as eagerly to the second sentence in this extract, even if he could not construe satisfactorily every phrase in it. *" What do we gain by that parsimony of faith which strives to deal out the Infinite in infinitesimal fragments, and to erect the largest possible superstructure of deductions, upon the smallest possible foundation of faith ?"* 'That sounds very grand language,' the reader will exclaim. 'And surely it *is* miserable par- ' simony not to trust a Being who has made known ' His Name to us, who has shown himself to be our ' Protector and Deliverer, righteous in all His ways, ' holy in all His works. If we do not trust Him, we ' shall be thrown back upon a trust in what is not ' true, not trustworthy,—in enchanters and miracle- ' workers, in notions of our own minds, in finite and ' feeble creatures like ourselves.'

How painful to Mr. Mansel must be such approbation as this ! He is aware that the faith for which he is contending, is not to be parsimonious, simply because it is beyond the region of all knowledge, because " the coexistence of the Infinite and the Finite in any manner whatsoever, is inconceivable by the reason," and because, since " Religion" demands their coexistence, faith is to admit it ungrudgingly, in any manner whatsoever.

This principle is affirmed in the next clause of the sentence. *" The only ground that can be taken for accepting one representation of it rather than another, is that one is revealed, and the other not revealed."* This statement also, taken by itself, would at once receive the applause of those who feel as English Christians generally feel. They would say, ' Unless ' God had revealed Himself to us in His only-begot- ' ten Son, how could we have discovered the relation ' which exists between us and Him ? We might have ' dreamt that we had a Father ; we could never have ' known that we had access to that Father, that He ' felt to us as children, if there had not been the ' revelation of the Son of God and the Son of Man, ' in whom He knows us, and in whom we may know ' Him. Yes, as Mr. Mansel says, it must be all ' revelation.' But the agreement here is even more hollow than in the other cases ; the difference between those who use the common phrases is wider. The ordinary British Christian accepts the Bible with unbounded thankfulness, as discovering to him the ground upon which he actually stands, the relation between the eternal Father and His family on earth, which existed in the Person of the only-begotten Son before the worlds were, and which was manfested in the fullness of time, when that Son, who was the brightness of the Father's glory and the express image of His Person, took flesh and dwelt among men, and when having by Himself purged our sins He sat down at the right-hand of the Majesty on high. Am I wrong in saying that this is the inmost, deepest faith of those who grow up under the influence of our prayers and sacraments, and who find in the Scriptures their daily food? Am I wrong in saying that they would feel the most utter revolting if they were told that any representation of the union between the Infinite and the Finite is just as suitable to the human constitution, is in itself just as reasonable, as that which they have believed to be the ground of all things in earth and heaven?

Mr. Mansel will say, however, ' I am not writing ' for simple Christians, but for those whose minds have ' been perplexed by philosophical doubts and specula- ' tions.' I apprehend that what is truth for the one is truth for the other. The union of the two natures in our Lord is either a mere notion or dogma contained in a book, or it is the deepest reality. It is either a mere representation of the union of the Finite and Infinite, to be accepted because we can know nothing about that union; or it is the actual discovery of what the Eternal Being is in the Person of a Man. Again and again I must repeat this proposition; again and again I must affirm that for every common wayfarer it is a question of life and death. But I am quite willing to start from the other ground. These statements are expressly intended for those who are perplexed with doubts about the Christian faith, with doubts even about the Being whom they are to wor-

ship, or whether there is any such Being. Shall I
trace the rise of some of these doubts? For Mr.
Mansel has not stated them; he is apparently ignorant of them. He has attributed a number of expressions which he has quoted from English writers
of our day to a craving for the license of German
Rationalism, to an impatience of faith, when I am
well persuaded that they have sprung from the impatience of a very hard Rationalism in which they have
felt themselves .pent up, from a desire for something
which they can believe.

I endeavoured to show you in my last Letter how
some of those who had felt their own personal affiance in Christ most strongly, who had owned Him
as their Deliverer and Reconciler, had perceived the
need of a foundation for that consciousness which was
liable to many fluctuations, and which could never be
its own foundation. The most vigorous of these men
became stern Calvinists. That which remained the
same amidst all their changes of feeling was the absolute will and purpose of God; to rely upon that was
to be at rest. They did rely upon it. They did find
rest in it. Yes; and they derived from it the power
to act bravely and nobly. How did they find out
what this Will or purpose was? That which made
them righteous they were sure must be righteous.
That which raised them out of their sin must be the
foe of sin. So long as they were only accounting for
what they found in themselves, here was, it seems

to me, a grand and a safe theology. But when they passed beyond themselves, the theology had to undergo terrible alterations. That Will which chose men in Christ before the worlds were, to be holy and unblamable in love, became emphatically a Self-will. Its absolute right to choose some and reject others was more and more regarded as its fundamental characteristic. When the first generation of those excellent men to whom this theology was really an interpretation of what they had experienced had passed away,—when it was transmitted as a formal bequest to men who cared for it chiefly as an interpretation of the condition of the world,—it assumed a horror which must be felt before it can be described. And yet the attempts to mitigate it by feeble Arminian or semi-Calvinistical statements, were equally offensive to the logical intellect and the practical conscience. They were felt to be poor compromises that could never clear away any actual difficulty, or be any source of action. Men might acquiesce in them just because they did not care for them; because they found a real principle upon which they could stand, and which had the smallest possible connection with the notion that pretended to represent it.

Those who could not acquiesce in these middle ways, these nothings of popular or scholastic dogmatism, began to ask whether there was not some basis to be found somewhere that was not merely arbitrary, or, as Mr. Mansel expresses it more diffusely, "*not raised on the shifting base of an arbitrary resting-place.*" Possibly that basis might be found in a religion within the bounds of the pure reason. It was surely worth while to inquire. I believe, as far as I understand what that religion is, that they will not find what they seek there, that they will never be satisfied with any religion at all, or aught save a living God ; that they will find the pure reason to be the purified eye of the spirit which sees Him, and that they will not desire to enclose Him within its limits more than they would enclose the sun within the limits of the bodily eye. Nevertheless I rejoice that they should make a trial which I believe will lead to this result; I rejoice that they should ask whether there is not a Will and Purpose to all Right and Good. I am sure that when they perceive there is, they will be more in harmony with their old and revered fathers than ever they were. I dare not doubt that those fathers are themselves, in various ways unknown to us, aiding them in the search. I rejoice also that they should feel that this Will to all good must stand in the closest and most intimate connection to the good will that is in them, in most direct opposition to the evil will that is in them. And seeing that I find this perfect manifestation of the Will to all Good, of the Light in which is no darkness at all, of the eternal, unchangeable, perfect Being, of the Father of our spirits, in Him who was made of a woman and died upon the cross, seeing in the union in Him of the divine nature with the human, I perceive the full relation which must exist between the Infinite and the Finite, the good in God and the good in man,—seeing that I find here a ground for each man's goodness and salvation from evil to rest upon, and at the same time a ground for all humanity to rest upon—I do believe that through all perplexities and confusions, after all attempts to eliminate the idea from the fact or to take the fact without the idea, God will bring these questioners back to the old, childlike faith in the divine humanity of Christ, and will show them and will show us that that is a rock which will not be shaken, which will prove its strength by every *'wind of controversy that blows against it and every flood of unbelief that descends upon it.'*

How much comfort these inquirers will derive from Mr. Mansel's assurance that they can find out nothing about the Infinite and the Eternal, that the Ruler of all may be the mere sovereign they have been told He is, that the Incarnation of Christ affords no clue to His inmost Nature, I leave you to judge. He will answer, perhaps, that he never dreamed of giving them comfort, he wished to teach them their absurdity. No doubt; but what I contend is that it is our absurdity as well as theirs. It is the absurdity of our English faith, of our English education. It is the absurdity of our Prayers and our Creeds; it is the absurdity not of the German national character,—

2 c

of that which is said to be ' savage in reason ' and to
' feed on chimeras,'—but of that character which is
the most indifferent to theories, the most contemptuous of chimeras, under the sun. This is a point
upon which I must dwell a little longer, because it
connects this subject with the one which comes next
under Mr. Mansel's review.

While I was tracing the steps by which men
whose minds are especially *Christian* have been led
to seek for a Divine and Eternal Will, as the root
of their faith and hope, I could not help suspecting
that some would say, ' There are such persons, as-
' suredly; we have met with them; they form a re-
' markable element in modern English society. But
' we cannot say that they are *characteristic* of Eng-
' land; their faith and experience, though most real,
' and touching at certain points on what we all are
' or would wish to be, we suspect are alien from our
' national habits. John Bull did not look kindly
' upon them formerly. Even now he welcomes them
' rather surlily; he accepts them as the antagonists of
' another class of feelings which he dislikes more.
' He is willing to encourage the Methodist or the
' Calvinist against the Romanist; that is all that can
' be said.'

Such statements as these have a meaning, though
it is one which is liable to great perversion. The
purely Christian movement of the last century—I
mean that which led to the sense of the individual

relation of men to Christ—unquestionably encountered a tremendous opposition, not only from the unbelief but from the faith which had been existing
in the land previously. I use the words advisedly
There was a faith in God as a Creator, a faith in
Him as the God of Righteousness and Order, which
if not always deep, was real. It was shaken by a col-
lision with the new thoughts which seemed to start
from a different ground, to begin from the sense of
personal evil and the need of personal forgiveness.
Those old convictions easily passed into a mere Physico-Theology, or into a thin modification of Unitarianism. They took no hold of actual sinners; of
human beings who wanted to find out a Father of
themselves, not a Creator of the Planets. But they
were convictions. They eagerly welcomed those arguments from Design and Adaptation which came in to
confirm their own weakness. Those who held them
were glad to acknowledge the Gospels as setting
forth the character of a Man who must have been sent
from a divine Being, must have been His chief messenger, because He was so good. They were glad to
think that He had brought adequate attestation of
His mission by doing very good and wonderful works.
The further proofs that those persons who spoke of
Him were not likely to deceive or be deceived, har-
monized all with their previous dispositions. A people used to discriminate by practical tests rogues
from honest men, valued such proofs when they were

skilfully drawn out. The direction of the thoughts
of Englishmen towards physical and mechanical studies favoured what I may call the less human side
of this Theology; their domestic habits redeemed
it from mere coldness, and led them gladly to think
of God as a Parent, even when their arguments
pointed to little more than an *Opifex mundi.*

Before I speak of the way in which this faith in a
God of Truth and Order which our fathers cherished
may be reconciled with that which appeared to strive
with it and contradict it, and how each may contribute
to our moral strength, I must show you that Mr.
Mansel is as effectually undermining the one as the
other.   If the man of individual conscious faith, when
he seeks for some foundation for that faith in a
Righteous Will which is the eternal ground of things,
is met by the announcement that he has no faculties wherewith to take cognizance of such a Being,
the man who starts from the assumption of such a
Being and thinks that he discovers corroborative evidence of His existence in Nature, is equally thrown
aback by being told that his thoughts have taken an
unlawful spring; that for his finite mind to pretend
even to make plausible guesses about the Infinite is
monstrous.   And no discourses respecting 'the personal life of Jesus' can in the very least degree fill up
the void which you have created in this man's soul.
It is the belief of an Unseen God that he has clung to
amidst all difficulty ; a God exhibited to him, in some

degree, in the Order of the Universe, in some degree
in the Order of human Life. His knowledge of Him
may be imperfect, but such as it is, he clings to it as
the best thing he has, and he hopes for more. Mr.
Mansel, coming fresh with Kant's evidence that the
arguments from Nature prove nothing but only confirm a conviction already existing, casts away with
scorn and indignation Kant's assurance that the conviction itself is of infinite value, that that is worth
all the arguments in the world. He strips the man
bare of that upon which he might ground a faith in
the God-Man, in Him who reveals the God of Order
and Righteousness. He refuses him the opportunity
of considering whether that God of Order and Righteousness could have made Himself known to a creation intended to exhibit the image of His Order and
Righteousness in another way than this. He will
not let him ask himself whether, if this Perfect Man
is the standard of good to man, he has not erred and
strayed from that standard, and whether he does not
want a Spiritual Restorer and Renovator. He cuts
the ground from under the feet of the Naturalist as
well as of the Humanist. If each is in some way
confessing a God and feeling after Him, the orthodox
believer prays him with the most vehement urgency
to desist; he is wasting his time; his business is to
acquiesce in everything that is told him, and to take
it for granted that he can know nothing. I must
say the words with all solemnity: the confirmed, self-

satisfied atheist is the one person who can receive
such tidings without a protest, with perfect complacency.

Surely those cannot, who have been taught in their
infancy that the Absolute and Eternal God has taken
them to be His own children, the members of Christ,
the inheritors of the Kingdom of Heaven.   Surely
that old English education is based not upon notions, but upon the assumption that we are actually
united to the Father of all in His Son; that He is
actually guiding us by His Spirit to a consciousness
of our own wants : at last, to a knowledge of Him
who is the satisfier of them.   Such education assumes an actual relation to be the ground of all consciousness of it ; an Actual and Living Being to be
the ground of the relation.   That assumption brings
our common human life into harmony with our life
as connected with the Kingdom of Heaven; each
illustrates the other.   The relation to the father and
the mother precedes all consciousness of it ; the father and the mother have a life of their own, besides
their relation to us.   Their feelings to us are discovered first; then we seek to be acquainted with themselves, to know their minds, characters, purposes.
That relation to a Heavenly Father, which is the
ground of our relation to them, is unfolded to us in
like manner, amidst the consciousness of disobedience,
distrust, wilfulness, forgiveness.   As the common education is pursued, we rise to the awful perception of

a personal self—of a personal existence which is not merged in our existence as brothers and sisters. The sense of a law binding our acts is awakened; the the sense of laws also which bind our speech, and which bind the things about us,—laws that we and they did not create. With that information, comes the discovery of social bonds, of ties to our fellows which our self-will is always ready to break. The higher spiritual lessons interpret these. We have ties to other men, because there is a Son of Man who unites us all together; we begin to perceive that the Lord of us and of our family must be the Lord of Nature. Then comes the rite of Confirmation, the witness of a Spirit guiding our spirit. When we are no more under the guidance of apparent, visible teachers, we are assured of the Presence of a Spirit, who will awaken our human sympathies, show us the root of them in the Will and Mind of God, who will bring us into awful communion with that Loving, Just, Self-sacrificing Will, the ground of all Love and Justice and Self-sacrifice among us.

I am not speaking of this education to those who despise it, but to those who wish us to preserve our English institutions, and to withstand all foreign innovations. To those, I would say, ' See whether it does not contain the greatest and most serious protest that can be borne against Mr. Mansel's teaching. See whether it does not lead us at every step from the notional to the actual, from phenomena to things, from rules to principles. See whether it does not lead us to seek our interpretation of the difficulties of the finite and the human, in the Infinite and Divine. See whether it does not treat the union of the infinite and the finite, the divine and human in Christ, as the foundation of our practical life.'*

The last subject discussed in this last Lecture, is the relation of special *Interpositions* to *general Laws*. The text of Mr. Mansel's observation, is a passage from Mr. Greg's 'Creed of Christendom,' in which he speaks of a belief in the efficacy of Prayer as incompatible with a deeply grounded belief in a God of Order. It would not be easy to express how much I differ from Mr. Greg's conclusion. It would not be easy to express how important I feel his premiss to be. The blank in an Englishman's mind when the sense of Order is taken from it, when he ceases to associate Order with the Being he worships, is greater than we can dream of. Atheism must enter in and take possession of that empty house. But I will speak especially in refe-

---

* A number of causes have tended to make Englishmen less attached to this education than they were. The chief I believe are, that it has been made notional by our comments when it is so essentially personal, (*What is thy Name? Who gave thee thy Name?*) and that it has been supposed to have some connection with what are called "High Church doctrines." That these doctrines put the Church before God, and suppose the Church to be our teacher respecting God, not God respecting the Church, is the real, earnest English objection to them. But they do so by turning the Creed upside down, and therefore, by changing the whole character of the Catechism. I know no greater witness against that abuse, than is to be found in them when faithfully used.

rence to the particular topic under discussion. I
should have no hopes of ever leading a man who had
been robbed of this anchor of his soul, to feel what
Prayer is, or why we are permitted and commanded
to pray. For prayer is surely a cry to the Judge of the
earth against the disorders of the earth,—to the Father
of our spirits, against the disorders of our spirits.
Because we believe that God is the enemy of such
disorders, and that it is His purpose to remove them,
—because we believe that man is both the cause of
them, and is intended to be God's instrument in removing them,—because we believe that the Son of
Man has come into the world to redress disorders,
and that in His name we have access to Him who
upholds order, therefore we have a warrant and encouragement to pray without ceasing. And secondly,
I could never hope to convince any one whom I had
robbed of this faith in a God of Order, of the end
and intent of the acts revealed in Scripture, which
we call miraculous, especially those which are attributed to our Lord, or of the difference between them
and any miracle spoken of in any Pagan, or mediæval, or modern legend. For, as I have endeavoured
to show in a sermon which accompanies these Letters, the characteristic of our Lord's acts appears to
be especially this, that they are acts for the restoration of order, not for the disturbance of it,—precisely
such acts as would show Him to be the King of Men,
the source of Life and Health to Men.

Not starting from this idea of Christ's Incarnation, —viewing it simply as a strange dogma to be received as any other representation of the relation between the finite and infinite might be received,—Mr. Mansel naturally cannot regard the miracles of our Lord in this light. And therefore it is very consistent in him to think that the more difficulties and perplexities he can throw in the way of a believer in divine Order, the more he is promoting the interests of Christianity. It is that unhappy opinion which gives his arguments all their danger. Stripped of their attraction as apologies,—exhibited as mere pleas for scepticism,—any man, with a hundredth part of Mr. Mansel's ability, would be able to expose their fallacy; the study of Butler would beget a love of Order, a belief in a Source of Order, which would make them powerless. But men whose minds are trembling in a balance, may be determined by them either to reject the Gospel as false, or to accept it as coming from some other God than Him of whom it testifies. And those who are only wanting excuses for an acquiescence that will demand of them no exercise of faith, disturb them in no evil course, rouse them to no duty, may be cast by such pleas for Christianity as these, into a deep mesmeric trance from which nothing will rouse them but the thunders of the Last Day.

Truly yours,

F. D. M.

LETTER X.

—◆—

MORALITY.—KANT.—THE HUMAN REPRESENTA-
TION OF ABSOLUTE MORALITY.—MR. MANSEL'S
METHOD OF DEALING (1) WITH THE ATONE-
MENT; (2) WITH THE DOCTRINE OF FORGIVE-
NESS; (3) WITH ETERNAL PUNISHMENT; (4)
WITH THE EXISTENCE AND IMMORTALITY OF
EVIL.

My dear Sir,

We have come to the Lecture which is to test the
soundness of all that have gone before. Mr. Mansel
cares nothing for speculation. He wishes only for
rules to guide action. Now we are to know whether
he has found them. Our subject is Christian Morals.

The Lecture begins with the old topic of Kant's
delinquency. That "inconsistency scarcely to be paralleled in the history of philosophy," of which we
have heard so often, is here held up again to still
stronger reprobation. It is a topic which causes so
much sensitiveness in Mr. Mansel that I desire to
pass it by as quickly as I can. I have said already

that I regard our interest in it as being merely this, that Kant accorded to us vulgar men, in the name of Philosophy, rights which we had always claimed for ourselves, without being able to make good our title to them by any formal proofs.

Three remarks I must make respecting the criticism on Kant in this Lecture, but they shall be brief, and they will be for the sake of Englishmen, not of Germans. (1.) Mr. Mansel appears to regard it as an especial inconsistency in the German, that the moral sense is " elevated above the conditions of " human intelligence . . . in that Philosophy which " resolves Time and Space into forms of human con- " sciousness, and limits their operation to the field " of the phenomenal and the relative." Now I apprehend that it was just because Kant had convinced himself that Time and Space are merely forms of human consciousness,—and because he was convinced that Moral Principles are *not* forms of human Consciousness,—because he had convinced himself that the understanding has only to do with the field of the phenomenal and relative, and because he was assured that Moral Principles must have to do with that which is,—that he supposed the moral sense to be above the conditions of the intellect. So doing, he maintained that identity of the Eternal with the Substantial which Theologians had always assumed ; the temporal he connected, as they are wont to do, with the changeable and the apparent. Whether he was

right or wrong, I cannot see the inconsistency.
(2.) Mr. Mansel imputes to all who agree with Kant
in affirming the existence of a practical Reason or
moral sense which deals with things as they are and
not with phenomena, with the eternal and not the
changeable, a determination to make our morality the
measure of the Absolute Morality. A more unjust
assertion, or one more directly refuted by his own
statements in this and his other Lectures, it is
scarcely possible to conceive. Evidently, if we take
merely his representations—coloured and caricatured
as they always are—of his opponents, the aim of
them, one and all, is to find some absolute morality
which is *not* measured by human morality. Evidently
their strong conviction is, that if the conditions of
our intellect, the conditions of time and space, are
applied to morality, it must cease to be absolute, it
must be brought to our level. Every one may have
his own opinion whether they have succeeded or failed
in their attempt to discover something more stable
and permanent than their own finite judgments and
conclusions ; but to deny that this is their object, is
to take away the point from at least one-half of Mr.
Mansel's arguments and scoffs.

(3.) He discovers however in Kant a fiction "which
is so manifest as hardly to need exposure." Perceiving that there must be a standard which is the measure of our morality and which cannot be twisted
and distorted by our individual feelings and appre-

hensions,—perceiving also that if it is the standard
for mankind, there must be the closest and most intimate relation between it and that which is human,
—Kant hinted at a " Universal Consciousness," a
Consciousness belonging to humanity itself.   Such a
notion strikes Mr. Mansel as supremely ridiculous.

" The fiction of a moral law binding in a parti-
" cular form upon all possible intelligences, acquires
" this seeming universality, only because human in-
" telligence is made the representative of all.   I can
" conceive moral attributes only as I know them in
" consciousness : I can imagine other minds only by
" first assuming their likeness to my own. To construct
" a theory, whether of practical or of speculative rea-
" son, which shall be valid for other than human in-
" telligences, it is necessary that the author should
" himself be emancipated from the conditions of hu-
" man thought.   Till this is done, the so-called Ab-
" solute is but the Relative under another name :
" the universal consciousness is but the human mind
" striving to transcend itself."—(*Bampton Lectures,*
2nd ed., p. 203.)

I spoke of my comments being for " Englishmen,
not for Germans."   That remark I meant to apply
especially to this last passage.   I think you will see
at once how it applies. And yet you will have a right
to find some fault with it.   The principle is true for
all human beings or for none, that we must *either
make God in our image, or admit that we are made*

in His image. That, I take it, is the doctrine of the Bible; that is the meaning of idolatry, and the explanation of the steps by which men have been led out of idolatry. But since we boast more of receiving the Bible and the whole Bible than the Germans, we ought to be more possessed and penetrated with this principle than they are. And since we take credit to ourselves for admitting the union of the two Natures in Christ more fully, as a fundamental article of faith, than some of them do, we ought more distinctly to allow, first, that there is a divine standard for human morality; secondly, that this standard is in such direct affinity with humanity in its highest form, that the one is the exact reflex of the other; thirdly, that it is not a fiction, but the most pregnant of all facts, that there is a universal human morality, transcending the particular morality of each man, and yet capable of being brought to bear upon that morality in all the circumstances and details of our lives.

This is our old English faith, the faith, as I tried to show you in my last Letter, which is the foundation of our old English education, not merely of that which we call technically our religious education, but of the whole education of the man. What I desire is, that before we accuse any of departing from this faith, or produce ingenious arguments to show why they are foolish or wicked for doing so, we should seriously consider what is involved in it for ourselves, what notions of ours it must scatter, to what results it must lead us.

To this test I would in the first place bring such statements as I find in the following passage :—

" That there is an Absolute Morality, based upon,
" or rather identical with, the Eternal Nature of God,
" is indeed a conviction forced upon us by the same
" evidence as that on which we believe that God
" exists at all.   But *what* that Absolute Morality
" is, we are as unable to fix in any human concep-
" tion, as we are to define the other attributes of
" the same Divine Nature.   To human conception it
" seems impossible that absolute morality should be
" manifested in the form of a *law of obligation ;* for
" such a law implies relation and subjection to the
" authority of a lawgiver.   And, as all human mo-
" rality is manifested in this form, the conclusion
" seems unavoidable, that human morality, even in
" its highest elevation, is not identical with, nor ad-
" equate to measure, the Absolute Morality of God.

" A like conclusion is forced upon us by a closer
" examination of human morality itself.   To main-
" tain the immutability of moral principles in the
" abstract is a very different thing from maintaining
" the immutability of the particular acts by which
" those principles are manifested in practice.   The
" parallel between the mathematical and the moral
" sciences, as systems of necessary truth, holds good
" in this respect also.   As principles in the abstract,

" the laws of morality are as unchangeable as the
" axioms of geometry. That duty ought in all cases
" to be followed in preference to inclination, is as
" certain a truth as that two straight lines cannot
" enclose a space. In their concrete application both
" principles are equally liable to error :—we may err
" in supposing a particular visible line to be perfectly
" straight; as we may err in supposing a particular
" act to be one of duty. But the two errors, though
" equally possible, are by no means equally impor-
" tant. For mathematical science, as such, is com-
" plete in its merely theoretical aspect ; while moral
" science is valuable chiefly in its application to prac-
" tice. It is in their concrete form that moral prin-
" ciples are adopted as guides of conduct and canons
" of judgment ; and in this form they admit of va-
" rious degrees of uncertainty or of positive error.
" But the difference between the highest and the low-
" est conception of moral duty is one of degree, not
" of kind ; the interval between them is occupied by
" intermediate stages, separated from each other by
" minute and scarcely appreciable differences; and
" the very conception of a gradual progress in moral
" enlightenment implies the possibility of a further
" advance, of a more exalted intellect, and a more
" enlightened conscience. While we repudiate, as
" subversive of all morality, the theory which main-
" tains that each man is the measure of his own
" moral acts ; we must repudiate also, as subversive

" of all religion, the opposite theory, which virtually
" maintains that man may become the measure of
" the absolute Nature of God."—(*Bampton Lectures,*
2nd ed., pp. 206–208.)

" *There is an Absolute Morality, but what it is we
are unable to fix in any human conception.*" I feel
myself as utterly unable to fix relative morality in
any human conception as absolute morality. If a
man's duty to wife and child is caged in a human
conception, I believe it will never come out of that
cage into any living action. What we have been
taught in our Creed is, that because Absolute Morality could not be fixed in a human conception, or in
any letters that express human conceptions, it came
forth in the life of a Person, in His acts, His sufferings. The unbounded Righteousness and Truth and
Goodness—so our fathers told us—showed themselves
forth in Him. In Him we might see what that
Being was who had made the worlds and all that
dwell in them.

We have always been instructed also that this manifestation of the Absolute Goodness in a man was
the removal of that perplexity respecting a *Law of
Obligation,* which Mr. Mansel appears to treat as
hopeless. A Son who perfectly delighted to do his
Father's will,—who obeyed Him because His law was
in His heart,—would seem to set forth the very meaning and nature of obligation, the sense in which it is
the submission of a Will and the power of a Will.

The readiness of that Son to fulfil all righteousness, to submit to all ordinary precepts, would seem to show how the inward obligation determined the outward conduct. And, if this is so, "the conclusion seems unavoidable that human morality"—because "in its highest elevation . . . it is manifested in this form" of filial obedience—"*is* one which is adequate to set forth" (I believe this language to be less equivocal than "identical with, and adequate to measure," though I do not object to that) "the Absolute Morality of God."

But it is to the second paragraph in this extract that I would especially invite the reader's attention. "*To maintain the immutability of moral principles in the abstract, is a very different thing from maintaining the immutability of the particular acts by which those principles are manifested in practice.*" Assuredly, very different indeed. The Gospel of St. Luke supplies us with a remarkable instance and illustration of the difference. "*And behold, a certain lawyer stood up, and tempted Him, saying, 'Master, what shall I do to inherit Eternal Life?' He said unto him, 'What is written in the Law? how readest thou?' And he answering, said, 'Thou shalt love the Lord thy God with all thy heart, and with all thy soul, and with all thy strength, and with all thy mind; and thy neighbour as thyself.' And he said unto him, 'Thou hast answered right; this do, and thou shalt live.' But he, willing to justify himself,*

said unto Jesus, ' And who is my neighbour ?'" Here
the 'immutability of the moral principle' asserted in
the book of Deuteronomy, is maintained ' in the abstract,' by the lawyer, with the greatest vigour. It
is just as applicable to his own time as to the time of
Moses. He would have confounded any member of
an opposing school who said otherwise. But ' the particular act by which that principle is manifested '—
here was the difficulty. He could find no letter about
that, or none which might not be explained to be
applicable to other times, and not to his own. He
was ' unable to fix' the Neighbour ' in any human
conception.' ' Who is he ? Of course I am to love
' him as myself, if I meet with him ; but where shall
' I meet with him ?' The parable which we all know,
was (so we have been used to suppose) an answer
to this question. The priest, the representative of
the Jewish nation before God, appointed to bless the
people in His Name,—the Levite, the authorized interpreter and defender of the Law which was given to
Jews,—see a stripped and wounded Jew lying on the
road, and never discover that he comes within the
scope of the rule, ' Thou shalt love thy neighbour as
thyself.' A Samaritan, with little of this legal knowledge, a suspected heretic, sees that same Jew, the
member of a race with which he has no dealings, and
at once acts as if he were his neighbour. The law is
within his heart ; he is obeying a principle, and not a
rule ; it is not an individual principle ; it is not one

which he has learnt from his fathers. It is human; the Son of Man owns it as His. He bids the ruler " *Go and do likewise.*"

Compare this divine record with Mr. Mansel's next position, which is only the former differently worded. " *As principles in the Abstract, the laws of morality are as unchangeable as the axioms of geometry. That duty ought in all cases to be followed in preference to inclination, is as certain a truth as that two straight lines cannot enclose a space. In their concrete application both principles are equally liable to error; we may err in supposing a particular visible line to be perfectly straight; we may err in supposing a particular act to be one of duty.*" The dogma that duty ought to be followed in preference to inclination, is as unlike as possible to the divine maxim which the ruler quoted so readily respecting the love of the neighbour. ' That duty ought to be followed,' means that ' we ought to do what we ought to do.' So very harmless a proposition is not likely to beget a very energetic course of action. The questions, ' What is duty?' ' What is inclination?' start up even more quickly than the question, ' Who is my neighbour?' Let us go all lengths with Mr. Mansel. Let us confess that this morality in the abstract is the poorest, most miserable, most helpless of all unrealities. We have heard much of the great evil of Slavery in the abstract. What man of sense listens to such stuff? Who cares for an abstract slavery, a slavery which has nothing to do with the concrete driver, the concrete drivee, the concrete lash ? Who would not endure such a slavery himself? Who can feel the least concern that those who are dearest to him should endure it ? Or again, who is better for the abstract benevolence which crosses abstract seas, to visit abstract soldiers, in abstract Scutaris, to place abstract plaisters on abstract wounds ?

But must not this abstract morality be the very opposite thing to that law of life, that royal law, that law of liberty, of which Apostles and Evangelists speak ? Must not that mean something which actually governs human beings, which they are created to obey ? Is it analogous to certain axioms, or propositions in books of ours, or to the law which the planets obey in their courses, which every tree and flower obeys in its budding and bearing fruit ? If there is to be a morality which bears upon action, 'the duty and destiny of man,'—a morality which cannot be explained away 'as liable in its concrete form to various degrees of uncertainty, or of positive error,'—must it not be of this kind? Can there be a greater proof of the radical feebleness of a mere regulative morality, than that which Mr. Mansel himself has given us ? The abstract proposition from which we start,—the logical generalization,—is a truism admitted at once, and cast aside as soon as admitted. The special application of this truism, that which is to bring it into contact with the actual doings and sufferings of men, is liable, as it must needs be, to endless debatings, before its propriety or impropriety can be settled. 'Who is my neighbour,' must be argued with profound skill between opposing casuists, the man who has been left half dead, dying altogether during the discussion. But let us hear the Lecturer again.

"God did not *create* Absolute Morality; it is co-
" eternal with Himself; and it were blasphemy to
" say that there ever was a time when God was and
" Goodness was not. But God did create the human
" manifestation of morality, when He created the
" moral constitution of man, and placed him in those
" circumstances by which the eternal principles of
" right and wrong are modified in relation to this
" present life. For it is manifest, to take the sim-
" plest instances, that the sixth Commandment of the
" Decalogue, in its literal obligation, is relative to
" that state of things in which men are subject to
" death; and the seventh, to that in which there is
" marrying and giving in marriage; and the eighth,
" to that in which men possess temporal goods. It is
" manifest, to take a more general ground, that the
" very conception of moral obligation implies a supe-
" rior authority, and an ability to transgress what
" that authority commands; that it implies a com-
" plex, and therefore a limited nature in the moral
" agent; the intellect, which apprehends the duty,
" being distinct from the will, which obeys or dis-

" obeys. That there is a higher and unchangeable
" principle embodied in these forms, we have abun-
" dant reason to believe; and yet we cannot, from
" our present point of view, examine the same duties
" apart from their human element, and separate that
" which is relative and peculiar to man in this life
" from that which is absolute and common to all
" moral beings. In this respect, again, our moral
" conceptions offer a remarkable analogy to the cog-
" nate phenomena on which other systems of neces-
" sary truth are based. Take, for example, the idea
" of Time, the foundation of the science of Number.
" We find no difficulty in conceiving that this present
" world was created at some definite point of time;
" but we are unable to conceive the same moment as
" the creation of Time itself. On the contrary, we
" are compelled to believe that there was a time be-
" fore as well as after the creation of the world : that
" the being of God reaches back in boundless dura-
" tion beyond the moment when He said, Let there
" be light, and there was light. But when we at-
" tempt to unite this conviction with another, neces-
" sary to the completion of the thought;—when we
" try to conceive God as an Infinite Being existing in
" continuous duration,—the contradictions, which be-
" set us on every side, admonish us that we have
" transcended the boundary within which alone hu-
" man thought is possible. And so too, while we are
" compelled to believe that the creation of man's

" moral nature was not identical with the creation of
" morality itself;—that the great principles of all
" that is holy and righteous existed in God, before
" they assumed their finite form in the heart of man;
" —we still find ourselves baffled in every attempt to
" conceive an infinite moral nature, or its condition,
" an infinite personality; we find ourselves compelled
" to walk by faith, and not by sight;—to admit that
" we have knowledge enough to guide us in our
" moral training here; but not enough to unveil the
" hidden things of God."—(*Bampton Lectures*, 2nd
ed., pp. 208–210.)

Now here we have the most distinct assertion I
can imagine, that the Gospel does *not* explain what
was left unexplained by the law,—that the manifestation of Christ in the fullness of time, does *not* remove
the veil which was over the minds of men in the old
dispensation. 'God could not create Absolute Morality,' that is admitted. I rejoice that it is,—the
Absolute Morality must be in Him, His own Nature. 'But God did create the human manifestation
of Morality.' What, is not Christ the human manifestation of Morality? Or does Mr. Mansel mean to
set aside the words of the Creed, 'Not created, but
begotten?' He need not be afraid that I should
impeach him of heresy. Happily, I should be very
little listened to if I did. And I prize those words
of the Creed too much, for their positive worth, to
degrade them by turning them into excuses for dis-

covering flaws in the faith of other men. But the loss we suffer from treating the unity of the Son with the Father as a formal tenet, not as an Eternal principle, becomes very evident in the next passage.

The commandments in the Decalogue are quoted to prove that they refer to a condition of things in which there is Marriage, Property, Death. Who ever thought otherwise? Moreover they belong to a condition of things in which there are transgressions against Marriage, against Property, against Life. The law, St. Paul says, is added because of *transgressions*. This law then, by the author's own showing, presumes a certain order anterior to its own existence. And the order demands an interpretation which the law cannot give. What is this wonderful union of man and woman, which is said in Scripture to have been involved in the Constitution of the Universe as it came from the Creator? What is this Life which He has given us, and which He watches over so jealously? What is this property of man in things? whence comes it? The Law does not answer these questions, does not attempt an answer to them. It simply says, " Thou shalt not murder, thou shalt not commit adultery, thou shalt not steal." But, because the *Thou* is a real man capable of entering into the command, of obeying it or disobeying it, —because he recognizes the command as coming from some one who has a right to utter it, and who is right Himself,—he craves from Him the answer which the

Law refuses. He asks after the source of that mysterious life which is in him and in all men. He asks after the ground of Marriage, the foundation of Property. If history speaks truly, these have been questions which have been awakened in men's hearts wherever they have not been brutal, wherever there have been impulses of family affection, desires for national union, an impatience of anarchy, a perception of Law and Government. The Jewish people were reminded by the solemnest precepts of their law that precepts were not the ground of their morality. They were told in the Fourth Commandment that they were to work because God worked, to rest because God rested. ' Be ye holy, because I am holy,' was repeated to them as the sanction of the prohibition of the most outrageous crimes. Their Prophets admonished them that their indifference to Life, Marriage, the boundaries of thine and mine, were all traceable to their idolatry, to their indifference about Him—the God of Righteousness—whom the eye cannot see. We have been used to suppose that the Sermon on the Mount unfolded those principles which lay beneath the precepts of the old time; that ' Be ye perfect as your Father in Heaven is perfect ' fulfilled the words ' Be ye holy, for I am holy;' that the Son of God translated these words into Life; that His Spirit was promised to write them in the hearts and minds of those whom he was not ashamed to call His brethren. All this old teaching may be set aside; but if Mr.

Mansel means to set it aside, should he not say so? Should he stand forth as the condemner of those who pronounce it unsatisfactory and obsolete, when his own philosophy appears utterly to ignore it?

The observations respecting Creation with which this passage closes, seem to show that Mr. Mansel had a sense of this earlier order; otherwise they would be out of place. They are bewildering; will prove more and more bewildering to the consciences of his readers; will darken all practical principles to them; will make action as impossible as belief; so long as we revile other persons for rejecting the plain words of Scripture, and refuse to accept those words as the guides of our own thoughts. Mr. Mansel tells us, " *When we try to conceive of God as an Infinite Being, existing in continuous duration, the contradictions which beset us on every side admonish us that we have transcended the boundary within which human thought is possible.*" Certainly, when we try to conceive of the Eternal Life of God as an existence in continuous duration, we transcend the bounds of thought by uttering words that mean nothing. But do those words of St. John mean nothing? Do they lead to nothing? " *That which was from the beginning, which we have heard, which we have seen with our eyes, which we have looked upon, and our hands have handled of the Word of Life. For the Life was manifested, and we have seen it, and bear witness, and show unto you that Eternal Life, which*

*was with the Father, and was manifested unto us.
That which we have seen and heard declare we unto
you, that ye also may have fellowship with us : and
truly our fellowship is with the Father, and with His
Son Jesus Christ.*" I, for myself, accept this as the
most perfect wisdom, as the deepest philosophy. And
so accepting it, I am bound to say 'that we have
not knowledge enough to guide our moral training
here,' if the 'hidden things of God' have not been
unveiled to us.

Mr. Mansel having shown to his satisfaction that
we have no means of knowing the hidden things of
God, no discovery of an Absolute Morality, proceeds
to answer the objections which have been raised in
different books against the Atoning Sacrifice of Christ.
To some of these objections he introduced us in the
First Lecture ; I said then what I thought of them
and of his treatment of the whole subject. But I
am thankful to be recalled to it again.

" The Atoning Sacrifice of Christ has been the
" mark assailed by various attacks of this kind ; some
" of them not very consistent with each other ; but all
" founded on some supposed incongruity between this
" doctrine and the moral attributes of the Divine Na-
" ture. By one critic, the doctrine is rejected because
" it is more consistent with the infinite mercy of God
" to pardon sin freely, without any atonement whatso-
" ever. By another, because, from the unchangeable
" nature of God's laws, it is impossible that sin can be

" pardoned at all. A third maintains that it is unjust
" that the innocent should suffer for the sins of the
" guilty. A fourth is indignant at the supposition
" that God can be angry; while a fifth cannot see
" by what moral fitness the shedding of blood can do
" away with sin or its punishment. The principle
" which governs these and similar objections is, that
" we have a right to assume that there is, if not a
" perfect identity, at least an exact resemblance be-
" tween the moral nature of man and that of God;
" that the laws and principles of infinite justice and
" mercy are but magnified images of those which are
" manifested on a finite scale;—that nothing can be
" compatible with the boundless goodness of God,
" which is incompatible with the little goodness of
" which man may be conscious in himself."—(*Bampton Lectures*, 2nd ed., pp. 211, 212.)

Is it not strange to hear these different objections
quoted, as if they were the special imaginations of
some particular writers, German or English? Have
they never presented themselves to Mr. Mansel's own
mind? Has he not had to fight his way through
them? Because, if so, he is unlike any other earnest religious man that I ever read of or met with.
All that it has been my lot to encounter in biographies, or in the world, have spoken of these questions as having once been torments to them. Nor
have they concealed the fact that the doubts rose up
before them again and again, or that it was God

who answered them to their minds, and not man.
And what was the answer ? So far as I could gather
from their statements,—which met all the deepest
convictions and experiences of my own soul,—they
found the belief of an Atoning Sacrifice growing more
dear and sacred to them in proportion as they took
the words that express it more literally. They believed that God in Christ had actually removed the
obstacles which separated them from Him; that in
the Sacrifice He was declaring Himself to be at one
with them, and inviting them to be at one with Him.
As St. Paul puts it, ' *God was in Christ, reconciling
the world to Himself,*' therefore ' *we, as ambassadors
of Christ, beseech you in Christ's stead, be ye reconciled to God.*'   Or as the Church expresses it in the
consecration prayer at the Eucharist,—" A full, perfect, and sufficient sacrifice, oblation, and satisfaction
has been made for the sins of the whole world.
On which ground she invites her sons to draw nigh
and enter into real and actual communion with their
Father in Heaven. Believing that Gospel,—partaking of that Communion,—Christian men declare that
they feel God's mercy to be infinite in the putting
away of sin; that sin is the separation from God;
that Christ is union with God. They can rejoice,
they say, in contemplating that Unchangeable Nature which never can be satisfied with any Perfec-
tion less than its own, with any Love less than its
own. They can hail the sacrifice of the Innocent, as

the highest and most practical exhibition of that love
—as revealing to them the perfect fellowship of the
Will of the Father with the Will of the Son,—as
showing them why God's Spirit is awakening them
to offer themselves as sacrifices to God,—sacrifices
to do His work for the guiltiest of His creatures.
Such persons learn, they tell us, that the anger of
God against Sin is not a detraction from His love,
but the proof of it; they are sure the anger could
not be less without the love being less; they wish to
feel more and more how hotly it is burning against
the evil which is in them and in the world. They
say further, that the more they think of this Atonement, the more it connects itself with an actual participation of the nature of Him who died for them ;
that what once seemed to them the greatest of all
puzzles, how the shedding of blood should be the
doing away of sin, seems to them now—while they
recognize an actual union with Christ as the secret of
their peace—the most living and practical of truths.
I am not going to defend these statements; I leave
them to defend themselves. I merely ask which
seem most in accordance with the belief that the
Atonement is the fundamental principle of the Gospel, the key-stone of the Christian arch,—these statements, or the apologies which are grounded upon the
assumption that it is presumptuous to connect our
thoughts and acts and life with His thoughts and
acts and life; which, in fact, excuse (!) the finished

Sacrifice of Christ, by maxims which might have afforded some explanation of the Heathen dreams of a sacrifice, if the Son of Man had never offered His. I wrong those dreams in saying that the maxims would have afforded this explanation. The very worst of them presumed that there was some union between the worshiper and the object of his worship, some relation between the human morality and the divine, some correspondence between the sin of which the creature was conscious, and the nature of the Being against whom he had sinned. All foretold that this union would be revealed, that the contradictions which interfered with it would be put away. It is the last achievement of Christian orthodoxy in the nineteenth century, to prove that the separation is hopeless, the contradiction irremovable. This is the way of refuting Rationalism ! This is the way of bringing young men to accept the Gospel of the atoning Sacrifice of Christ ! This is the way of preparing them to preach it to the world !

If you think that my language is strong, and that there is not really that opposition between the morality of the Gospel and Mr. Mansel's statements which I have supposed, consider seriously the following passage :—

" It is obvious indeed, on a moment's reflection,
" that the duty of man to forgive the trespasses of
" his neighbour, rests precisely upon those features
" of human nature which cannot by any analogy be re-

" garded as representing an image of God. Man is
" not the author of the moral law : he is not, as man,
" the moral governor of his fellows: he has no au-
" thority, merely as man, to punish moral transgres-
" sions as such. It is not as sin, but as injury, that
" vice is a transgression against man : it is not that
" his holiness is outraged, but that his rights or his
" interests are impaired. The duty of forgiveness is
" imposed as a check, not upon the justice, but upon
" the selfishness of man : it is not designed to extin-
" guish his indignation against vice, but to restrain
" his tendency to exaggerate his own personal injuries.
" The reasoner who maintains, 'it is a duty in man
" 'to forgive sins, therefore it must be morally fitting
" 'for God to forgive them also,' overlooks the fact
" that this duty is binding upon man on account of
" the weakness and ignorance and sinfulness of his
" nature ; that he is bound to forgive, as one who
" himself needs forgiveness ; as one whose weakness
" renders him liable to suffering ; as one whose self-
" love is ever ready to arouse his passions and per-
" vert his judgment."—(*Bampton Lectures,* 2nd ed.,
pp. 214, 215.)

" *Forgive us our trespasses, as we forgive them that
trespass against us.*" " *Forgiving if ye have a quarrel
against any, even as God for Christ's sake hath forgiven you.*" " *O thou wicked servant, I forgave thee
all that debt because thou desiredst me; shouldest
not thou also have had compassion on thy fellow-ser-*

vant, even as I had pity on thee?"—*"It is obvious, on a moment's consideration, that the duty of a man to forgive the trespasses of his neighbour, rests precisely upon those features of human nature which cannot, by any analogy, be regarded as representing an image of God."* Can you conceive a more direct and literal opposition than you find here? But penetrate below the letter—connect our Lord's words with the whole Evangelical history, with the doctrine of the Apostles, with His own words on the Cross,—and see whether the contrast becomes less or greater. Is it not evident that we have here a war, if ever such were, of principles, of the most practical principles, of those which most determine the whole life and conduct of human beings? These maxims cannot co-exist. Each of us must say by which he will hold.

I admit at once the 'obviousness' of Mr. Mansel's conclusion. It is just as 'obvious' as that the sun is moving about the earth. It is the first impulse of every one to respond to his proposition, as to the Ptolemaic proposition, 'Of course; a man must be a fool to think otherwise.' But there were perplexities about the 'obvious' theory of the heavens— practical difficulties—which suggested doubts about it, even before the 'unobvious' law had been demonstrated to be the actual one. And there are moral perplexities—practical perplexities—in the 'obvious' theory about the features in human nature that are the foundation of our forgiveness, which make it most embarrassing even to those who do not hold, as I do, that our Lord's acts and words and sufferings— if they are what we say they are—*demonstrated* the doctrine which Mr. Mansel rejects to be the only tenable, the only possible, one.

"The duty of forgiveness is binding upon man on " account of the weakness and ignorance and sinful- " ness of his nature." But what if the weakness, igno- rance, and sinfulness of my nature dispose me *not* to forgive ? What if one principal sign of the weakness, ignorance, sinfulness of my nature is that I am un- forgiving ? What if the more weak, ignorant, and sinful my nature is, the more impossible forgiveness becomes to me, the more disposed I am to resent every injury and to take the most violent means for aveng- ing it ? It is my duty to forgive, because I am " one " whose self-will is ever ready to arouse his passions " and pervert his judgment." To arouse my passions ; to what ? To anything so much as to acts of revenge ? To pervert my judgment ; how ? In any way so much as by making me think that I am right and other men wrong, and that I may vindicate my right against their wrong ? And this is the basis of the duty of forgive- ness !—The temper which inclines me at every moment to trample upon that duty, to do what it forbids !

The obvious conclusion then has some obvious dif- ficulties. Obvious indeed ! They meet us at every step of our way ; they are *the* difficulties in our moral progress. Forgiveness is ' to be a check on the selfishness of man.' Where does he get the check? From his selfishness. It is the old, miserable, hopeless circle. I am to persuade myself by certain arguments not to do the thing which I am inclined to do. But the inclination remains as strong as ever; bursts down all the mud fortifications that are built to confine it; or else remains within the heart, a worm destroying it, a fire consuming it. Whence, oh whence is this forgiveness from the heart to come, which I cry for? Is it impossible? Am I to check my selfishness by certain rules about the propriety of abstaining from *acts* of unforgiving ferocity? God have mercy upon those who have only such rules, in a siege or a shipwreck, when social bonds are dissolved, when they are left to themselves!

All men have declared that forgiveness, real forgiveness, is *not* impossible. And all have felt that it is not impossible, because it dwells somewhere in beings above man, and is shown by them and comes down as the highest gift from them upon man. I say, in every nation there has been a sense of the duty of forgiveness, and there has been also the sense of its being a divine quality, of its being imparted to man in spite of the weakness, ignorance, selfishness of his nature. If it comes along with a feeling of weakness, ignorance, selfishness,—along with a feeling that we are not to judge lest we should be judged,—that feeling is itself owned as a gift, a light proceeding from the forgiveness which is manifested towards

us. But these common feelings have been worked
into the heart of *Christendom* Morality; they have
expressed themselves in every form of its Society; they
have impressed themselves on its Literature. How
could it be otherwise, if the Lord's Prayer was anything but an idle form of words, if it was really a
prayer to a Forgiving Father that His will might be
done in earth as it is in heaven?

> "Why all the souls that are were forfeit once;
> And He that might have best the advantage took
> Found out the remedy,"—

this has been the maxim, the habit of thought which
breaks forth unawares into words, because it is so
deeply imbedded in the very existence of Society; because Society is recognized as standing on the principle which it embodies. And whenever the idea of
Forgiveness has been severed from this root,—whenever the strong conviction that we are warring against
the nature of God and assuming the nature of the
Devil by an unforgiving temper, has given place to a
sentimental feeling that we are all sinners, and so
should be tolerant of each other,—there has come
that weakness and effeminacy over Christian Society,
that dread of punishing, that unwillingness to exercise the severe functions of the Ruler and the King,
which has driven the wise back upon older and sterner
lessons, has made them think the vigour of the Jew
in putting down abominations, the self-assertion of
the Greek in behalf of freedom, was manlier than the

endurance and compassion of the Christian. Which I should think too, if, referring the endurance and compassion to a divine standard, I did not find in that standard a justification of all which was brave and noble in the Jewish protest against evil, in the Greek protest against tyranny. Submission or Compassion turned into mere qualities which we are to exalt and boast of as characteristic of our religion, become little else than the negations of Courage and Justice. Contemplated as the reflections of that Eternal Goodness and Truth which were manifested in Christ, as energies proceeding from Him and called forth by His Spirit,—submission to personal slights and injuries, the compassion for every one who is out of the way, become instruments in the vindication of Justice and Right, and of that Love in the fires of which all selfishness is to be consumed.

For this is what I meant by the demonstration which the Cross and Sacrifice of Christ have made of the nature and ground of Forgiveness. It is, I hold, impossible to maintain what our Christian Creeds have maintained respecting the Union of the two Natures in Christ,—impossible to think that His human Forgiveness was the perfect image of the divine Forgiveness,—without adopting that belief which has pervaded all the thought and dialects of modern Europe, and which involves, Mr. Mansel tell us, a *primâ facie* absurdity.

Either (1) Christ's forgiveness was the highest ma-

nifestation of the Divine character, and, being such,
becomes effective through the gift of His Spirit for
working the like forgiveness in us; or (2) He has
not set us an example that we should follow in His
steps; or (3) His forgiveness, like ours, was—I dare
not quote the words in this connection; you have
heard them already. If we think that Christ has died
and risen again, we think He has demonstrated that
Forgiveness is mightier than Unforgiveness, Good
than Evil, Life than Death; if we think He has not
died and risen again, we ought not to invent plausible
arguments for keeping up a profession the meaning of
which we have renounced.

Mr. Mansel proceeds to treat the question of Pre-
destination and Freewill as he has treated all other
questions which have agitated the human heart and
conscience. "The controversy, whether viewed in its
" speculative or moral aspect, is but another example
" of the hardihood of human ignorance. The ques-
" tion, as I have observed before, has its philosophical
" as well as its theological aspect; it has no special
" difficulties peculiar to itself; it is but a special form
" of the mystery of the coexistence of the Infinite
" and the Finite." Many such things have we heard;
miserable comforters are ye all! This question, in its
moral or practical 'aspect,' does present itself to every
man and woman; does connect itself with action and
suffering, with life and death. My dear friend, what
does it signify? "It is but a special form of the

" co-existence of the Finite and the Infinite." What I
said before, I must repeat. Butler's experience that
man is dealt with as free, Luther's experience that
man is dealt with as a slave, are both veritable experiences which cannot be ignored : neither of which is less
sure or less important to life than the other. Where
do we find the resolution of the problem ? I find it
in the revelation of that Eternal Nature of which Mr.
Mansel tells me I can know nothing. When I am
poring over my own mind, the contradiction faces me
at every turn, darkens all my course to me. When
I acknowledge God as a Deliverer,—a deliverer of
the Will out of that bondage into which it has cast
itself by denying Him,—a Restorer of the Will to
its true, reasonable, human state of subjection to Him,
—I confess that I am meant for a Service which is
perfect Freedom, I confess also what that bondage
and prison-house of Self is, in which I must stay till
that is dead wherein I am held.

These last words, which I use with the deepest certainty of their truth, with the most entire conviction
that a man shut up in self must be miserable,—must
be eternally miserable,— introduce the next topic in
Mr. Mansel's Lecture. Let him have all the advantage which can be derived from being allowed to state
his own case and his opponent's case also.

" And is not the same conviction of the ignorance
" of man, and of his rashness in the midst of igno-
" rance, forced upon us by the spectacle of the arbi-

" trary and summary decisions of human reason on
" the most mysterious as well as the most awful of
" God's revealed judgments against sin,—the sen-
" tence of Eternal Punishment? We know not what
" is the relation of Sin to Infinite Justice. We know
" not under what conditions, consistently with the
" freedom of man, the final spiritual restoration of
" the impenitent sinner is possible; nor how, with-
" out such a restoration, guilt and misery can ever
" cease. We know not whether the future punish-
" ment of sin will be inflicted by way of natural con-
" sequence or of supernatural visitation; whether it
" will be produced from within or inflicted from with-
" out. We know not how man can be rescued from
" sin and suffering without the co-operation of his
" own will; nor what means can co-operate with that
" will, beyond those which are offered to all of us du-
" ring our state of trial. It becomes us to speak
" cautiously and reverently on a matter of which God
" has revealed so little, and that little of such awful
" moment; but if we may be permitted to criticize
" the arguments of the opponents of this doctrine
" with the same freedom with which they have cri-
" ticized the ways of God, we may remark that the
" whole apparent force of the moral objection rests
" upon two purely gratuitous assumptions. It is as-
" sumed, in the first place, that God's punishment of
" sin in the world to come is so far analogous to
" man's administration of punishment in this world,

" that it will take place as a special infliction, not
" as a natural consequence. And it is assumed, in
" the second place, that punishment will be inflicted
" solely with reference to the sins committed during
" the earthly life;—that guilt will continue finite,
" while the misery is prolonged to infinity. Are we
" then so sure, it may be asked, that there can be no
" sin beyond the grave? Can an immortal soul incur
" God's wrath and condemnation, only so long as it
" is united to a mortal body? With as much reason
" might we assert that the angels are incapable of
" disobedience to God, that the devils are incapable
" of rebellion. What if the sin perpetuates itself,—
" if the prolonged misery be the offspring of the pro-
" longed guilt?"—(*Bampton Lectures*, 2nd ed., pp.
220-222.)

I quite agree with Mr. Mansel, that it is extreme
ignorance and presumption to use the word Eternal in
connection with one subject or another,—with life or
death, with reward or punishment,—if by the conditions of our mind we can attach no signification to
that word. To join it with solemn duties and responsibilities, with the hopes and fears of man,—if this is
the case,—must be the most egregious trifling. My
reason for adhering to the expressions Eternal Life,
Eternal Death, Eternal Punishment—for desiring that
we should meditate on them far more earnestly than
we have ever done, and that we should introduce
them into our discourses, not for oratorical purposes,

not to move the nerves of our hearers, but to raise and deepen all their thoughts of their own destiny, and of human destiny,—is that I believe these phrases have been rescued from vagueness, have been translated into life, by the words and acts of our Lord Jesus Christ. Believing, as our fathers did, that He came to reveal the Eternal God, Him who is, and was, and is to come,—believing that He did manifest that life of Righteousness, Love, Truth, which is not and cannot be limited by Time,—believing that these are the invisible things which St. Paul opposes to the visible things that are temporal,—believing that the Gospel means the admission of men in Christ, into the possession and enjoyment of these Eternal Treasures, which men in the ages before His coming were feeling after, and in which they were sure that they had an interest,—believing that to be without these Eternal treasures, is to be in the state which the Apostles describe as Death, Eternal Death, that to possess them in any measure is to have a taste of Eternal Life, that to possess them altogether, to live and dwell in them, to go no more out of them, to sink no more back into our own evil nature, is the reward which God has prepared for those that love Him, the fullness of joy which is at His right-hand, —believing that this is the teaching of the Bible, and that the more we read it, the more that teaching explains to us all the capacities of good as well as of evil in ourselves,—I am not afraid of Christ's own language. I desire to look more into it, I desire to take it more literally, more and more in the length and breadth of its spiritual significance. I cannot take it literally if I change the force of it at my pleasure, if I assume the adjective to have one sense when it is applied to God, and another when it is applied to Life or Death or Punishment. I take it as having the same force wherever it occurs; its highest application being the only measure of all the others.

To speak of God as 'without beginning or end,' and to say that punishment or death only means ' without end,' is to play with Scripture, to bring Christ's awful revelations down to our sense because we will not permit Him to raise our sense to His revelations. If He comes to unveil God to us, if He comes to make us partakers of the life of God, the absence of that life must be eternal death. A lost soul must be, as all Evangelical teachers have said, in a state of death, — not in a state of temporal death, of bodily death, but of eternal because of spiritual death. To say that a soul in this world cannot be raised out of this death is to say that there is no gospel nor salvation for human beings at all. There is a deliverance from eternal death, in the strict Scriptural sense of eternal death. Whether that deliverance is *only* in this world, whether the threescore years are barrier beyond which Christ's Gospel does not reach, is a question which cannot be determined by the use of *that* word. By all means let the question be discussed with the ut-

most earnestness whether the Scripture has settled it
by the use of any *other* language. I long that all you
who are preparing for orders,—that we who are in
orders,—should enter upon that inquiry in the most
serious temper, invoking the help of God's Spirit to
guide us in it, utterly distrusting the conclusions
of our minds, ready to receive, and believing that we
shall have His Light. How important it is I have
long felt. I see clergymen turned away from it by
which the notion that morality must suffer if the
check comes from the despair of the future is taken
away. And I see them spending their strength for
nought,—utterly failing to penetrate the mass of evil
which is around them while they *are* using that
check. Men seem to think that there is nothing better for them than to eat, drink, and be merry here,
seeing that they have so little chance of not perish-
ing with the immense majority of their race hereafter.
I see some of more serious minds trembling lest they
should strip such awful words of any of their force
for themselves as well as for their hearers. And it
seems to me that they *do* strip them of the awe
which they ought to have for each one of us. When
we look down into our own spirits we discover a pit
of lovelessness, of atheism, there, which tells us, I
think, more of what eternal death is—more of our
own nearness to it—than all the rhetoric in the
world. It is not well to speak much of such revelations; no serious man would care to do it. But

are they not given us that we may not use rhetorical phrases for the frightening of others; that we may not trifle with God's Word; that we may turn ourselves, that we may turn others, to His infinite Love as the only deliverance, for us or for them, from an infinite despair. Oh, my friend, you may be compelled to ask some day, What is this eternal horror of which I have been preaching to my people? Is it in some distant, unknown world? Is it not here? God grant that then you may be able to say, 'Thou who hast revealed, in the Cross of ' Thy Son, a Love which is stronger than Death, ' the Grave, and Hell, art not Thou, too, here? Is ' there not an Eternal Life which I may claim that ' is mightier than the Eternal Death?' When a man has been driven—not once, but again and again —to find that this is the only refuge for himself, he learns that he must not confine the message he brings from the Cross and Sepulchre and the Resurrection morn, by any terms or forms of his understanding. If St. Paul's words about the length and breadth and depth of the Love of Christ are too vast for him, as he knows they are, he must yet proclaim them to beggars and outcasts. If it sounds dangerous to say that God willeth all men to be saved, and to come to the knowledge of the truth, and that His Will shall one day be done, we must leave Him to justify the language; since we cannot, at least let us not contradict it.

But if I held the conviction before, that this question must be faced boldly in God's strength, whatever shrinking there may be in our minds from it, I cannot tell you how this conviction has been deepened in me by the passage of Mr. Mansel's Lecture which I have just quoted. I need scarcely point out to you how utterly he has mistaken the whole difficulty which has startled the consciences of those who have listened to the popular statements on this subject. He says, " We know not how man can be rescued " from sin and suffering without the co-operation of " his own will, nor what means can co-operate with " that will beyond those which are offered to us all " during our state of trial." Why I *do* know most certainly, if I believe the Scripture and the warrant of my own conscience, that no man can be rescued out of the state of sin and suffering without the co-operation of his own will; because Sin is the very revolt of man's will from the true will, and because to speak of being delivered from a disease in the will without the will itself being set right, is more monstrous than to speak of being cured of a disease in the liver without the liver being set right.

What is the whole Gospel but a message to the Will? What is Redemption but a redemption of the Will? But if this is so,—if we may at once concede to Mr. Mansel all that he asks with so much timidity, what becomes of the next inquiry? Do we ask any more means to co-operate with the Will besides those which God has provided? What we say is, that the revelation of that deliverance which God has wrought out, of that power by which He acts upon the Will of men, has nothing in its nature which fixes death as the limit of it, but everything which defies and breaks through that limit. What we say further is, that it is a cruel fiction to speak of the knowledge of that power by which God acts upon men's Wills to raise them, as being offered to us all during this state of trial. To say that the prostitutes in our streets, that the Hindoos, that the Australian Bushmen, have had the same means of learning what power there is to reform and regenerate the Will, as Mr. Mansel and I have had, is to outrage all sense. To insist that the Scripture obliges us to utter so monstrous a contradiction of fact, is to blaspheme it as no German Rationalist ever did. The fear—I must repeat it—is for ourselves. Those who have seen and known most of the love of God, must feel most what there is in their wills which resists it, how they have fought and do fight against it. If we think God's grace can overcome *us*, I am certain there is no obstinacy or rebellion in others which we can conclude must prove too mighty for it.

Mr. Mansel apologizes very humbly for venturing " to criticize the arguments of the opponents of the " doctrine with the same freedom with which they have " criticized the ways of God." The last clause would be highly commendable in an Old-Bailey advocate;

whether it is equally admirable as coming from a
Clergyman and a Gentleman, I leave to the author's
conscience. I will say nothing of myself, but I declare that I have never met with *any* objector to the
popular statements respecting Eternal Punishment
(and I have met with many from whose opinions and
arguments I entirely dissented), who did not desire
to vindicate the ways of God from what seemed to
him unlawful and injurious criticism. But waiving
that point, the tenderness of Mr. Mansel towards us
—his dread lest he should entirely crush us with
the severity of his criticisms—was quite uncalled for.
He may pour on ; we can endure many more such as
these ; for there is not one of the points upon which
he insists, which I, at least, have not always taken for
granted. That punishment is not a special infliction
for Sin, but the necessary consequence of it—following upon it, as Butler points out, because the world
is subject to a righteous moral Governor ; that Sin is
not dependent upon the existence of a body,—supposing the body did cease to exist in a future state ;
—that sin perpetuates itself ;—that prolonged misery
must be the offspring of prolonged guilt ;—these are
data of the Conscience, which, so far from wishing
to suppress, I complain of our popular teaching about
punishment for suppressing ; which I desire should
be brought out into far greater prominence than they
have been. For then the belief of a Lamb of God who
taketh away the Sin of the World, will not be frit-

tered and explained away into the belief of a Lamb of
God who taketh away the punishment of a certain
portion of the world ; then it will be confessed in our
theological theories, as every Christian confesses in his
practical experience, that Punishment is one of God's
blessed instruments for making us aware of sin, and
for making us feel that it is from *that* we need to
be delivered ; then we shall understand something of
the battle which God has been waging against Evil,
something of His triumph over it when He gave His
Son to die for our sins, and raised Him again for our
Justification.

But no ! we are not to believe in that triumph.
The following paragraph is nearly the most tremendous I ever read in a Christian writer.

"Against this it is urged that sin cannot for ever
" be triumphant against God.   As if the whole mys-
" tery of iniquity were contained in the words *for*
" *ever !* The real riddle of existence,—the problem
" which confounds all philosophy,—ay, and all reli-
" gion too, so far as religion is a thing of man's rea-
" son,—is the fact that evil exists *at all;* not that it
" exists for a longer or a shorter duration.   Is not
" God infinitely wise and holy and powerful *now ?*
" and does not sin exist along with that infinite holi-
" ness and wisdom and power ?   Is God to become
" more holy, more wise, more powerful hereafter ;
" and must evil be annihilated to make room for His
" perfections to expand ?   Does the infinity of His

" eternal nature ebb and flow with every increase or
" diminution in the sum of human guilt and misery?
" Against this immovable barrier of the existence of
" evil, the waves of philosophy have dashed them-
" selves unceasingly since the birthday of human
" thought, and have retired broken and powerless,
" without displacing the minutest fragment of the
" stubborn rock, without softening one feature of its
" dark and rugged surface."—(*Bampton Lectures,* 2nd
ed., pp. 222, 223.)

I was beginning to comment on these words. I
was trying to tell you what impression they made on
me. I cannot. I can only say, ' If they are true,
' let us burn our Bibles; let us tell our countrymen,
' that the Agony and Bloody Sweat of Christ, His
' Cross and Passion, His Death and Burial, His Re-
' surrection and Ascension mean nothing.' But oh,
friend! do not let us lose the lesson which this language is to teach us. What I was, in my haste, about
to condemn in Mr. Mansel, is in you and me. *We*
have been tolerating evil; *we* have been believing
that because it exists, it may just as well be immortal.
This is the unbelief which has paralyzed all our arms
and all our hearts. This it is which makes us patient of baseness and cowardice in ourselves, which
makes us indifferent how much of moral corruption
there is in the world. We have said to ourselves,
What is there in that little word ' for ever'? Is not
God good now? Yet He suffers evil. We who are

pledged by the vows of our Ordination, as well as by
the vows of our Baptism, to resist evil to the death,
—we have been actually propagating this accursed
denial, we have been investing it with sacred names,
we have been making it a part of our orthodoxy. Do
you think that this can go on ? Is not this habit of
mind destroying the vitals of the Nation, the vitals of
the Church ?

After speaking with so much complacency of the
possibility that evil may last for ever and ever,—after
showing that if we admit its existence at all, there
is no further difficulty in entertaining the cheering
faith that nothing can overcome it,—Mr. Mansel al-
ludes "to the great and terrible mystery of Divine
Judgment." What ! to a Divine Judgment between
good and evil, between light and darkness; that
Judgment for which Christians in Scripture are encouraged to wait and hope and long, however searching and terrible it may be, because it will show that
the Prince of the world is judged, that all things are
gathered up in Christ, that to Him all things in
earth and heaven are subject ? Such a Judgment,—
that which is called, in the New Testament, the unveiling of the Son of Man, the discovery of the real
Head and Source of all Life, Order, Peace, in God's
Universe, the overthrow and destruction of all Death,
Disorder, War,—the Judgment which has cheered
the heart of the sufferer on sick-beds; the lonely prisoner, the martyr at the stake, not because he ex-

pects some reward for himself, but because he shall
see Righteousness and Truth triumphant; because he
hopes to hear his prayers answered, that God's Will
may be done at last throughout His Creation ; such
a Judgment we must banish from our thoughts.   By
proclaiming that all the Divine Government and
Education of mankind have not been necessarily
tending to this issue, that the contradictions which
every true man feels to be agonizing may be immortal, the idea of Judgment is destroyed.   A shrivelled remnant of it may survive in the feeble, flick-
ering expectation that we who have led tolerably
respectable lives, shall be paid for our good beha-
viour hereafter, and that the disreputable will have
endless wailings for their portion.   But, thanks be to
Almighty God, He will. by the goadings of His Spirit, by kindling in us a sense of *our* infinite evil,
drive us from that refuge of lies, that beggarly hope
which must make us ashamed, that He may restore
to us that other and more glorious hope of a full revelation of His Kingdom, of the "*restitution of all
things which God hath spoken by the mouth of all His
holy prophets since the world began*." I believe, if we
lose that hope altogether,—if God gives us up, as He
may, for our rebellions, to such an entire extinction
of it as there never has been in any period of the
world yet,—we shall not stop at Mr. Mansel's point ;
we shall be certain that Evil *must* reign for ever and
ever, *must* drive out all that is opposed to it.   We

shall praise thee, O Devil, we shall acknowledge thee to be the lord. And those who still retain the conviction that Christ has come into the world, will realize Jean Paul's tremendous dream. They will suppose that His message to men was, "Children, you have *no* Father."

Yet I am glad that this dreadful language has been used, and used in a Christian pulpit. It will bring the thoughts of many hearts to light. It will show who can and who cannot bear this prospect. And those who cannot, it will lead to reconsider some of the language into which they dropped through conformity to the habits of their time, though it has corresponded very ill to their inmost convictions, and to the teachings of God's Spirit. Among many questions which will occur to them, this I am sure will be one. Has not the language we have used respecting the hopeless division between the world on this side death and the other, deprived us of some of St. Paul's most elevating as well as most practical lessons? It may be well for Mr. Mansel to scoff at the notion of one moral law for all intelligent beings. But St. Paul speaks of Him in whom we say the Moral Law was embodied, *as the head of all principalities and powers;* speaks of *the manifold wisdom and love of God* being made known to those powers *through the Church.* When he bowed his knees, it was to the *" Father of our Lord Jesus Christ, in whom the whole Family in Heaven and Earth is named."* Are Protestants afraid of such passages,—afraid of accepting the full force of them,—lest they should fall into Romanist notions, either about Purgatory, or our communion with the spirits of just men made perfect? Has not St. Paul always been the great deliverer from Romish notions? Do we tremble lest he should lead us into them? May not some on the right hand and the left be falling into them just because we have not confessed the truth of which they are the counterfeits?

And if private Christians may discover that the notions they have cherished on the subject of the future world, its joys and its terrors, have darkened the Universe, as well as the Gospel of God's Kingdom to them,—surely the preachers of that Gospel have more need still to be inquiring whether they have not entertained theories which go near to make their preaching utterly vain, a tissue of empty truisms, or flagrant contradictions. Mr. Mansel's words may be most effectual for bringing this question to a trial. Can I tell my congregation that God wills them to be saved and not damned? Can I tell them that they may trust His Will absolutely to conquer that which resists it in them? Can I preach Christ as a real deliverer of mankind, as a real conqueror for mankind? Compromises on this controversy must as much come to an end, as compromises about forgiveness when Tetzel preached his sale of pardons. We must determine what we have to declare, or for ever hold our tongues.

So far, then, we have not discovered in this Lecture many rules which can guide us in dark hours of trial, or help us in the action 'which is our duty and destiny.' We have only been taught that we are not to believe in any relation between human forgiveness and Divine forgiveness, that we must not look forward with any hope to the extirpation of evil. These are the great moral pole-stars which are to guide us over the deep ; these are to be substituted for any " principles satisfying to the Reason." Still there is one subject upon which it might have been hoped that a disciple of Butler would throw light. In a Lecture on morals, the Conscience was entitled to some notice. It *is* noticed in the last paragraph. We are told that " the very Philosopher whose wri-
" tings have most contributed to establish the su-
" preme authority of conscience in man, is also the
" one who has pointed out most clearly the existence
" of analogous moral difficulties in Nature and Reli-
" gion, and the true answer to both,—the admission
" that God's government, natural as well as spiri-
" tual, is a scheme imperfectly comprehended." This is actually the only recognition we find of a fact which Butler esteemed so profoundly important to practical morality. A very strange one certainly ! How astonished Butler would have been to hear that his writings ' established the authority of that conscience in man' which he affirmed had been established there by the Creator and Lawgiver of the Universe,

—which he said that each man was obliged by the very constitution of his nature to confess. And this is no slip of the pen, no carelessness of language which it would be unworthy to notice even in a careful writer and a professed logician. It is in strict harmony with all Mr. Mansel's teaching. The Conscience is something which we are told about in a book : we are to admit there is such a power, because a great philosopher found it indispensable for his system. How little it is suffered practically to exert itself, the whole course of Lectures bears witness. Mr. Mansel refers with triumph to an exposure which Mr. Rogers has made of the contradictions of the Moral Sense when it tries to utter its voice in protest against anything which seems to it immoral; no writers command so much of his admiration as those who disparage its testimonies, and prove its conclusions to be worthless. I may indeed be told that this incapacity of distinguishing right and wrong refers only to representations of the Divine nature. When I am called to settle what it is unjust, dishonest, treacherous for me to do, it may start into full vigour. At least the distinction should have been illustrated and explained in a treatise which professedly exalts action above speculation. It should have been shown how this faculty acquires a sudden clearness just at the very moment when all motives and inclinations are most likely to bewilder it; how that which cannot be trusted to give an honest verdict at other times, will do its work effectually, and assert its supremacy just when some hungering lust or great argument of covetousness is assailing us. It may be so, doubtless, but a little effort might have been spared to explain a perplexity which may strike others than Rationalists and Mystics as a very serious one.

I cannot help thinking that we have here decided evidence in support of a remark which I ventured to make when I was speaking to you of Butler before, that his great fame will not be maintained by those who servilely copy his opinions or adopt his nomenclature; that to vindicate it for our time,—to preserve the principles which he asserted from becoming dead letters,—we must be content to acknowledge some facts which the conditions of his age did not permit him to acknowledge. I have for many years felt this strongly about his doctrine of the Conscience; I never felt it so strongly as since I have read Mr. Mansel. Evidently those grand phrases— which I am sure have done good, which when translated into life and action are of immense worth,— about the supremacy of the conscience, are in infinite peril. They are exposed to the deadliest wounds in the house of his friends. And those who wish to defend him most are obliged to ask how they may do it without overlooking other facts which also have made themselves clear. What has been said and felt and suffered by those who have found that in themselves, that is, in their flesh, dwelleth no good thing, has worked more than all the logic and ridicule of Mr. Rogers and Mr. Mansel—though these may contribute their quota—to make men distrust that testimony to which Butler attached such worth. The difficulty must have a solution; talk about the finite and infinite is no solution at all. To me the solution has come through that very experience of evil which has led many to cast aside the idea of a Conscience, or to rob it of all its significance. The protest against that evil, whence does it proceed? It is in me, yet I cannot call it mine. Must I try? Must I adopt Butler's phraseology, if the word Conscience itself, if the lessons of Scripture, will help me to a better, and so will save his practical principle from the contempt of his own professed disciples? Does not what was said of Consciousness apply with deepest emphasis to Conscience? Is not that the witness—not of some part of the man, but of the man himself—to a Word nigh him, even at his heart; to a divine Teacher from whose sentence he cannot fly; who judges him, whose judgment he owns, even when he is resisting it most, to be according to truth?

It is the entire failure to recognize the presence of such a teacher as this within man, which renders Mr. Mansel's moral teachings at once so unscriptural and so unpractical. Because he differs from St. Paul and St. John, he must deal unfairly with the witness in our hearts; he must set at nought the lessons even of his own chosen master. For the same reason he is obliged to treat the doctrine of a Universal human Consciousness with mere contempt. The fact of such a Consciousness is forced upon us not by the dogmas of philosophers, but by the commonest observation of life. It works itself into our very dialect. Orators talk of appealing to the great common human heart. They may practise great cheats in the use of such phrases, but the cheats would be impossible if there were not a truth at the bottom of them. Pascal says that it is as dangerous to think basely of ourselves as to think highly of ourselves. Butler commands us to reverence Human Nature when we are most aware of our own evils. How can these sayings be good for anything if there is not some standard which men do confusedly recognize, which we should strive that they may recognize not confusedly but clearly and fully? How is it but because an individual selfishness—that which severs us from communion with our kind—is the great sin of the world? How is it but because Christ, who took away the sin of the world, is the bond between every man and his fellow, as well as the perfect manifestation of the Eternal and Absolute Goodness. Oh, may God make us ready to fight even to the death against the mere Public Opinion of an age which crushes the freedom of thought, which erects itself into the Judgment of God! But may He teach us to fight against it, not on behalf of some private opinion of ours, but on behalf of that great human standard which He sets before us, which justifies whatever is strong and vital in all our partial judgments, which confounds whatever in them is unsocial and dividing!

Faithfully yours,

F. D. M.

LETTER XI.

MY DEAR SIR,

Thus far Mr. Mansel has taught us these lessons : That it is not right to be Dogmatists or Rationalists, or Mystics. That it is not possible to know anything about the Absolute and the Infinite. That it is not possible to rise above our own Consciousnesses and Conceptions. That it is not right to pray as the eclectical philosopher Schleiermacher prayed. That it is not right to think about the union of the Divine and human natures as Hegel or Marheinecke thought about it. That it is not in any department good to seek for principles satisfying to the Reason. That it is not possible for us to know that which is. That Philosophy does not teach us, any more than Religion, about the Many or the One. That we are not to esteem one Representation of the union of the Finite with the Infinite above another, except because it is revealed, since one is as impossible for us to conceive of as another. That we are not to know anything of an Absolute Morality. That there is not a general human Consciousness. That Forgiveness in man is not the image of God's forgiveness. That we are not to hope for the final extinction of Evil. Thus far we have advanced at present. The Regulative Morality and the Regulative Revelation have brought us to this point. What remains must be contained in the Lecture we are now entering upon. If there is anything positive in the course, it will be there.

Mr. Mansel is fully aware that as yet he has established nothing. He admits that his demonstrations, however conclusive, are only preliminary. Preliminary to what? To a study of the 'contents' of the Scripture? By no means. To a study of the evidences in favour of their authenticity and inspiration. When we have finished Mr. Mansel, we are in a condition to enter upon the study of Paley. The object of this final Lecture is therefore to complain of the indifference which is shown in our days to external evidences—to show within what very narrow limits any argument grounded upon internal evidence must be confined; to give a summary of those points of evidence with which we are most familiar; to guard us against the danger of attaching any weight to plausible reasoning on the other side after we have once admitted that the probabilities on our own predominate; to warn us that the Scriptures must be taken altogether or rejected altogether; to propound a theory respecting *Moral Miracles,* which disposes of all objections to particular acts as not being in accordance with the moral character of God; to repeat what has been said before respecting the impossibility of our arriving at any conclusion about what is or is not in accordance with His character; to moderate the reasonings of some theologians of Mr. Mansel's own school, who, he thinks, have too hastily affirmed that there is *no* relation between human qualities and divine; to deepen by these very cautions the sense of our incapacity to pronounce anything certain concerning the relation; finally, to urge the duty of our cultivating self-knowledge, as we can have no other knowledge.

I. I do not feel the temptation which Mr. Mansel deems is characteristic of our age, o undervalue Paley for being too historical. The more I meet those whose passion is for logical formulas and intellectual abstractions, the more I reverence that quality of his mind. It was connected with the transparency of his style, and with that simplicity of character which co-existed with a northern shrewdness, with a utilitarian creed, and with notions about moral honesty which would have disturbed it if it had not been part of himself. His love of evidence was cultivated in him, as it is in all Englishmen, by our institutions, especially by our jury system. It was not in the spirit of an advocate chiefly that he desired to make use of his skill in weighing the worth of testimony. He shared the feeling which now and then induces a young nobleman to throw aside his conventional dignity that he may wrestle or box with a mechanic, perhaps with a professional prize-fighter. It seemed to him that it was scarcely fair play to meet the objector to Christianity, or even to Theism, with a weight of traditional opinion, with the prescription of centuries on our side. He would do his best to cast off these advantages. He had confidence that his case could dispense with them. There was an apparent justice and manliness in this course which his countrymen, in whose habits of mind he so largely partook, were able to appreciate. The feeling that it was a homage to truth not to profit by assumptions, worked powerfully, if somewhat confusedly, in those who read the 'Natural Theology,' the 'Evidences of Christianity,' or the 'Horæ Paulinæ.' With respect to the first, even those who, like me, yield to the opinion of Kant and Mr. Mansel, that he has not proved anything, may yet be most thankful to him for having given them reasons for adoration which their coldness wants, the *proof* being sought and found elsewhere; may rejoice that any corrections which later discoveries have made in his science will not diminish but increase these reasons, however fatal they might be if we supposed we could not confess the Author of Nature till we understood His works. Again, the books which turn upon the authority of documents, will always suggest a number of thoughts even to those who read the books themselves, and find in them lessons which they prize more, and which carry more conviction to their minds than the most subtle observation of coincidences ever did or could impart.

II. Why then are Englishmen of this day, as Mr. Mansel complains, more indifferent to these evidences, even as they are presented by this able writer, than their fathers were? One very strong reason appears to me to be this, that the quality which recommended them to Paley and to men of his character, has been found signally wanting in them. The objector has not a clear stage for fighting his battle on. It has proved altogether an illusion that in managing these evidences no favour is shown to one side. I must speak what I have seen and know,—in some degree, what I have felt. Young men at College are *taught* these evidences; they learn them by heart, and must be able to produce them. They are reminded while they learn that a certain conclusion is to be reached; they are told that it is exceedingly perilous if they arrive at any other than that. The statement of Butler, which has been dwelt upon till it has almost extinguished in some minds every other passage in his writings,—till it has made three parts of them out of four unmeaning,—that in a question of safety a very low amount of probability ought to satisfy us, is thrown in to make up for any deficiences in Paley's reasoning; it is accompanied in many cases with serious warnings against rash meddling with adverse arguments. Now whatever may be the justification for such suggestions, they are utterly incompatible with that profession of putting ourselves on the level of opponents with which we started. A young man soon becomes keenly, bitterly, sensible of this contradiction. He says when he goes out into the world, 'The Christian ' evidences with which I was supplied at college do ' not answer in the very least degree to the idea of ' evidence which prevails in the law courts, or which ' I find recognized by men of science. The maxim ' *Audi alteram partem* is not one upon which I was ' encouraged to act; I was warned against it. Why, ' then, was I deceived by a promise to the ear which ' was belied in fact? Why was I not told the thing ' that I was to receive, as people are told it in other ' countries? Why did they give me sham argu-' ments which I was to swallow under that name, in-' stead of merely thrusting the conclusions down my ' throat simply and frankly? Was this what Paley ' meant?' The amount of infidelity among young laymen of the upper and middle class which proceeds from this discovery is, I believe, incalculable.

And how is it with the Clergy? We hear that the conflict which Paley provoked,—which he had courage to believe would turn out for the honour of the Bible,—has been carried on fiercely in another country. We hear that documents, the genuineness and authenticity of which we thought were proved by our evidence, have been assailed. We have not, most of us, leisure to inquire how they have been attacked, or how they have been defended; perhaps we know that the gifts,—very peculiar gifts,—which fit men for this special work, have not been bestowed upon us, that there is other work we can do better. And yet there is an uneasy feeling, which our education —I mean our recent education—has fostered, that our whole faith depends on the settlement of these points; that if any one of them should be determined the wrong way, we should have nothing left us to stand upon. Therefore we practically come to the conclusion, that they must not and shall not be determined the wrong way. In other words, we take Paley's evidences for granted as if they were divine. Nothing must be permitted to shake their authority in our minds. Yet we know all the while that they are not divine, that they are mere ordinary, clever, human arguments, any one of which is liable to be sifted, has a right to be sifted, and may turn out to be worthless. Of course we have all heard a thousand times what Mr. Mansel tells us for the thousand and first, that if there is the least balance of probabilities in favour of a conclusion, that conclusion must be received, however many there may be on the other side. But are we prepared to rest all on which we lean for life and death, all which we tell others is necessary for them, on the cast of a die? Whatever logicians may say, every practical man feels that he does not, and that he cannot. If this is the ground of our faith, it must fall. And therefore, to give it a ground, we throw in the consideration that it is safer to hold some opinion than not to hold it. We all know how that argument works; we all know whither it leads. 'The safety of an infallible Church, oh, will ' you not seek that, poor youth, tossed by a thousand ' arguments about this document and that! Con- ' sider the repose of receiving whatever you are told ' to receive! You can find out nothing that *is*. Oh, ' take these probable *seemings* to save your soul!' How many clergymen and laymen have listened to the voice of this Siren! If all have not listened to it, we have not our books of evidence to thank for stopping our ears to it.

III. But the book to which those evidences refer— that book, so far as we have opened it, so far as we have cared for the contents of it more than for proofs about it, so far as we have thought of it as our fathers thought of it, that *has* been a protection, for that has testified to us of One who is, of One from whom men fled in the old times to gods on hill altars and in dark groves for the safety of their souls, of One

who delivered them from the miserable darkness and
captivity into which they came when they forgot
Him who was not far from any of them—the Infinite and Eternal, the Father of their spirits—and tried
to make Him anew out of their conceptions of the
finite and the temporal. It testifies of a God of Righteousness and Truth, ruling in the armies of Heaven,
and among the inhabitants of earth. It testifies of
the way in which that Being has discovered Himself
through the actual doings and sufferings of nations,
through the doubts and struggles of individual hearts,
through the discomfiture and overthrow of those
who were appointed to be the witnesses for Him,
but who refused to own Him when He came near to
them and showed Himself forth in a living and suffering man. Therefore did our fathers find in the Bible a refuge from dark superstitions and moral evils;
therefore did they regard it as the pillar of their national and daily life; therefore did they call it the
word of God. The Bible pointed them to a ground
of Certainty, not of Probability, beneath them, beneath itself. Its power rested on no arguments about
the origin of documents. It proved itself in another
way,—by the facts of life, by sore and blessed experiences. They could trust these proofs. They could
trust God to show forth His mind and purpose, which
they believed to be unchangeable, in their day as
in other days, through common events, through the
righteous or the foul doings of men, through mighty

deliverances and mighty judgments. They felt that they understood the Bible very imperfectly, but it helped them to understand all that was passing around them.

IV. In the last century, during the lull that pre-ceded the tempest which closed it, the Bible was not thought of much as an interpreter of *political* events. At one time it had almost ceased to be regarded as an interpreter of the problems of *personal* life. As it was smiled at by men of wit and fashion in London, rejected in the salons of Paris, the divines supposed that their function was to extol its beauties or to al-lege signs of its inspiration. But there were men at that time also who said, ' The Bible has shown itself ' to us to be the Word of God by other than this ' evidence. It has come to us with a demonstration ' of the Spirit and of power. It has changed the ' purpose of our lives. It has enabled us to become ' witnesses to others of that which we have found ' to be true ourselves. We cannot convince people as ' we have been convinced, but God can. His Word ' will not return to Him void. It will accomplish that ' for which He has sent it.' This brave and manly language, or rather the deep conviction which it ex-pressed, kindled a feeling respecting the Bible which all the arguments about authenticity and inspiration in the world could not kindle. It prepared our people for the shock that was to try the nations of what sort they were, whether they had anything better than

their own opinions and decrees and the traditions of
the past to rest upon ; whether they believed in anything, or only believed that there was something in
which it was exceedingly desirable, for various interests here or hereafter, that they should believe.

V. It is owing to such men as these that what is
called internal evidence has, to Mr. Mansel's great
sorrow, so much displaced what he calls external or
historical evidence.   There was no intention on the
part of these believers in the Bible to set up one
against the other.   They were merely testifying of
what they had seen and known ; they were exalting
the contents of the Book above talk and arguments
about the Book.   In his able summary of Christian
evidences (p. 248), Mr. Mansel speaks of the " ina-
" bility of human means to bring about the results
" which Christianity actually accomplished ; its anta-
" gonism to the current ideas of the age and country
" of its origin; its effects as a system on the moral
" and social condition of subsequent generations of
" mankind ; its fitness to satisfy the wants and con-
" sole the sufferings of human nature."   Well, the men
of the last century, to whom I have alluded, believed
all this about the primitive time, but they believed it
also about their own.   They found human means
quite unable to bring about the results which the Gospel actually accomplished in them.   They found, that
when they tried to act upon its principles they were
in antagonism to ideas that were current in their age

and country, and that were even strong in themselves. They felt that if it had produced moral and social effects upon other generations,—for instance, in breaking the chains of slaves,—it was capable of producing the same in their own. And they deemed it very unnecessary to *prove* its fitness for satisfying the wants and consoling the sufferings of human nature, because they could actually offer it to satisfy those wants and console those sufferings which were as real, and were to all intents and purposes the same, in their time as in the time of the Apostles. Arguments about these things become very important when the things themselves are dead; as long as they are alive, the things take the place of the arguments.

VI. In reference to the strife about documents, the battle of books, in Germany and elsewhere, Mr. Mansel knows much better than I do how these feelings about the internal worth of the truths contained in the Scriptures have operated. He must be conscious, I think, of some unfairness in his way of representing to his English readers the sentiments of those whom he calls Naturalists, or Neologians, or Rationalists. He has not concealed the fact of their being very different from one another; but he has endeavoured to make capital out of their differences, by showing that they could not agree because they had departed from our quiet and uniform standard. Would it not have been fairer to confess, that the mere Naturalists, who looked at the doctrines and events of

Scripture as altogether external to themselves, had been driven from a number of their strongest holds by men who had felt that all true criticism demanded an examination of the meaning and purport of the books and of their relation to human beings, as well as of their origin and outward structure? Might it not have been right to remind us that *we* stimulated that eager inquiry into the origin of the books, that we in some sort were the authors of their Naturalism, and that a spiritual conviction, of which our writers upon Evidences had taken little account, restored much of that affection for the Bible to the German mind which characterized it at the time of the Reformation? The statement of these facts might have been inconvenient for the purposes of Mr. Mansel's argument; it might have been humbling to our vanity. But would it not have been a consolation to some perplexed thinkers to have tokens that God can take better care of His Revelation than we can, and that the criticism which we might have desired to stifle, may, after all, have done more to bring the actual power of the Bible to light than our apologies for it?

VII. I am, however, convinced that there was a weakness in the English asserters of internal evidence, as well as in the Germans who applied that same evidence to documentary criticism. I would adopt Mr. Mansel's phrase, though in a somewhat different sense, and say they were too indifferent to the historical evidence for the Bible,—to the external proofs, that we must resort to other than human means for explaining its wonderful power of " satisfying the wants of human nature, and consoling its sufferings." There has been a very loud cry, ever since the commencement of the French Revolution, for Principles of Political Justice and Order. There must be a Right, it has been said, beneath our laws and conventions. It cannot be measured by the habits and prejudices of particular races or nations. It ought to explain how those habits and prejudices have arisen. This demand was at first eminently unhistorical. It trampled upon history. It tried to find maxims of pure reason on which all society should be constructed and rebuilt. But it has given birth to a painstaking and earnest study of history ; a sense of its importance, and of its superiority to all abstract conclusions, such as I believe existed in no former day, prevails among us. The danger is that this historical spirit having become so lively in its apprehension of the tendencies of ages and races, should almost lose sight of the influence which first awakened it ; that it should too much overlook that deep craving in men for that which is not limited by special circumstances, but belongs to all. If, however, this danger becomes imminent for the *student*, it is met and counteracted by a demand—inarticulate generally—yet often expressing itself distinctly and loudly in that class of society which forms the bulk

of every nation; that class to which Paine addressed
his 'Rights of Men' and his 'Age of Reason.' This
class asks whether we do confess any foundations
deeper than those we have laid,—any laws not created for the interest of particular classes, — any to
which priests and kings are as much subject as other
men ?

VIII. These needs of human nature cannot be satisfied,—the sufferings which are associated with them
cannot be consoled,—by reference to what Christianity or the Bible did in former days. Are we
willing to ask manfully what it can do in these days
for meeting the questions which are disturbing all
hearts ? If we are, I believe numerous portions of
the Bible which lay almost in shadow from some of
the most earnest of our immediate forefathers, may
become an illuminated scroll for us. We shall prize
the Old Testament as much as the Puritans, or those
who argued against Puritans, prized it. But we
shall not dare to use it as they did, for the purpose
of proving that God is on our side, and against our
opponents ;—that we are the Israelites, and they
the Moabites or Hagarenes. We shall read in it
that a living God is sitting as our judge no less than
theirs ;—that He has been condemning in all ages
the unrighteous and cruel deeds of His servants, has
been showing forth in all ages His righteousness in
contrast to their evil. We shall not scruple to declare that He has dealt with priests and kings, with

Churches and kingdoms, in the modern as He did in the old world, justifying what was right in every pagan or Mohamedan land, condemning what was evil and accursed in every Christian land; no respecter of persons, of sinners or saints. If we have not courage to do this,—if we go on as we have done, pleading and arguing for our schools and our opinions,—I believe God will confound us in the sight of the people; that every day they will become more atheistical for our defences and apologies; that we shall become in our hearts as atheistical as they. If we enter humbly and in fear on that course, I do not say that we may look for any immediate results. I believe that the immediate result will be an experience of our own feebleness to crush opposition, of our own impatience with it; a discovery, to which others have been led before us, that the word is God's word, and not ours.   But see whether, if we work on, He will not confirm that word with signs following, whether He will not justify Himself in the eyes of men if He does not justify us.

IX. And if this is so with the poor and ignorant to whom the Gospel was first preached, I am satisfied that a result no less real and satisfactory may be looked for among the patient and conscientious students of history.   It has been a miserable part of our apologetic system to set up Sacred History as a kind of rival to Profane; to treat one as if it concerned God, and the other as if it was merely of

the earth. At the same time, there has been a dis-
creditable and faithless eagerness to catch at every
witness in favour of a Scripture narrative from a
profane author, as if we could not trust it without that confirmation; an eagerness which has led
us often to accept doubtful legends in Pagan his-
tories, which, when they were shown to be less probable than other statements of the same transaction, left those who had depended on that evidence
in great perplexity. Oh! shall we never do justice
to our own convictions? Shall we never try whether Scripture, by interpreting God's dealings with
one nation, may not expound His dealings with the
other nations? Shall we never consider whether the
witness which the Bible bears against the idolatry
to which Jews were so prone, does not explain the
temptation of every land; the forms under which
the temptation has presented itself to one and another; the *necessity* of idolatry, if we deduce the
Eternal from the Temporal, the Infinite from the
Finite; the protest against idolatry which there was
in the heart of every people under Heaven in the assurance that the Eternal must be the ground of the
Temporal, the Infinite of the Finite? Shall we never
ask whether the Day of Pentecost is not the explanation of the Constitution of human society, the interpretation of the difference between that Universality which is grounded upon a Spirit of Truth, who
binds together and quickens the spirits of men,—and

the Universality of Despotism, Imperial, Ecclesiastical, Democratical?—whether therefore the record of that day is not a key to the sins with which Church History abounds, as well as to the possibility that there could be a Church in the midst of them? Here, again, we can expect and desire no sudden conversions of modern historians to an acknowledgment of the Scriptures, which have seemed to so many of them a chain upon all free and manly investigation. Our clumsy efforts to connect the Bible with their studies may only display our imperfect acquaintance with both. If we think we have some wonderful new trick of fence, it will be laughed to scorn, as all such tricks ought to be, by those against whom they are used. But if we suffer the Bible to trample upon our tricks, and to speak its own speech, I am sure it will at last be found to 'satisfy the wants and console the sufferings' of those who have found in history most of those wants and those sufferings.

X. Those who have deduced the divine origin of the Bible from their own personal experience, though far more efficient than the mere reasoners about genuineness and authenticity, have failed, then, as I think, in appreciating the social and historical demands of their time, as well as the social and historical character of the Bible. It would have been a much less serious failure if they had not understood the demands of philosophers; for just so far as these

demands are special, just so far as they are not connected with what is universal, they may be fairly
overlooked by those whose message is not to classes
but to men.   Oftentimes, however, what appear to
be the reasonings of Philosophers point to the most
serious 'wants of human nature,' to its most intense
'sufferings.'   Such, I believe, is that demand for the
knowledge of the Infinite or Eternal which has occupied us in these Letters.   Mr. Mansel has said in
his third Lecture (p. 68), that " a belief in the ex-
" istence of an Absolute and Infinite Being appears
" forced upon us as the complement of our conscious-
" ness of the relative and the finite."   This is a very
good statement of a logical necessity.   The terms on
which he dwells so much indicate it; the term Finite
is unintelligible without the term Infinite. But translated from the formulas of logic into the forms of
life, this search for something to complement the finite
and relative is nothing less than the most awful demand in the nature of man; that which has been
expressing itself in every age; that which, as I have
just said, has been the witness against thinking that
the "*Godhead is like to gold, or silver, or stone, graven by art or man's device;*" that which has become
strongest and clearest in the great crises of human
history; that which in our days, though not for the
first time, has given birth to the fearful question, Is
this Infinite anything, or everything, or nothing?

  XI. If we set this question distinctly before ourselves, if we treat it as the question which God is awakening in all men's hearts, I believe the New-Testament will be read with an interest with which it has never been read ; that it will be taken more literally than it has ever been taken ; that the acts and words of Christ, His miracles, His parables, His death, His resurrection, His ascension, the descent of the Spirit, the preaching and letters of the Apostles, the final unveiling to the Beloved Disciple, will all come forth as parts of the answer to the question—as declarations that the Eternal and the Infinite is not the Nothing which it must be if it is a mere generalization from our conceptions of the Finite and the Temporal, but is that Love which was before the worlds were, which was manifested in due time in the Only-begotten Son, which is the ground of all that is loving and true in the hearts or in the acts of men. I do not say that this discovery can commend itself at once to any human being. It must have deadly battles to fight with that which is opposed to it in us and in every man. The battle, I think, will be such as it has never been in any other generation. No one can dare to say how he may comport himself in it ; no one who knows the depth of selfishness in his own heart can boast that he may not succumb to it ; no one who takes any measure of the struggle between good and evil, between light and darkness, or who reflects how often the opinion of the world—the religion of the world—has been ranged against that which he is sure must ultimately triumph, can help trembling lest he should yield to that opinion or resist it through selfwill, not in obedience to the Spirit of Truth. But looking at the question apart from these personal considerations, I cannot doubt that a more reverent and childlike faith in the lessons of the New Testament will result from its being brought side by side with this great inquiry. Nor can I doubt that that peculiarity of the Bible which we have all noticed,—that it is written in the language of the senses, and with such an absence of logical formulas as is to be found in no other book,—will explain itself by this comparison. Beginning from the Eternal, and descending to the Temporal, proceeding from the Infinite to the Finite, the forms of logic, which are abstractions from the Finite and the Temporal, have no place in it. The realities which are behind the veil express themselves through the forms of sense, because that is the order and principle of God's universe. The logical difficulty vanishes in its own nothingness. The real difficulty is felt more and more as we feel what we are in the sight of the Holy One who inhabiteth eternity. It disappears only in the awfulness of trust and adoration, only in the belief of an eternal Daysman between the creature and the Creator, who has borne our weakness and carried our sorrows, who dwells at the right-hand of the Majesty on high.

XII. But if this question is ignored, if it is treated

as insoluble, if there is a perpetual balance and equivocation between the real problem and the nominal one, then I am satisfied that the Old Testament and the New, as far as their contents are concerned, as far as any evidence is concerned which is involved in those contents, must be equally cast aside or explained away. It is one object of Mr. Mansel in this last Lecture, to show that we must either accept the whole Bible or reject the whole. I do not know that I have shown much desire to reject any part of it in these Sermons or Letters ; nevertheless I cannot pretend that I attach much worth to this kind of language. It sounds very well in the ears of the religious world; it has been quoted largely in the religious journals. But does it indicate faith that the Bible is God's word ? Does it not look rather as if we thought that it was our word? If the Bible speaks truly, if the experience of godly men in all ages speaks truly, He has guided them very gently and gradually, giving line on line, precept on precept, often through dark roads, to the goal which He meant them to reach. It looks rather as if we were taking the matter into our hands, as if we were assuming to be the guides of the spirits of men,—guides most ignorant of what these spirits are and what voices they obey,—when we cry, 'Now, you rebels! we have 'given you arguments such as ought to convince 'you. Take all, or reject all.' As long as I believe the Bible, I shall hate that mode of speaking, how-

ever orthodox and popular it may sound; I shall regard it as the proper dialect of inquisitors, which is
quite out of date when there are no swords to maintain it with. The utterer of it is complimented on
his faith. It turns the hearer into an infidel.

XIII. But when I am told that I must take all or
nothing, I am obliged to inquire whether the all is not
a very near approximation to nothing? I have read
carefully through these Lectures; I have marked
every instance in which Mr. Mansel has quoted a
text; I have considered especially those which he has
prefixed to his discourses; I must say I never saw
Scripture treated with so little reverence, its words
so recklessly employed, merely to point a sentence or
confound an opponent, without the least reference to
the occasion on which they were spoken, or to the
meaning which they must bear in the Sacred Volume.
I know that the habit of using mottoes to sermons has
prevailed greatly;—I hoped it was beginning to be
discarded; I hoped that in Oxford, whence we clergy
are to derive our models of preaching, it would have
been banished altogether. But Mr. Mansel has im-
proved upon the old practice: he has given his mottoes all their sting, by emptying them of *all* their original signification.

The first is taken from that magnificent chapter in
the Book of Deuteronomy, in which Moses begins to
set forth the privileges of his people, in that the Living God had come so near to them, in that He had

spoken to them out of the midst of the fire, in that He had given them ordinances which would make them a wise and understanding people in the sight of the nations, if they remembered Him, the unseen God, and did not bow down to the likeness of any created thing, *" Ye shall not add,"* he says, *" to the word which I command you ; neither shall ye diminish aught from it."* The word that proceeded out of the mouth of God is a religious system. Dogmatists add to it ; Rationalists take from it. Conceive such an application of the language of any legislator, whose sentences were *not* written in the Bible : who would not call it monstrous ?

The third Lecture is introduced by another passage from the Pentateuch. It is that in which Moses is told that *" He cannot see the face of God, for no man shall see Him and live."* If Mr. Mansel had acknowledged any connection between the Old and New Testament, would not this passage have led him to that in the third chapter of the Second Epistle to the Corinthians, in which St. Paul contrasts the Old Dispensation with the New in this very respect, winding up with the memorable words, *" And we all with open face beholding the glory of the Lord, are changed into the same image from glory to glory"?*

The fourth and the seventh Lectures also open with sentences from the Old Testament. The first is that from the sixty-fifth Psalm : *" O Thou that hearest prayer, to Thee shall all flesh come."* It is quoted in the course of the Sermon (p. 128), apparently to support the proposition "that it is not as "the Infinite that God reveals Himself in His Moral "Government, nor as the Infinite that He promises "to answer prayer." The second is the memorable passage from the tenth of Ezekiel: " *Yet ye say, The way of the Lord is not equal. Hear ye now, O house of Israel, Is not my way equal? Are not your ways unequal?*" I need not tell you to read the chapter. I need not tell you that this verse is connected with the whole argument of it. That argument, you know, is one which God holds with His people, through the prophet, to convince them that His course of government is just; He explains it to them. The prophet assumes them to have a standard by which they could judge of God's dealings with them. The object of the preacher is to show that as finite human beings they could have none.

Mr. Mansel's treatment of the New Testament is of the same kind; only in some cases there is a curious felicity in the quotation which one might almost call judicial. For instance, the second Lecture, in which there are more logical subtleties than were ever gathered into a sermon before,—for the purpose of proving that there can be no knowledge of the Infinite Being by a finite being,—opens with that address to young Timothy, the force of which some of the congregation may perhaps have felt. " *Keep that which is committed to thee, avoiding profane and vain babblings,*

*and oppositions of science, falsely so called; which
some professing have erred concerning the faith.*" The
persons aimed at are Rationalists and Mystics.

The fifth is taken from 1 Cor. i. 21–24. That text
declares that the Apostle preaches *" Christ crucified,
unto the Jews a stumblingblock, and unto the Greeks
foolishness, but unto them which are called, both Jews
and Greeks, Christ,* THE WISDOM OF GOD *and* THE
POWER OF GOD.*"* The Lecturer undertakes to show
that " in Religion God has given us truths... which
" do not tell us what God is in His absolute Nature,
" but how He wills that we should think of Him in
" our present finite state." Surely a most valuable
correction and mitigation of the Apostle's broad
statement of the truth which *he* declared to men !

The sixth is taken from that passage, in the same
Epistle, to which I have referred more than once :
*" For what man knoweth the things of a man save the
spirit of a man which is in him ? Even so the things
of God knoweth no man but the Spirit of God.*"* The
verse which immediately follows that text is this :
*" Now we have received not the spirit of the world, but
the Spirit which is of God, that we might know the
things that are freely given us of God.*"* And the
16th verse is this : *" For who hath known the mind of
the Lord that he might instruct Him? But we have
the mind of Christ.*"* The object of the sermon is, of
course, to show that we cannot know the mind of
God.

The Lecture before us is headed by a verse from the fifth chapter of St. John. It is this : *" The works which the Father hath given me to finish, the same works that I do, bear witness of me, that the Father hath sent me."* One of the sermons I have sent you is on a text closely resembling this, from the tenth chapter of the same Evangelist. It is on the subject of Miracles. I have endeavoured to show you how our Lord's works did each of them bear witness by its character of the Father who had sent Him.* I will not repeat what I have said, but I will apply it to a very remarkable passage, in this Lecture, on *Moral Miracles*. I could scarcely find a more complete illustration of the way in which an apologist may overthrow the principles of the book for which he is pleading, whilst he is demolishing the objections to it.

XIV. Many acts recorded in Scripture, especially in the Old Testament, have, you well know, been objected to as inconsistent with the moral character of God. The wars with the Canaanites are the most obvious example. These wars are clearly represented in Scripture as part of the conflict of a Righteous God with an unrighteous, filthy, and cruel people. They are set forth as acts of the God of Order in punishing disorder. Some may feel, as I do, that they were so, and

* It gives me great pleasure to find that so eminent a Biblical scholar as Mr. Westcott, in a course of sermons preached at Cambridge while I was preaching mine, has treated them as Epiphanies. I need not say that I do not hold Mr. Westcott answerable for any of my statements ; but this coincidence is peculiarly gratifying.

may find in them a key to later events in the history and government of the world. Some may be quite unable to take this view of the case; then their true course is, at all events, not to pretend that they think what they do not think. If they follow the example of the prophets, they will ask God to interpret His own ways to them; I, for my part, believe that they will not ask in vain. But what is Mr. Mansel's method of solving the difficulty? He assumes that these wars were not what Joshua manifestly assumes them to be, part of God's Order, but exceptions, or departures from that Order; not illustrations of His righteous dealings with men, but *Moral Miracles.* Thus, to save the credit of the Book, he destroys the testimony of the Book on that point; and, if I am not greatly mistaken, its testimony respecting the whole meaning and purpose of God's works, as they were manifested by Him who *" did the works which His Father gave Him to finish."*

XV. This, it seems, is the modern method of coming to inquire of the oracles of God; by this process they become a light to our feet, a lamp to our path! Accept the book as a whole, and then treat all the portions of it just as you like. Confess all its words to be words of the Lord, and then you may yourself be lords over them, and may perform moral miracles by turning the bread of life into stones for casting at your enemies! Far indeed am I from charging Mr. Mansel either with intending this irreverence, or with setting the first example of it. No disease is so prevalent in our times; there is no one of us who is not liable to the infection; none, who has not often caught it, and done something to spread it. That is my reason for entering upon this examination. If Mr. Mansel's were a new scheme for confuting infidels, or establishing a religious philosophy, one might trust our English Conservatism, or, I am afraid, our indifference, to extinguish it. But he appeals to our Conservatism; he enters into an alliance with our indifference. He promises us peace from foes that we are afraid of. He assures us that we shall be able to repose comfortably in our ancient opinions. The habits and tendencies which he finds prevalent amongst us, he condenses; our floating maxims he reduces into order, flatters our vanity for having entertained them, teaches us to laugh at all as unphilosophical, or to condemn all as irreligious, who do not accept them. He is sure therefore to be popular with us, for he gives us back our own judgments, looking far less incoherent than they commonly look. We have secretly thought that it would be a great relief if we could persuade ourselves that the Eternal lay entirely beyond us; that the doctrines of our creeds may be taken for granted because they treat of matters about which people have disputed to no purpose for centuries; that Morality cannot be brought to any absolute standard, but is a subject for rules and conventions, such as we can get; that certain services and duties are owing to God, and that certain things are to be believed about Him for the regulation of our lives, but that the truth of these things cannot be ascertained; that truth and falsehood are properties of our conceptions; that we are to admit the evidences of the Bible because it is safer to do so, and not to be anxious about its contents. We have all, I say, held these thoughts; but we have held them uneasily. We have said to ourselves, 'Is this then the faith once deli-'vered to the Saints,—the faith which has overcome 'the world, and is to overcome it?—the faith which 'lifts men above themselves, which unites them to 'God, which makes them partakers of Christ's risen 'life?' To have all such suspicions quelled; to be assured that we cannot have a faith which raises us above ourselves; to be told that to ascend above our own thoughts is the dream of Rationalists and Mystics; and that to stay on the level of our own thoughts is the duty of all sober Christians,—to have all this set forth to us in logical statements which we do not the least understand, but which we are sure must prove the case,—the old *ignotum pro magnifico* of superstition happily combining with the delight of thinking that we are in possession of the last result of school wisdom;—to have the testimony of a man who knows all about Germans and Philosophy, that we are not only much better, but very much wiser, than those who we were afraid were about to rob us

of our treasures—where can we look for comfort if
not here?

XVl. My answer is, Certainly not to the Bible,—
not to the book which Englishmen have cherished and
reverenced,—if this is the comfort we want! If we
turn to its words, and not to the words which wise
people have written about it, or in excuse for it, we
shall be robbed of this comfort. We shall be robbed
of our notion that we can have rest by suppressing
the doubts and oppositions of other men, or the doubts
and opposition in ourselves. We shall be taught that
truth has never thriven except in conflict;* that men
have never sought the true peace till they have rejected the false peace; that those who make the soul
a solitude, and call it peace, must part with the peace
which passeth understanding and dwells in the knowledge of God. We shall be robbed of the notion that
logic can set our minds at rest. It is of great value.
It tells us what we are when we are shut up in ourselves, in our own conceptions; how we abstract and
form notions from names; how they are to be distinguished from the things which they set forth; how
impossible it is for them to exhibit a single living
process. For every process of bodily life—seeing,
smelling, tasting, handling, walking, breathing—is an
act of rising out of ourselves. Not to do that is to
die. The Bible consistently and harmoniously shows

* I would exhort all clergymen to study a passage on this subject
in Mr. Mill's 'Liberty,' pp. 73–78.

us that every process of life in the man himself,—
every movement of thought, feeling, affection—is, in
like manner, a rising above ourselves, an ascent into
another region. The Bible tells us of the new man
who is created after God in righteousness and true
holiness, created for the knowledge of a righteousness and true holiness which are not in himself but
in Him. The Bible, in every song and prayer, is inviting us to leave the dungeon-keep of our own low,
grovelling thoughts; it affirms that the invitation
comes from the Creator of the Universe, the Father
of our spirits. That our dull ears will not hear this
music, that we are always seeking to gravitate into
ourselves, is what the Bible warns us of. It is this
accursed sloth we have to shake off, this spiritual
death from which we need to be delivered. Believing this, I thought it necessary to ask how far one
who urged that confinement within the limits of our
own thoughts could face the facts and lessons of the
Bible. This Lecture, it seems to me, is altogether
decisive on that point. The author defends the
Bible; the moment he approaches it, you feel that
he is at war with it. He must emasculate it—he
must reduce it from a word of God into a collection
of opinions—before it has any meaning for him. And
so the only moral he can leave us with is that which
Pope, educated in Romanism, matured by Boling-
broke, expressed, as perfectly as it can be expressed,
in the well-worn couplet,

> " Know then thyself, presume not God to scan,
> The proper study of mankind is man."

On which text I take this to be the true comment. We can know nothing of ourselves till we look above ourselves. We can see light only in God's light. The knowledge of man is possible, because the knowledge of God is possible.

Very truly yours,

F. D. M.

POSTSCRIPT.

It may appear to you and to other readers, that I have not done justice to some passages in Mr. Mansel's volume, wherein he holds out the hope that the knowledge which is impossible for us here, may be attained in a future state. A hint of this kind occurs in the peroration to the fourth Lecture. I give all weight to such remarks; I gladly accept them as proofs that the writer longs for that fruition which the Psalmist longed for. But taken in connection with the rest of his treatise, these passages, I must say, are utterly puzzling to me. If it is involved in the very condition of a finite being, that he should not know the Infinite, such promises must imply that hereafter we shall cease to be finite. If it is treason against the limitations which God has appointed for us, to suppose that we can transcend our own conceptions here, will it cease to be a treason in another world? Is then all that Butler has taught us about the relation between the two worlds, about the analogy between our pursuits and expectations here and that which is to be bestowed upon us when we have passed out of this world, a delusion? Is that which is evil here to be the good there? We have been used to think that all the restless ambitions and longings which we indulge in this imperfect state, will be quelled for ever in a perfect one. Far from it. These ambitions, which it is our duty to check on this side the grave, are to be indulged freely on the other. Mr. Mansel speaks as if it were a difference of *degree*. It *is* a difference of degree when St. Paul tells us that we see through a glass darkly here, and shall see face to face hereafter. The same object is presented to us in both cases,—is presented with equal truth in both cases; only the eye from the very contemplation is growing stronger,—is becoming more able to take in the vision. But it is a question of *kind*, not of degree, whether by faith we rise above ourselves, or whether to make that attempt is to be guilty of infidelity. Whatever is true upon that question now must be true for ever.